Winds of Change

Winds of Change

HURRICANES & THE
TRANSFORMATION OF
NINETEENTH-CENTURY
CUBA

LOUIS A. PÉREZ JR.

The University of North Carolina Press

Chapel Hill and London

© 2001
The University of North Carolina Press
All rights reserved
Set in Bodoni type
by Tseng Information Systems, Inc.
Manufactured in the United States of America
The paper in this book meets the guidelines for
permanence and durability of the Committee on
Production Guidelines for Book Longevity of the
Council on Library Resources.
Library of Congress Cataloging-in-Publication Data
Pérez, Louis A.
Winds of change : hurricanes and the transformation
of nineteenth-century Cuba / by Louis A. Pérez Jr.
p.   cm.
Includes index.
ISBN 0-8078-2613-8 (cloth : alk. paper) —
ISBN 0-8078-4928-6 (pbk. : alk. paper)
1. Hurricanes—Economic aspects—Cuba—History—
19th century.   2. Cuba—Economic conditions—
19th century.   I. Title.
QC945 .P47   2001
363.34'922'09729109034—dc21   00-046691

05 04 03 02 01   5 4 3 2 1

To the memory of Pepín

Contents

Acknowledgments

This book was completed as a result of the generous and expert assistance of the staffs associated with a number of research facilities in Cuba and the United States. I am grateful for the assistance of the staff of the Archivo Nacional de Cuba in Havana. The hospitality offered by Eliades Acosta, the director of Biblioteca Nacional José Martí, as well as by the Biblioteca staff is most appreciated. I am similarly grateful to director Nuria Gregori Torada for graciously facilitating consultation of the magnificent research collections housed at the Instituto de Literatura y Lingüistica in Havana. Graciela Milián, the director of the Archivo Provincial Histórico de Matanzas, was unfailing in her courtesy and helpfulness. The assistance provided by Manuel López, director of the Instituto de Historia de Cuba, and by Amparo Hernández Denis, also of the Instituto, was especially helpful in the arrangement of research on the island. In the United States, I benefited from the assistance of the staffs at the New-York Historical Society, New York Public Library, Library of Congress, and National Archives. At the University of North Carolina at Chapel Hill, I was the beneficiary of the expertise and assistance of the staffs of the Rare Book Collection and the North Carolina Collection at the Wilson Library and the Reference and Inter-Library Loan staffs at the Davis Library.

I benefited, too, from the insights and wisdom of friends and colleagues, who over the years have provided helpful suggestions relating to sources and research possibilities on the subject of hurricanes. I am particularly grateful to Ana Cairo, Jorge Ibarra, and Oscar Zanetti for the generosity with which they assisted my work. Francisco Pérez Guzmán was a constant collaborator during the course of this project and offered responses and practical suggestions to help the research along. His command of information was especially enlightening during our visit to the ruins of the Angerona coffee estate and aided in the completion of one key facet of this book. I especially appreciate the assistance of Gabino la Rosa Corzo, who generously shared with me his knowledge of the *cafetales* (coffee plantations) of the nineteenth century. The early section of the book benefited from a careful reading by Jay Barnes, whose own vast knowledge of the great storms added to the clarity of my own thinking about hurricanes. I very much appreciate the thoughtfulness with which K. Lynn Stoner and Luis Martínez-Fernández read the manuscript; their comments and suggestions were enormously useful in the preparation of the final draft. I owe a large debt of gratitude to Rebecca J. Scott for her careful reading of an advanced draft of the completed manuscript. A particular acknowledgment of gratitude is owed to Elaine Maisner of the University of North Carolina Press. Her counsel and collaboration all through the completion of this book and beyond are very much valued.

Marel García and Fidel Requeijo provided continuing support during the years this project was in its research phase in Cuba. Without their help, the completion of this book surely would have been postponed well into the far distant future. A long overdue acknowledgment of appreciation is also owed to Mayra Alonso, of Marazul Tours, who for many years has provided expert assistance in arranging travel between Cuba and the United States.

From my daughters Amara and Maya, I obtain a particular joy in knowing them as adult women and watching them move through life so full of confidence in who they are. They have a rightful sense of the things that matter—and act on it. And to Deborah M. Weissman, my appreciation for the constancy of her support.

LAP

Chapel Hill, North Carolina
September 2000

Winds of Change

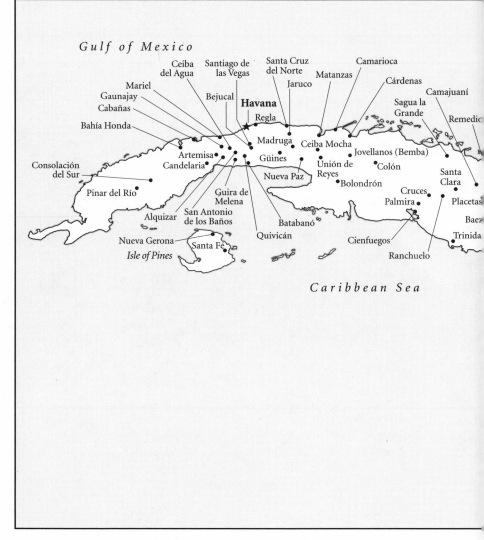

Gulf of Mexico

Ceiba del Agua
Santiago de las Vegas
Santa Cruz del Norte
Camarioca
Matanzas
Cárdenas
Camajuaní
Mariel
Jaruco
Sagua la Grande
Gaunajay
Bejucal
Havana
Remedic
Cabañas
Regla
Bahía Honda
Madruga
Ceiba Mocha
Artemisa
Güines
Jovellanos (Bemba)
Consolación del Sur
Candelaria
Unión de Reyes
Colón
Santa Clara
Nueva Paz
Pinar del Río
Bolondrón
Cruces
Guira de Melena
Palmira
Placetas
Alquizar
San Antonio de los Baños
Batabanó
Cienfuegos
Baez
Quivicán
Trinida
Nueva Gerona
Santa Fé
Ranchuelo
Isle of Pines

Caribbean Sea

Cuba

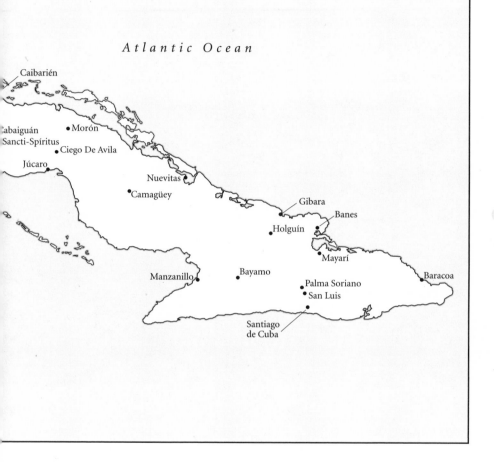

Atlantic Ocean

Caibarién

Cabaiguán
Sancti-Spíritus
Morón
Ciego De Avila

Júcaro

Nuevitas

Camagüey

Gibara
Banes
Holguín
Mayarí

Manzanillo
Bayamo
Palma Soriano
San Luis
Baracoa

Santiago
de Cuba

Introduction

"I was only three years old," Dolores María de Ximeno wrote of the 1870 hurricane in Matanzas, "and I remember perfectly well the roaring of that storm, the strident, frightful whistling. The painful recollection, the overflowing rivers, the horrifying storm causing ruin and desolation never before seen. I carry the memory of the innumerable deaths and sad scenes of desolation."[1] Inocencia Acosta Felipe was in Havana during the hurricane of October 1926. "I was young then but I remember it clearly," she reminisced fifty years later. "Now I'm more terrified of thunder and lightning. My face turns green and yellow and becomes so disfigured with fear that I look like someone else."[2]

Almost everyone in Cuba remembers one hurricane in particular—that one encounter with terror, often at an impressionable age. But, then, hurricanes have a way of making an impression at any age. No passage of time seems to dim the memory of the experience or its effects: it is something that people recall clearly and often. The episode can serve permanently to demarcate a lifetime, to persist as the reference point by which people make those profoundly personal distinctions about their lives as "before" and "after."

To firsthand experiences are often added secondhand accounts, tales transformed into legend and lore, of family tragedies and personal triumphs. The experiences become stories passed down and circulated from grandparents to parents to children, among kin and between friends, recounted so often that they insinuate themselves into the repertoire of reminiscences that others appropriate as their own memories. This is the stuff from which lasting bonds develop, the means by which people come to share those things that give resonance to the proposition of community.

This is also true of entire towns and cities. Almost every city in Cuba incorporates into local lore the experience of at least one hurricane that so totally ravaged the community that daily life was never quite the same again. It is often a defining experience and eventually passes into shared memory perhaps as much as folklore as history.

For communities, too, one hurricane in particular often stands out. For Matanzas, it was October 7–8, 1870, when virtually all the homes along the bay front were swept out to sea, most filled with their occupants. More than a thousand people lost their lives, and municipal authorities appealed to the army for assistance to bury the dead.[3] For many towns in the western half of the island, it was September 4–5, 1888, when a powerful hurricane razed vast stretches of western Cuba. "We cannot even begin to calculate the magnitude of the disaster," a military commander in Pinar del Río informed authorities in Havana several days later, "for the roads remain impassable and the rivers have not yet receded into their banks." Residents of Sagua la Grande also remembered September 1888. "There are no words to describe such anguishing moments," recorded the town historian. "The horrible whistling of the wind that sounded like the prolonged moaning of all of humanity, . . . the frightful crash of buildings collapsing, the clash of doors and windows and of zinc siding and tiles and a thousand other objects that whirled in the air crashing against one another driven by the raging elements. . . . And in the midst of all this despair, the screams and *ayes* that seconded the horrific noises made it sound that the way was being opened to reach the throne of Eternity."[4] Pinar del Río was struck again during October 13–17, 1910, by a storm that assumed legendary proportions as the "five-day hurricane." For Havana, the calamity of October 20, 1926, was etched into popular memory. Some even remembered the exact hour — 10:45 A.M. — when winds in excess of 150 miles per hour roared into the capital; more than six hundred people died and tens of thousands were injured. Pablo Medina recalled 1926 as the "worst of the cyclones [to] hit the city . . . , during which fishing boats floated down streets like deserted gondolas, dead cows dropped on rooftops, and houses flew overhead like birds."[5] The only solace was that the hurricane struck during the day. "Had [the hurricane] occurred at night, and in the dark," recalled one survivor, "the number of victims would have reached horrifying proportions."[6]

The small fishing village of Santa Cruz del Sur remembers November

1932, when a monumental storm wave estimated at more than twenty feet high washed the town away, carrying out to sea more than 2,500 of the total 3,000 residents. Havana was besieged again in 1944, and for hours the capital was buffeted by winds many believed to have approached two hundred miles per hour. Oriente province remembers seven days in October 1963 when Hurricane Flora rained down incalculable destruction; almost all of its rivers—the Cauto, Contramaestre, Salado, Bayamo, Cautillo, Yara, and Camasán—poured over their banks onto the surrounding countryside. Virtually everything in the path of the surging waters was swept away. "All the rivers, creeks, and marshes are out of their beds," Juan Almeida Bosque recorded in his diary at the time, "and now, as if they were a single body, form a vast moving body of water and cause havoc." More than 1,000 persons perished, 175,000 people were evacuated, and 11,000 homes were destroyed.[7]

The stories of hurricanes are thus passed from one generation to the next, as something lived and later as something learned. The stories develop over time into received knowledge that passes as conventional wisdom, is shared as a common experience, and eventually becomes "historical," hence all-inclusive. "Of the historic hurricane that devastated our native city of Matanzas in the year 1870," playwright Federico Villoch recalled, "we heard our parents recount horrific stories, and we still remember, notwithstanding how young we were, when the day after the storm, we looked from the window of our house on América Street, at passing carts loaded with the dead, victims of the overflowing Yumurí and San Juan Rivers: a horrible experience that we continued to relive in our memory in later years."[8] Bandleader Xavier Cugat also remembered a childhood moment, when his family had just moved into a new house outside Havana:

> We were hardly there a month when a hurricane, one of the most ruthless ever experienced, furiously struck. . . . The ones you've seen in newsreels were sunny days in comparison. Our house was not well built. Like a Hollywood rumor, it had little foundation. I thought surely it would be blown over. In fact, my childish fear had me believing the hurricane was the end of the world. When the wind let up somewhat, instead of bringing relief it turned the rain into torrents. Rivers and lakes overflowed. As the waters rose, hopes dropped. Luckily, we had little furniture and belongings to damage. What we had, floated around on the pond that was once our ground floor.[9]

The earliest European accounts of the encounter with Atlantic hurricanes are filled with incomprehension, occasionally assuming fully the form of metaphysical narratives, musings on the larger meanings of the realms of divine signs and malevolent spirits. It was an experience that could induce disquiet and doubt among even the most intrepid *conquistadores* and colonists.

Over time hurricanes were incorporated into the cosmology of the Caribbean, and the attending devastation periodically visited on the islands and mainlands was an eventuality contemplated with a mixture of dread and resignation. Storms intruded early in the history of European colonization and settlement. The first recorded European encounter with an Atlantic hurricane appears to have occurred in September 1494 during the second Columbus voyage to the New World. Samuel Eliot Morison suggests that the explorer had been forewarned of the approaching storm by the appearance of "a repulsive sea monster, big as a medium-sized whale with a carapace like a turtle's, a horrible head like a barrel, and two wings." When such creatures came to the surface, Columbus concluded, it was time to prepare for bad weather.[10]

Storms often destroyed early European settlements, thereby forcing residents to relocate and rebuild elsewhere. During the initial years of colonization, when Europeans did not know better, settlements were established directly in the path of oncoming hurricanes, with tragic outcomes. A hurricane in August 1508 destroyed Santo Domingo at its original location at the Ozama River. Early Spanish colonization efforts in the Gulf of Mexico under Tristán de Luna to settle Ochusa (Pensacola) were frustrated by a powerful hurricane in 1559.[11]

Hurricanes frequently disrupted maritime commerce and communication, both transatlantic travel and circum-Caribbean shipping. All through the early decades of the eighteenth century, hurricanes played havoc with the merchant fleets of Spain. Notwithstanding efforts to arrange the scheduled sailing of the annual treasure fleet around the Atlantic hurricane season, storms often took a heavy toll on Spanish shipping. In September 1622 almost all the 56 ships of the annual fleet were lost in the Florida Straits. All but one of a 15-ship convoy sank in a July 1715 hurricane. Nearly half of the 30 treasure ships went under in a storm in 1733, and another 5 vessels were lost during a hurricane in 1766.

The number of settlements across the Caribbean increased steadily, particularly at those coastal points desirable for their seasonal winds and prevailing currents, and for their maritime accessibility to Europe and to the other islands and mainlands. Bays and harbors filled with towns and cities and expanded into the surrounding countryside. But these were also precisely the zones most susceptible to the forces of the great storms. As European colonies developed and population centers increased, so too did the hazards of the Atlantic hurricanes. The colonial economies were exceedingly vulnerable to the vagaries of unpredictable meteorological furies. Indeed, hurricanes often served to set specific limits on the character and course of development by influencing the type of sustainable economic activity.

/ / / / /

Hurricanes played an important, often decisive, role in the social and economic development of Cuba. This book examines a time of transformation, the years between the end of the eighteenth century and the middle decades of the nineteenth century, with particular attention to the impact of a succession of three hurricanes during the 1840s.

Stunning economic development in early-nineteenth-century Cuba was accompanied by spectacular population growth. Land transportation improved, maritime traffic increased, and commerce expanded. The economy developed and diversified in a balanced fashion. Cuban agricultural production generated vast wealth across the island, bringing on one hand prosperity to many thousands of creole and *peninsular* families and on the other abject poverty and exploitation to hundreds of thousands of African slaves.

Cuban well-being was always subject to the unpredictable and unseen forces of distant markets. A decline by mere pennies in the world price of Cuban agricultural exports could mean instant ruin. Wars in Europe could have similar effects. So could wars in the New World. Colonial insurrection had rocked the European empires in the Americas, in British North America, in the neighboring French colony of Saint Domingue, and in the far-flung Spanish colonies on the mainland. Producers in Cuba contemplated unfolding political developments around them with deepening disquiet and were appalled on learning of the ruin and devastation attending the New World colonial wars of liberation. In the end, creole elites opted for prosperity over independence, economic security over national sovereignty. This does not mean they did not have grievances. Of course, they did. Rather, they were simply unwilling to risk economic ruin for political gain.

But it was also true that ruin came in many forms and from many sources, not the least of which were the wind-borne rain-driven calamities of the Atlantic hurricanes. Repeatedly the island was subject to ruinous storms. Hurricanes, though unpredictable, were fairly common occurrences and time and again resulted in staggering losses to life and property.

What made the hurricanes of the mid-nineteenth century noteworthy were their timing and intensity. During a crucial period in Cuban development, against a larger backdrop of shifting world market forces, the island was struck by three destructive hurricanes in succession—in September 1842, October 1844, and October 1846. These storms permanently changed some of the dominant features of the colonial economy, including land tenure forms, labor organization, and production systems. No less important, many social relationships around which colonial society had developed were reconfigured with lasting consequences.

Virtually every facet of Cuban life was affected by the great nineteenth-century hurricanes. The storms rearranged the terms by which social classes defined their place in the colonial order and hence transformed their relationship to everything else. They set in relief the colony's relationship to the metropolis and, more significant, placed in full public view many of the assumptions governing the peninsula's administration of the island.

/ / / / /

The objective of this study is to insert the phenomenon of mid-nineteenth-century hurricanes into the larger circumstances of the Cuban condition as one more variable in the formation of nation. This is an exploration of environmental history within the framework of the national experience. Specifically, this study examines the ways that the catastrophic storms of the 1840s shaped socioeconomic developments in nineteenth-century Cuba, by which, too, the limits of human agency were defined even as the circumstances of human choice were refashioned. Hurricanes must be viewed as factors—sometimes decisive factors—shaping the options and outcomes to which huge numbers of people were obliged to respond and to which they were often required to reconcile themselves. Indeed, it was precisely at the conjuncture of response and reconciliation that some of the more notable facets of Cuban national development assumed form. Hurricanes and their aftermaths loomed large in the sequence of factors influencing social and economic developments in nineteenth-century Cuba and were deeply implicated in the ways that the nation evolved.

These were not solely matters of human loss and material destruction, of course, although these consequences should not be minimized or, worse yet, ignored. Just as important are the ways that hurricanes shaped the strategies of economic development, influenced the organization of labor systems, and acted on the social determinants of nationality. This has much to do with the circumstances by which people were bound together as a nation in the face of forces beyond their control, often even beyond their capacity to conceive, in cooperative efforts of long-term recovery and the collective will to prevail.

Under certain circumstances, the calamities visited on Cuba exposed new realities and larger truths about the colonial condition; about the role of the state, the nature of class structures, the character of slavery and race relations; about kinship and community; and, in the end, about the people that Cubans were becoming. This work considers the hurricane as a flash point by which to illuminate the colonial landscape during a brief but revelatory moment, when complex relationships — between the moral and material, between production systems and political structures, between national character and historical context — suddenly appeared with a clarity never before imagined.

The material foundations and the well-being of tens of thousands of people, free and slave, were subject to the power of natural forces capable of destroying in a few hours the work of many decades. Urban residents and rural folk alike, their way of life, their occupations and routines of daily existence, were changed permanently and in the process transformed the course of Cuban history. The hurricane entered the cosmology of Cuba as a fact of life, a specter against which people were obliged in the ordinary course of events to mediate the possibility of potential catastrophe with the needs of daily life.

Because hurricanes were recurring phenomena, they played an important role in forging a people into a nation. They loomed as forces of vast proportions, larger than human effort and negating the proposition of humans as the center and measure of all things, but in relation to which people developed inexorable reciprocities in ways large and small, in shared grief and adversity, in individual triumph and collective recovery.

The preponderance of the historical literature has correctly assigned a privileged place to the proposition of human agency: that people, for example — or cultures, or nations — act upon each other as a function of power or in response to powerlessness, with kindly intent or with mischievous purpose, with volition if not always with perfectly understood purpose. The range of this interaction is, of course, endless, but the historiography of the human condition shares common assumptions about the dominant place of human initiative. This study suggests another possibility. That is, there are occasions when human agency is overwhelmed or altogether negated by larger forces against which people are simply powerless to resist and which have the capacity to affect the well-being of communities — both local and national—in ways that are both dramatic and decisive, immediate and long-lasting.

How individuals responded to adversity as a shared experience—how misfortune and misery were transacted and in the end transformed into a source of empowerment—offers insights into the origins of nation and the character of nationality. These circumstances converted acts of individual heroism into facets intrinsic to the meaning of nation and in the process served to inscribe heroism and sacrifice as commonly shared characteristics by which a people represent themselves to one another and to the outside world. It was also out of this experience that the proposition of national will was forged, in terms accessible to almost all, for the experience was common to almost all. The resolve to put together shattered lives and, more important, the determination to prevail over disruption and disarray, gave decisive form to normative hierarchies by which Cubans would negotiate adversity of all types.

Hurricanes thus offer an opportunity to examine the larger social circumstances of colonial society in times of stress, the points at which the routines of daily life were interrupted and suspended, when "normal" became impossible. Nothing, perhaps, escapes the searching gaze of the historian as readily as the habits of everyday life, those practices and behaviors so ordinary that they cease to be apprehended at all, even—and, indeed, especially—by the very people who ordered a large part of their quotidian existence around the rhythm of routine. In Cuba, actions repeated day after day, over long periods of time, gave order to the structures by which people organized their daily lives and in the aggregate validated the very appearance of normality of colonial social structures. It was the repetitiousness of the act that etched the grooves by which the boundaries of daily life derived public form and private meaning.

These were precisely the conditions that were impossible to sustain during the disarray occasioned by the fury of a hurricane. Because people longed to return to routine, previously taken for granted, they could summon up the cognitive categories around which to articulate the ordinary with a newfound sense of self-interrogation—and often urgency—as something to which they sought to return. In that process they gave ordinary life a clarity and texture unimaginable under any other circumstance. Hurricanes disrupted the conventions of custom and made patterns of common practice all but impossible to continue. By shattering the assumptions governing the workings of everyday life, hurricanes thus revealed the social tissue that gave form and function to the Cuban condition.

///// /

Not as well known are the larger ecological consequences of the great storms. These issues lie beyond the scope of the present study, but the question merits raising. Long before the Europeans arrived in the West Indies, perhaps even before human life itself appeared on the islands, and certainly throughout the many centuries that followed, Atlantic hurricanes shaped the definitions by which the Caribbean would develop into a distinct historico-geographic region. Storms played a part in the formation of shared regional characteristics. The fauna and flora of the latitudes of Middle America were often dispersed and distributed over the water and across the islands by powerful winds. Winds bearing seeds and spores and transporting birds and insects were the means by which the landscape and ecology of the region were formed over long stretches of time.

Unknown, either, is how hurricanes of the past, especially the fearsome storms of the nineteenth century, affected resident and migratory birds, no less than local species of wildlife. The hurricanes tore open the canopy of the tropical forests, stripping extensive stretches of trees of leaves, flowers, and fruits. That these developments were simultaneous with the expansion of sugarcane cultivation, which occurred also at the expense of vast acreage of virgin woodlands, combined to contribute to the deforestation of immense regions of central western Cuba. Hundreds of thousands of acres of forestlands were thus affected, with untold if unknown evironmental consequences.

1. Where Winds Gather

Every street was impassable, every roof was gone, every lane closed up, shingles and immense pieces of wood, stone, and bricks were knee deep in the streets. . . . The greater number of the houses were levelled with the earth or unroofed; the largest trees were torn up by the roots, or their branches were twisted off them. . . . The wind rushed under the broad verandahs, tore off the roofs, demolished the walls, and the pillars were levelled in rows. . . . The country villas were no more, and the once beautiful and smiling scenery was now also gone. No vestiges remained of the woods and the groves of palms, and even the soil which produced them was washed away; almost all the public buildings were razed to the ground.

  James E. Alexander, Transatlantic Sketches *(1833)*

Parents beheld their children, and children their parents, husbands their wives, and wives their husbands, buried in the ruins, or strewn around them disfigured corpses; others, with fractured limbs, and dreadful mutilations, were still alive, and many of them rescued from under the fallen buildings; and it was dreadful to hear their heart-piercing cries of agony. Many streets in the town were totally impassable, from the houses having been lifted up from their foundations, and thrown in one mass of ruins into the roads. Masses of rubbish, broken furniture, ships spars, packages of merchandise, huge blocks of mahogany, seemed to have been washed up, and carried by the wind or the tide to great distances, so as completely to block up the streets and highway.

  Andrew Halliday, The West Indies *(1837)*

The tempest rages with such fury that trees are uprooted, buildings thrown down, and ships lifted high on the beach. So vivid and incessant is the lightning that the whole heavens seem in conflagration; appalling thunders mingle their stormy music with the roar of the waves, the shriek of the winds, and the frantic cries of those are in expectation of almost immediate death. The roof of a house may be torn away, and its doors and windows be driven in, yet there is little hope of safety in flight, for there is danger being blown over a precipice, or struck by the boards and shingles, which are drifted to and fro as if they were light as threads of gossamers. . . . The island from end to end is one scene of desolation. . . . Cane fields and provision grounds are as thoroughly devastated as if a troop of wild elephants had rushed over them.

   Jabez Marrat, In the Tropics *(1884)*

It is not given to the pen, Your Excellency, to paint with such frightful colors the terror experienced on that horrible night. . . . I know of no other instance of inhabitants drowning in their own homes as a result of water driven by the wind through the doors, windows, and the roofs, whose tiles flew about like feathers. Many fled into the streets, envisioning their imminent death by being buried alive in the ruins of their homes or drowning by the raging waves of the sea that invaded the town, carrying their children in desperate search for another place of shelter. . . . The scene we confront is one of anguish and widespread destitution.

   Manuel de Mediavilla, Cienfuegos, to Governor General *(June 8, 1832)*

The winds originate from the eastern waters of the Atlantic, from somewhere on the vast oceanic expanse between the Cape Verde Islands and Barbados, at the point where the prevailing northeasterly breezes above the equator converge with southeasterly breezes from below the equator. The strongest winds begin to stir during the months around the autumnal equinox, the time of the equatorial doldrums, in the still region of moist air between the steady trades. Catastrophic winds begin as calm air.

   The still air, well moistened by evaporation, starts to churn under the strong sun, becoming unstable and unpredictable, forming low-pressure systems by which the warm air is driven inward and upward by convection into cooler zones, there to spiral and swirl. Warm vapors rise and in the process cool and condense into billowing clouds. Evaporation and conduction transfer immense quantities of heat and moisture into the atmosphere and eventually give definition and direction to the mass of moving air.

   The churning winds migrate westward, driven by trade winds, often on a journey of thousands of miles, over many days—sometimes weeks, gaining momentum and velocity as they draw strength from warm moist air pulled over the tropical waters. Bands of squalls and thunderstorms swirl in alignment with the direction of the winds, often three hundred to four hundred miles in advance of the approaching center. It is possible to speak broadly of a corridor extending from longitude 56° west to 96° and from latitude 10° to 30° north—the area otherwise known as the Caribbean Sea—and extending upward into the Gulf of Mexico and Atlantic Ocean, over which these winds most frequently traverse the New World.

/ / / / /

The signs of approaching winds assumed recognizable form for early European settlers in the Caribbean, for in these times all that was available were signs. First, there was a stillness in the air, experienced as moisture-laden air and as a sultry, heavy atmosphere. Breezes began to stir often days in advance, shifting daily as erratic movement from land to sea and back again. Falling temperatures were at times accompanied by indigo blue skies. Winds pushed in their advance long rolling waves, often a thousand miles ahead of the center, at speeds slightly less than the velocity of the winds that produced them. Then there appeared the unmistakable signs: a thin cirrus haze, followed by the true cirrus: magnificent clouds shaped as long white feathery plumes brushed across a clear azure sky—a phenomenon early associated with approaching atmospheric mass—and often converging to a point on the horizon suggesting the center of the approaching disturbance. Solar and lunar haloes often accompanied the cirrus haze, mostly as spectacular crimson skies at sunrise and sunset.

The early Europeans quickly learned to divine the meaning of these signs. Information was obtained first from Native Americans. Colonists in St. Christopher, wrote John Oldmixon in 1708, were tutored by one elderly Indian in the "Prognosticks to know when a hurricane was coming":

If it will come on the full Moon, . . . then observe these Signs: That day you will see the Skies very turbulent, the Sun more red than at other Times, a great Calm, and the Hills clear of Clouds or Fogs over them, which in the High-Lands are seldom so. In the Hollows of the Earth or Wells, there will be a great Noise, as if you were in a great Storm; the Stars at Night will look very big with Burs about them, the North-West Sky very black and foul, the Sea Smelling stronger than at Other Times . . . and sometime that Day for an Hour or two, the Wind blows very hard Westerly, out of its usual Course.[1]

The winds reached the Caribbean mostly in August, September, and October—although they were known as early as June and July or as late as November—entering through well-defined paths, usually by way of the northern Windward Islands, moving at a speed of 12 to 15 miles per hour. By this point they may well have expanded to a radius exceeding hundreds of miles, driven by counterclockwise winds attaining sustained velocities between 75 and 150 miles per hour, sometimes more. The course as well as the intensity of the winds generally coincided with the season. Early in the summer they recurved northward out of the western Caribbean. In August and September the winds typically swept in a northwesterly direction through the eastern Caribbean; in October they roared northward over the waters and islands of the southern Caribbean. Their frequency varied from year to year: sometimes there were as few as one or two a year, sometimes none; other times as many as ten to fifteen.[2]

They may have been unexpected, but they were not unfamiliar, and the arrival of each new season raised a specter of danger looming just beyond the horizon. A brooding disquiet descended on the Caribbean in anticipation of the destructive fury of the winds from the east. It has always been thus, since the Native American peoples dispersed among wide-flung islands of the Caribbean archipelago.

/ / / / /

The word *huracán* passed into the Spanish vernacular from indigenous usage. The Taíno Indians used "huracán" to mean malignant forces that took the form of winds of awesome proportions and destructive power, winds that blew from all four corners of the earth. The word was found in a variety of derivative forms, including *hunrakán*, *yuracán*, *yerucán*, and *yorocán*, and appeared in use among the pre-Columbian peoples of Mexico, Central America, and the northern coast of South America. All forms signified the name of a malevolent god, possessed of the capacity to inflict immense destruction.[3] Among the Maya, *hurakán* was the name of one of the mightiest gods; *hurakán*, *cabrakán* (earthquake), and *chirakán* (volcano) constituted the three most powerful natural forces in the Mayan culture.[4]

Among the Taíno in the Caribbean, "huracán" was the name of a powerful demon given to periodic displays of destructive fury. Indeed, the Taíno explanation of the creation of the Antilles held that huracán had shattered the coastline of the mainland and subsequently scattered the land fragments into the Caribbean archipelago.[5] Hurakán was one of the principal deities of the pre-Columbian pantheon, to be periodically placated, typically by

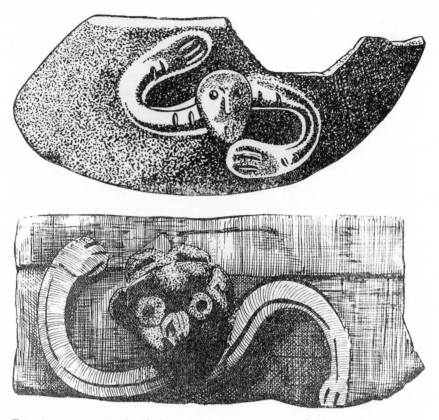

Taíno images associated with the representation of hurricanes. The similarity to the modern meteorological icon of the hurricane is suggestive. Reprinted from Fernando Ortiz, El huracán: Su mitología y sus símbolos *(Mexico, 1947).*

ritual supplication of music, song, and dance. In *Historia general y natural de las Indias, isla y tierra firme de la mar océano* (1535), one of the earliest European accounts of the indigenous population of the Caribbean, chronicler Gonzalo Fernández de Oviedo, who resided in the Caribbean intermittently between the 1510s and the 1530s, wrote of the terror inspired by huracán: "[T]he way the devil . . . is depicted assumes a variety of colors and ways. When the devil wishes to frighten [the Indians] he threatens them with huracán, which means storm. These storms are so fierce that they topple houses and uproot many large trees. . . . [I]t is a frightful thing to see, which without doubt appeared [to the Indians] to be the work of the devil."[6]

One of the earliest known European uses of huracán appears in Pedro Mártir de Anglería's 1511 chronicle *Décadas del Nuevo Mundo*. He wrote of "a monstrous whirlwind [*inaudito torbellino*] from the east that lifted even the heavens" and continued:

> The violence was of such force that it lifted up by the roots the largest of trees. . . . Many affirm that the sea extended itself further inland and rose higher than ever before. The islanders thus muttered among themselves that our people had disturbed the elements and brought on such portentous developments. The islanders call these tempests of winds *huracanes*, which they say strike that island often, but never before with such violence and fury. None of those alive had ever in their time seen or heard the elders speak of a comparable storm capable of uprooting the largest of trees.[7]

Huracán, acknowledged explicitly as a word of Indian origin, also appeared in the *Historia de las Indias* by Bartolomé de las Casas, published in 1575. "At this time," Las Casas wrote of a storm in 1495, "four ships . . . in the port were lost in a great storm, what the Indians called in their language *huracán*, and which we now also call *huracanes*, something that almost all of us have experienced at sea or on land." Fernández de Oviedo observed firsthand what the Indians meant by huracán and recorded the episode in his chronicle. "*Huracán*, in the language of this island," he wrote, "properly means an excessively severe storm or tempest; for, in fact, it is nothing other than a powerful wind and an intensive and excessive rainfall, together or either one of these two things by itself." Oviedo added: "No one on this island who lived through these storms will ever forget the experience."[8] Pedro Simón discovered the word "huracán" in use among Indians on *Tierra Firme*. "In the language of these regions," Simón recorded, "the wind is called *huracán*, from which the Spaniards took the word, improving the vocabulary to call the turbulence of winds *huracán*. . . . Every effort was made to learn the language of the Indians with whom they deal, committing to memory among others this word *huracán* and what it signified, and they used it to refer to tumultuous winds."[9] The word "huracán" appears to have obtained English language usage for the first time in Richard Eden's 1555 translation of Mártir de Anglería's account as "furacanes," and it appeared during the next one hundred years in various forms — including "herycano," "furicano," "hericano," "huricano," "heuricane," and "hurican" — before assuming its present form, "hurricane," in the late seventeenth century.[10]

/ / / / /

Before hurricanes passed into the realm of the European familiar, they dwelled in a place of fear and foreboding. Certainly Europeans before Columbus had direct knowledge of storms. The mariners and maritime merchants of the Mediterranean had accumulated a vast store of information on storms at sea. But nothing in the weather of the Mediterranean could prepare Europeans for the New World tropical hurricane. "Of the terrible storms believed to exist in all the oceans of the world," Las Casas declared, "the ones of these seas in these islands and *tierra firme* are apt to be the worst." William Strachey wrote in awe of his encounter with a tropical hurricane in 1609, contrasting it with previous experiences in the Mediterranean:

> [A] dreadful storm and hideous began to blow from out the northeast, which, swelling and roaring as it were by fits, some hours with more violence than others, at length did beat all light from Heaven; which like a hell of darkness, turned black upon us, so much the more fuller of horror as in such cases horror and fear use to overrun the troubled and over-mastered senses of all. . . . What shall I say? Winds and seas were as mad, as fury and rage could make them. For my own part, I had been in some storms before, as well upon the coast of Barbary and Algiers, in the Levant, and once, more distressful in the Adriatic gulf in a bottom of Candy. . . . Yet all that I have ever suffered gathered together, might not hold comparison with this.[11]

Knowledge of the hurricane phenomenon did little to calm European dread. On the contrary, it only deepened apprehension. "It is . . . in the interval between the beginning of August and the latter end of October," Bryan Edwards observed as early as the eighteenth century, "that hurricanes, those dreadful visitations of the Almighty, are apprehended. The prognostics of these elementary conflicts, have been minutely described by various writers, and their effects are known by late mournful experience to every inhabitant of every island within the tropics, but their immediate cause seems to lie far beyond the limits of our circumscribed knowledge."[12]

Surviving first-person accounts of the early encounters with hurricanes convey a sense of disbelief and horror. It was difficult for Europeans to imagine that such force could be released from unstable atmospheric conditions, and all who witnessed it struggled mightily to give narrative structure to the experience. "Good God!" exclaimed a young Alexander Hamilton to his father after a hurricane struck St. Croix in September 1772, "what horror and destruction. Its [sic] impossible for me to describe or you to form any idea of it." To him,

> It seemed as if a total dissolution of nature was taking place. The roaring of the sea and wind, fiery meteors flying about it in the air, the prodigious glare of almost perpetual lightning, the crash of the falling houses, and the ear-piercing shrieks of the distressed, were sufficient to strike aston- ishment into Angels. A great part of the buildings throughout the Island are levelled to the ground, almost all the rest very much shattered; sev- eral persons killed and numbers utterly ruined; whole families running about the streets, unknowing where to find a place of shelter; the sick exposed to the keeness [sic] of water and air without a bed to lie upon, or a dry covering to their bodies; and our harbours entirely bare. In a word, misery, in all its most hideous shapes, spread over the whole face of the country.[13]

Eight years later a monstrous storm laid waste to Barbados. "It is im- possible to express the Dreadful scene it has Occasion'd at Barbadoes and the Condition of the miserable Inhabitants," wrote Admiral Lord George Rodney of the hurricane of October 1780. "Nothing but occular demonstra- tion could have convinced me it was possible for Wind to have caused so total destruction of an Island remarkable for its numerous and well built Habitations." In fact, the magnitude of the damage persuaded Rodney that it had actually been produced by an earthquake:

> And I am convinc'd that the Violence of the Wind must have prevented the Inhabitants from feeling the Earthquake which certainly attended the Storm. Nothing but an Earthquake could have occasion'd the foun- dations of the Strongest buildings to be rent, and so total has been the devastation that not one house or one Church, as I am well inform'd but what has been destroy'd. The whole Face of the Country appears an entire ruin, and the most Beautiful Island in the World has the appearance of a Country laid waste by Fire, and Sword, and appears to the Imagination more Dreadful than it is possible for me to find Words to express.[14]

The Reverend George Wilson Bridges described in graphic detail another hurricane of the 1780 season as it passed through Jamaica. "[T]he sea seemed mingled with the clouds," Bridges wrote, "while the heaving swell of the earth, as it rolled beneath its bed, bore the raging floods over their natural boundaries, overwhelmed the coasts, and retreating with irresistible force, bore all before them." He continued:

> To the distance of half a mile, the waves carried and fixed vessels of no ordinary size, leaving them the providential means of sheltering the houseless inhabitant. Not a tree, or bush, or cane was to be seen: universal desolation prevailed, and the wretched victims of violated nature, who would obtain no such shelter, and who had not time to fly to the protecting rocks, were either crushed beneath the falling ruins, or swept away, and never heard from more. The midnight horrors of the scene were viewed as the last convulsions of an expiring world. . . . The scattered remains of houses, whose tenants were dead or dying—the maddening search for wives and children, who were lost—the terrific howling of the frightened negroes, as it mingled with the whistling but subsiding winds—and the deluged state of the earth, strewed with the wreck of nature, and ploughed into deep ravines, was the scene which day-light ushered in; and, as if to mock the misery it had caused, the morning sun was again bright and cheerful.[15]

Some eyewitness accounts provide detailed information about the effects of hurricanes on agriculture. British planter Christopher Jeaffreson had been in St. Christopher five years when he experienced his first hurricane. "It bore downe strong stone walled houses before it," he wrote in November 1681, "as well as trees and timber buildings. It left me not a house or sugar-worke standing on my plantation. It broke and twisted my sugar-canes, rooted up my Cassava, and washed the graine and new-planted puttatoes."[16] A newspaper account of the hurricane of August 1831 in Barbados depicted a grim landscape: "Were you to ride through the country you would actually be shocked. . . . Not a dwelling-house, not a set of sugar-works, and but few pieces of even the walls of the mills are to be seen on the road. . . . Scenes of ruin and devastation are everywhere to be met with. For the last two days the living have been employed in burying the dead; this is a most distressing sight; wherever one turns, there are coffins to be met with. . . . All is in desolation and ruin."[17]

/ / / / /

Hurricanes caused destruction in many forms. The winds exerted a powerful force on the ocean surface and generated enormous swells often far in advance of the approaching storm. Gale-force winds lashed the coast as the hurricane moved out of deep water. The enormous force transferred to the sea by wind turbulence was deployed on land with devastating effect.

The immediate power of the hurricane was contained in the storm surge, as winds drove tides, currents, and waves against the shoreline, pounding the exposed coast. The combination of mighty winds and low barometric pressure acted literally to lift the water from the ocean basin in the form of a huge mound sweeping atop the sea, gaining height and momentum as it moved across shallow coastal waters in its approach to land. This towering dome of water sometimes extended as long as fifty miles across and served as the base on which high waves were able to penetrate low-lying regions farther inland. A hurricane that made landfall at or near the mouth of a river often drove existing water back in upon itself deep inland, resulting in widespread flooding to the surrounding low-lying countryside. The larger effect of the storm surge, moreover, depended on the phase of the lunar tide at the time of the impact. The combination of a storm surge and a normal high tide could produce a catastrophic storm tide. Some hurricanes created storm surges along coastlines and bay fronts that rose twenty or more feet above sea level and were capable of extending ruination along flat land surfaces miles inland.[18]

The destructive power of the storm surge was heightened by flooding caused by a rising sea level in combination with the violence of the surf pounding the land. Swelling ocean waves crashed on coastal settlements, along bay fronts, and up inland rivers. Waves seemed to explode upon landfall, erupting into colossal plumes of white spray. Devastation was marked at those points where shallow estuaries stretched upriver, in which the rising hurricane tide surged inland and inundated riverside communities. Similarly, low-lying land, including zones of less than two or three feet above sea level, sometimes extending miles inland from the coast, was especially vulnerable to the storm surge. Productive coastlands were often damaged by flooding saltwater, leading to defoliation of interior watersheds. Oldmixon described the great Jamaica hurricane of 1722 this way:

> The inhabitants had some Prognostick of it before they felt its Fury. The Weather being very unsettled, the Wind often shifting, and more than both these a prodigious uncommon Swell of the Sea, which threw them into a terrible Consternation, it throwing up the Day before several hundred Tons of Stones and large pieces of Rocks over the Wall of the East End of Port-Royal, though at the same time there was very little if any

Wind. The Town was overflowed with Water the Night before, occasioned by the driving of the aforementioned Swell.[19]

Under such circumstances, the wave action was similar to a battering ram pounding on all surfaces. The combination of powerful currents and coastal waves uprooted trees and undermined building foundations, making land structures all the more susceptible to the impact of winds blowing in excess of one hundred miles per hour. With the weight of water approaching two thousand pounds per cubic yard, protracted pounding over an extended period of time had other devastating effects. Swells filled with floating wreckage and heavy debris, carried forward by currents that accompanied the storm surge. Lurching and pitching with the hurricane tide and wave action, accelerated by the wind, they added to the force of the water that battered other land structures. Floating debris, often carried miles inland, and airborne refuse added to the general destruction. This is what Bryan Young recalled best of the shifting gales during the storm of 1831 in Barbados: "[T]he hurricane again burst from the western points with a violence beyond conception, hurling before it thousands of missiles, the fragments of every unsheltered structure of human art. The strongest houses were caused to vibrate to their foundations."[20]

The ferocity of the winds added to the terror of the storm. Winds often reaching 150 miles per hour, sometimes capable of gusting to 200 miles per hour or more and occasionally spawning localized tornadoes, released enormous forces that were capable of sheering the landscape of raised surfaces of all types, natural as well as man-made. Hurricane winds had devastating effects on fields of standing crops, especially corn, sugarcane, and banana plants. The wind-borne debris had predictable effects. "At midnight the clouds burst in a severe squall," recalled Captain James Alexander:

> Then the work of destruction commenced; every succeeding five minutes there was heard in the town the dreadful crash of falling trees, chimneys, roofs, and houses themselves, above the roaring of the gale. Those who had cellars to their houses took shelter in them, overpowered with feelings of intense agony; they were helpless, and could only commit themselves to the care of a merciful Providence. Huge pieces of timber, tiles, and bricks would continually strike the frail tenements, and the inhabitants whose houses had been overwhelmed, would be heard wandering about the streets crying for shelter. . . . The air was filled with shattered fragments, threatening with instant death those exposed without shelter

to the pelting storm. The majestic palms would be tossed to and fro as a withe, then snapped off with an appalling crash, or uplifted from the earth with terrific force, and dashed against the buildings they were wont to shade.[21]

Rain-soaked winds driven inland delivered still more destruction. Salt-saturated air was particularly harmful to the vast expanses of forests, groves, and orchards. Towering walls of white foam crashed against the shore, where the salt spray was lifted by driving winds and swept miles inland over agricultural zones. "The sea all this time rolled in mountain waves towards the shore," as Captain Alexander described one hurricane in 1833, "and was lashed into one immense sheet of white foam. As the quick rising billows uplifted their heads, the wind carried the salt spray into the troubled air, and swiftly bore it on its pinions over the ill-fated island."[22]

Agricultural lands were frequently rendered useless for an entire planting cycle or longer, until sea salt was leached from the soil. Robert Schomburgk recalled his experience with a hurricane in Tortola in 1831: "I was residing . . . at St. Bernard's, a hill the summit of which is about 1000 feet above the sea; the dwelling-house, however, is at an elevation only of 920 feet. The day after the gale the leaves of the trees and plants in the garden which had remained became black, from the contact with the sea-water spray . . . and the rain-water in the cistern and vats, which was to be used for domestic purposes, was rendered brackish." This was the same phenomenon that Alexander Hamilton described in St. Croix, where he noted: "it was observed that the rain was surprizingly salt [sic]. . . . Indeed the water is so brackish and full of sulphur that there is hardly any drinking it."[23]

Vegetation bore the dramatic effects of hurricanes. Trees that were not uprooted or truncated were often totally defoliated. Shrubs, bushes, and plants pounded by raging winds appeared as if scorched by fire, bearing the combined effects of the saltwater spray and the pounding of sand and dirt driven by powerful winds, resembling sandblasting. Foliage singed by wind-driven saltwater could be found forty-five miles from the ocean.[24] "The whole face of the country was laid waste," Andrew Halliday wrote with astonishment in 1837, "scarcely any sign of vegetation existed, and what did remain was of a sickly green. The surface of the earth appeared as if fire has passed over it scorching and burning up everything. The few trees that were still standing were stripped of their boughs and foliage, and appeared as withered trunks," Sir Gilbert Blane had witnessed something similar in October 1780: "All the fruits of the earth, then standing, have been destroyed; most of the trees of the island have been torn up by the roots; and (what will give as strong an idea of the force of the wind as anything) many of them were stripped of their bark." [25]

The destructive force of hurricanes was also contained in torrential rains, particularly in the inland regions and perhaps nowhere with greater devastation than in mountainous zones. Heavy, continuous rainfall set the stage for the next series of adversities. Rainfall of fifteen to twenty inches or more caused localized flooding in some areas and deadly flash floods and mud slides in others. In mountainous regions, where drainage was downward along slopes and hillsides, the effects were often frightful. Long after the winds had passed, rain continued for hours, often days, and resulted in extensive damage through inland flooding.

And when the winds had subsided and the rains had ceased, perils of other kinds descended on the stricken land. The specter of disease and epidemics cast a dark shadow over the ravaged communities. Famine threatened. In the absence of shelter, adequate food supplies, or potable water, the survivors faced a new round of hardships. [26]

/ / / / /

Expanding European settlements in the West Indies—all along the coastal regions, around the bays and harbors, and inland along rivers and streams, in the fertile foothills and the interior valleys—inevitably meant an evermore populated landscape, with the accompanying architecture of colonialism and the development of agriculture and commerce. This growing European presence situated itself in those zones most subject to direct encounters with hurricanes.

In fact, losses had less to do with the character of the hurricane than with the nature of European development of the local economy and population centers. The hazards of storms increased in direct proportion to the expansion of the European presence and in relationship to the sites selected for settlement, the growth of towns and cities, and the increase and diversification of economic activities. Settlements at the confluence of inland rivers meant that populations were concentrated in zones most vulnerable to hurricane flooding.

The greatest intensity of a hurricane's destructive power—that is, the point of maximum intensity—occurred at the moment of landfall, as the storm transferred energy from sea to land. The expansion of coastal towns and cities along bays and river estuaries, so prominent an aspect of colonial economies wholly dependent on maritime traffic, the increase of trade and commerce, and the development of agriculture and ranching all produced conditions that were especially vulnerable to hurricane damage.

European architectural styles were also inimical to the well-being of communities located in hurricane zones. Captain James Alexander perceptively observed that in the British colony of Barbados "the style of building throughout the island was . . . very badly adapted to the clime," adding: "Instead of flat roofs, the houses were covered in with a lofty and clumsy structure, quite disproportionate to the rest of the building, and offering a resistance to the wind, which too often has occasioned their destruction." Indeed, in the 1780 hurricane more than 4,500 residents were buried alive under the ruins of their own homes.[27]

Spanish colonial architecture was similarly ill-adapted to specific properties of the hurricane. Towns and cities planned around central plazas, which expanded outward in square grids along narrow streets, were exposed to the winds and wind-driven rains of hurricanes, as was the typical rectangular construction of the buildings, often with overhanging barrel tile roofs. In discussing the relationship between architecture and hurricane damage, engineer James Power suggested that the "simple box type structure[s]" in close proximity to one another with roof overhangs, such as was found in Spanish colonial settlements, were especially vulnerable to hurricanes.[28] These were precisely the conditions that traveler James Phillippo observed during his visit to Havana in the early 1850s. "The streets of Havana are formed generally at right angles," Phillippo wrote, "and are narrow, confined, irregular, unpaved and undrained. . . . Many of the thoroughfares also are, in wet weather, dirty and muddy, to the no small inconvenience of pedestrians. . . . Some of the more public streets are paved, though very indifferently, and the frequent rains, or rather cataracts, washing away the soil and sand from between the huge stones, render the footing insecure." One foreign resident of Havana was astonished by conditions in the capital: "The streets are not paved; there is no drain for the water; the ground continues in the state in which it was originally created."[29]

/ / / / /

Hardly anything, it seemed, could withstand the combined fury of the storm surge, winds, and flooding. Port facilities, including wharves and piers, cargo docks, shipyards, and berths, as well as vessels in anchorage, were ravaged. Residential dwellings were notably unprotected against wind; if located along the coast or on rivers or streams, they were susceptible to flooding. Often, the humbler the dwelling the more complete the destruction. Farm buildings, including storage facilities and curing houses, often of lighter construction, were exposed to driving winds. Loss of human life by drowning was especially high along coastal zones as well as inland rivers and streams. Domestic fowl and livestock, too, suffered the effects of winds, rain, and flooding. Trees were toppled by the combined force of rain and wind, as heavy rain preceding hurricane winds often saturated the ground, thereby weakening the capacity of the soil to retain root systems.

Hurricanes were the seasonal scourge of the Caribbean. Between 1493 and 1885, no less than four hundred hurricanes were recorded in the region.[30] They were anticipated with dread and entered the realm of the popular familiar through local folklore and received wisdom, and thereupon expanded into the realm of knowledge of the European world. In 1609 nine ships carrying five hundred English colonists bound for Virginia were dispersed by a midsummer hurricane. One vessel separated from the others was driven onto the reefs of the Bermudas; it subsequently became the basis on which England advanced its claim over the small island chain. But at least as noteworthy, one survivor's account served as the source of William Shakespeare's *The Tempest*, and thus was the hurricane of 1609 immortalized:

> The sky, it seems, would pour down stinking pitch,
> But that the sea, mounting to th' welkin's cheek,
> Dashes the fire out. O, I have suffered
> With those that I saw suffer: a brave vessel —
> Who had, not doubt, some noble creature in her —
> Dashed all to pieces! O, the cry did knock
> Against my very heart — poor souls, they perished.
> Had I been any god of power, I would
> Have sunk the sea within the earth or ere
> It should the good ship so have swallowed, and
> The fraughting souls within her.[31]

/ / / / /

All through the early decades of Spanish conquest and colonization in the Caribbean and the adjacent mainlands, hurricanes disrupted maritime traffic, interrupted reconnaissance and exploration, destroyed vessels both at sea and at anchorage, and devastated coastal settlements. Maritime authorities in Spain quickly learned to avoid the peak period of hurricane activity through carefully planned transatlantic departures and punctual returns.

That Cuba experienced Atlantic hurricanes in disproportionate regularity was related largely to circumstances of geography. Stretching 750 miles in length, the long axis of the island lies east and west along the middle latitudes of the New World, extending lengthwise across the most frequented trajectories by which hurricanes traversed the Caribbean into the Gulf of Mexico.

Cuba was particularly vulnerable on two counts. Extensive coastal settlements, centered principally around two hundred harbors, bays, and inlets on both coasts, were directly exposed to the immediate impact of the storm surge.[32] The interior faced adversity of another kind. Cuba's fluvial network originated from the center of the island along two watersheds: north and south. More than two hundred rivers, and at least as many streams and creeks, drained three principal mountain systems, periodically subjecting tens of thousands of residents to the hazard of inundation and flash floods. Ordinary spring rains, the Reverend Abiel Abbot learned during a visit in 1828, routinely threatened residents with loss of life and property. "In the rainy season," Abbot explained, "the water falls in a deluge, the brooks roar from the mountains, and the rivers are full. The fields are almost a sheet of water, and the roads are almost impassable."[33]

Over the course of 350 years between the 1490s and the 1840s, hurricanes large and small are known to have struck Cuba, often annually, sometimes repeatedly in the same year, resulting in inestimable property damage and the loss of countless thousands of lives. Alvar Núñez Cabeza de Vaca provided one of the more complete descriptions of an early sixteenth-century hurricane from the port of Trinidad (Casilda). "An hour after I came in from the sea," Núñez Cabeza de Vaca recalled years later, "the sea began to rise furiously and the north wind [*el norte*] was so violent that ships dared not to approach land . . . because of the head wind." He continued:

> At this time, the rain and the storm began to increase to such an extent that there was no less agitation in the town than on the sea, for all the houses and churches collapsed and it was necessary for us to move about seven or eight men locking arms at a time to prevent the wind from carrying us off. . . . We wandered all night through this tempest and danger without finding any part or place where we might be safe for even half an hour. . . . Nothing as terrible as this has ever been seen before in these parts. . . . We went to the harbor but did not find any vessels. We saw their buoys floating in the water, from which we deduced that the ships were lost. We turned into the forest and walking a quarter league in water we found a small boat of a ship on the top of some trees. . . . We remained

thus for some days surviving through dire need and with considerable effort, for all the food and provisions of the town were lost. . . . It was lamentable to behold the condition in which the land remained: the trees fallen, the woods blighted, stripped of leaves and grass.[34]

An estimated 1,500 persons lost their lives in the hurricane of October 1644; more than 1,000 residents of Havana perished in October 1768. Official estimates calculated that more than 3,000 deaths resulted from the hurricane of June 1791.[35] "The effects of the hurricane were so deplorable," nineteenth-century historian Jacobo de la Pezuela wrote of the 1786 hurricane around Havana, "that on the following days there were neither seedlings nor nursery beds that had not been flooded. . . . The harvest of an entire year was thus lost and the farmland of many tillers was left without resources, not only the needy classes but also many planters of substantial fortunes."[36]

Late-season storms of September and October visited the greatest devastation on the island. October hurricanes were especially dreaded, for they usually recurred at the precise latitude of the island, where they crossed from south to north through the most productive agricultural zones of western Cuba with an intensity that approximated their full strength over the open sea. Of the 69 dated hurricanes known to have struck the island between 1494 and 1850, 44 hit in the three months of September (14), October (24), and November (6) (see Table 1.1).[37] "The month of October is the one that inspires the greatest terror among the inhabitants of Cuba," chronicler Félix Erenchún wrote in 1859, "for it is the time of the greatest frequency of hurricanes, those that lay waste to everything that is found in their destructive path, as much on land as at sea."[38] In September 1588 a fearsome hurricane pounded Havana, leaving the city with critical food shortages that were met only through emergency relief supplies from New Spain.[39]

Hurricanes struck both coasts and all provinces of the island. A storm in late September 1616 devastated the town of Bayamo in Oriente. Jacobo de la Pezuela described the resulting catastrophe in graphic terms: "So persistent were the rains in the autumn of that year, that at the end of September the Cauto [River] and its tributaries overflowed producing formidable flooding. The countryside was converted into lagoons, and its farm lands, its factories, its animals, disappeared almost completely. Palm trees and cedars [were] uprooted by the violence of the waters, and more than thirty ships, some crashing against others, were smashed to pieces and were destroyed."[40] Devastation in eastern Cuba continued with recurring hurricanes in 1744,

TABLE 1.1. Hurricanes in Cuba, 1494–1850

Year	Date	Location
1494	May 19–21	Southern coast (Oriente)
1494	July 25–27	Southern coast (Oriente)
1512	NA	Cuba
1515	NA	Occidente
1519	NA	Cuba
1525	October	Occidente
1527	October	Trinidad
1537	NA	Havana
1551	NA	Havana
1554	November 14	Oriente
1557	October 27	Occidente
1588	September 23	Havana
1600	September 26–27	Northern coast (Occidente)
1616	September	Oriente
1622	September 5	Northern coast (Occidente)
1623	October	Havana
1634	October 5	Occidente
1640	September 11	Occidente
1641	September 24	Northern coast (Occidente)
1644	October	Occidente
1687	October	Southern coast (Occidente)
1692	October 24	Havana
1705	NA	Havana
1712	October	Pinar del Río
1714	September 11	Southern coast (Occidente)
1730	September 2–3	Occidente
1731	August 13–14	Puerto Príncipe
1733	July 16	Northern coast (Occidente)
1744	November	Oriente
1751	NA	Occidente
1754	November 1	Oriente
1756	October 2–3	Occidente
1759	September	Central Cuba
1767	NA	Oriente
1768	October 11	Occidente
1772	August 16	Santiago de Cuba
1773	July 18–2	Oriente
1774	NA	Cuba
1778	October 18	Havana
1778	October 28	Oriente
1780	October 4	Puerto Príncipe
1780	October 16–17	Pinar del Rio

TABLE 1.1. Continued

Year	Date	Location
1791	June 21–22	Occidente
1791	September 27	Oriente
1792	October 29	Occidente
1794	August 27–28	Havana
1796	October 2–3	Southern coast (Occidente)
1796	October 23–24	Occidente
1796	November 2	Havana
1799	NA	Southern coast (Occidente)
1800	November 2	Oriente
1804	September 3–9	Cuba
1807	September 5	Cuba
1810	September 28	Oriente
1810	October 25–26	Havana/Pinar del Rio
1812	October 14	Trinidad
1819	NA	Southern coast (Occidente)
1821	NA	Havana
1825	October 1	Trinidad/Cienfuegos
1826	NA	Southern coast (Occidente)
1831	August	Central Cuba
1832	June 3	Cuba
1833	October 16	Occidente
1837	October 26	Cienfuegos/Trinidad/Santa Clara
1841	November 28	Santa Clara
1842	September 4	Occidente
1844	October 4–5	Occidente
1846	October 10–11	Occidente
1850	August 21–22	Havana

Sources: Félix Erenchún, *Anales de la Isla de Cuba*, 4 vols. (Havana, 1856); Marcos de
J. Melero, "Los huracanes de la Isla de Cuba: Bajas y ondas barométricas observadas," *Anales
de la Academia de Ciencias Médicas, Físicas y Naturales* 7 (November 1870): 329–35; José
Carlos Millás, *Hurricanes of the Caribbean and Adjacent Regions, 1492–1800* (Miami, 1968).

1751, 1767, and 1778.[41] In October 1780 a frightful storm devastated Puerto
Príncipe. "The destruction experienced by the buildings of the town and
the estates of the five districts [*partidos*] of its jurisdiction has been grave,"
reported Lieutenant Governor Juan de Quesada. As he explained:

> Damage-related costs have risen to 278,000 *pesos*, without taking into
> consideration the immense scarcity of food supplies in which the people
> find themselves. . . . As a result of the hurricane, diverse diseases have
> claimed the lives of many people. An immense number of cattle, pigs,

and horses have perished. Houses are in ruin. All the fruit trees, all the banana plants, and all the sugar cane fields have been leveled, leaving us without fruits to eat or seeds to plant. The price of jerked beef, honey, sugar, and salt has risen. The poor endure these scarcities with mounting bitterness. I end my report by saying the needs are urgent and the scarcities falling upon the poor are unbearable.[42]

Occidente was not spared. A succession of hurricanes ravaged the northern coast of western Cuba in October 1692, again in October 1712, and once more in September 1730, resulting in extensive damage in Remedios, Sagua la Grande, Matanzas, Havana, and Pinar del Río. The western provinces were particularly hard-hit in September 1791. In his nineteenth-century history of the Caribbean, Captain Thomas Southey recorded vivid impressions of Havana in 1791:

> It began to rain near Havana . . . with such force as to cause the greatest flood ever remembered in that country. The royal tobacco mills, and the village in which they stood, were washed away, and 257 of the inhabitants killed. . . . Four leagues thence, the torrent was so great, that none of the inhabitants within its reach escaped. All the crops of corn and growing fruits were carried away. Three thousand persons, and 11,700 head of cattle, are said to have perished in the flood.[43]

Hurricanes pummeled the western provinces in October 1768, October 1796, and once more in 1799. More than a thousand perished in October 1768. Captain General Antonio Bucareli reported devastating damage to tobacco warehouses in Batabanó and Trinidad, adding that inland communication was impossible. He wrote: "The roads are totally obstructed by trees felled by the wind and that make travel impossible." News from the Havana hinterland in October 1796 was also bleak. "The storm has destroyed all the plantain farms [*platanales*], the corn fields, and the rice farms"; according to the Real Consulado y Junta de Fomento, "it has caused major damage to sugar cane, so much that the harvest is expected to be reduced by two-thirds. The scene is one of desolation."[44]

Hurricanes in the early nineteenth century were no less noteworthy. Two hurricanes in September and October 1810 led to widespread damage from flooding in Pinar del Río. Hurricanes in 1812, 1819, 1821, 1825, and 1837 caused havoc in Cienfuegos, Trinidad, and Santa Clara. The storm in 1812 pummeled the southern coast, damaging or destroying more than a thousand homes and leaving more than six thousand people homeless. "There are few living people born this century," the Real Sociedad Económica de La Habana later wrote, "who have not heard something about this [1812] hurricane. Not a single house escaped some destruction. The countryside surrounding the town presented a horrific sight, as if it had been razed by a desolating fire." The 1819 storm all but annihilated the newly founded town of Cienfuegos, which was rebuilt only to be demolished in 1825 and again in 1832 and 1837. "This newly reborn port that was recovering in its agriculture, the certain base of prosperity and its principal source of its happiness," reported Lieutenant Governor Manuel de Mediavilla of Cienfuegos in June 1832, "has for the foreseeable future returned virtually back to its primitive condition. . . . The surrounding region is found in truly horrendous conditions. Outside the city huge trees have fallen, the banana plantations are destroyed and all other plants have been totally ruined. The rivers have risen out of their banks flooding the surrounding countryside. It is impossible to describe the scene."[45] In August 1831 a powerful storm swept through Puerto Príncipe, resulting in widespread devastation in Nuevitas, Ciego de Avila, and Morón. In October 1837 a hurricane entered the southern coast through the port of Casilda, moving northwesterly and causing extensive wreckage all along that coast, including Cienfuegos, and through central Cuba, especially the region around Santa Clara and Sagua la Grande.[46] Of a memorable moment in Havana in 1833, Captain James Alexander wrote:

> In turning out, after the manner of an ancient mariner, to see how the sky looked, there was a certain wildness in the heavens which was not particularly agreeable to behold — the clouds collected in mass, then suddenly dispersed, and the moon had a greenish aspect. I lay down: presently the wind began to whistle through the shutters; then it came in gusts; then it howled round the dwelling, as if evil spirits were in the blast. It increased in force till it became a perfect roar; doors and shutters were blown in, and tiles fell from the roofs; the rain lashed the trembling walls in ceaseless torrents.[47]

Hurricanes became a familiar occurrence in colonial Cuba, a circumstance of the Cuban condition that early insinuated itself into popular sensibilities and insular culture. It was only a matter of time before Spanish colonists, like the Taíno before them, came to associate hurricanes with demonic spirits. Las Casas affirmed outright that "demons possess means to cause storms and atmospheric disturbances." Gonzalo Fernández de Oviedo's experience with a hurricane stirred deep religious misgivings. "Truly whoever would have seen and walked through a forest after a hurricane has passed, where once stood great and dense trees," Oviedo wrote of a storm in 1509, "would have seen much to inspire awe and frightful revulsion." He explained:

> Innumerable huge and thick trees were fully uprooted, their exposed roots as high as the loftiest branches of some of them; others broken in half and in parts, broken into pieces from top to bottom; others piled one on top of another in such a manner that it seemed to be the work of the devil. . . . It is something to marvel to see some of them so torn asunder and so distant from the site where they matured, and with their upturned roots, some upon the others, in such a way locked together and piled and interweaved, that it appears, as I have said, to be by design, a work in which the devil or some part of hell has taken part. There are no Christian human eyes that can behold this sight without experiencing horror.[48]

By the end of the sixteenth century, with the onset of the hurricane season, the colonial church had adopted the practice of annual supplication for divine protection and enjoined local clergy to recite the prayer "Ad repellendas tempestates" at every Sunday mass during September and October.[49] The practice, too, of giving each hurricane the name of the saint's day on which it occurred appears to have been well established by the mid-eighteenth century. Hurricanes were thus named, for instance, Santa Teresa (1768), San Narciso (1792), San Agustín (1794), San Rafael (1796), San Evaristo (1837), and Santa Rosalía (1842).

The immediate impact and indeed the larger implications of hurricanes were in direct relationship to demographic and economic developments. It is unlikely that hurricanes either occurred with greater frequency or struck with greater intensity after the mid-seventeenth century. Nor is it probable that the forty-three years between 1641 and 1687, for example, or the thirty-one years between 1557 and 1588 would have passed without a single hurricane. Making allowances for annual meteorological variations, in which in any given year storms may have occurred more often or with greater intensity, or indeed not struck at all, the apparent increase in hurricanes after 1750 appears to be related to better reporting methods—specifically, advances in scientific methods and improved collection and recording of data.

The eighteenth century was a time of intellectual and scientific advances in almost all forms of learned inquiry. Cuban elites were very much products of the Enlightenment; they were at home in the marketplace of ideas if only to seek ideas for the marketplace. They embraced scientific knowledge entirely on pragmatic grounds as they sought practical knowledge for instrumental purposes—to improve agriculture, to foster industry, and to promote commerce. The weekly *Papel Periódico de La Habana* commenced publication in 1791. Unlike the periodical format most prevalent in the eighteenth century, which served mainly as a forum for disseminating official notices, the *Papel Periódico* was devoted to the dissemination of information and opinion, with particular attention to new developments in agriculture, commerce, and industry.[50] Founded at about the same time was the Sociedad Económica de Amigos del País to collect and disseminate information on industry, ranching, mining, commerce, but most of all agriculture. The Sociedad had a special interest in gathering and distributing information in those fields with the potential to aid agricultural production, including agronomy, botany, chemistry, mineralogical sciences, and technological advances in sugar production. Considerations of meteorology, especially the understanding of hurricanes, was an integral part of these developments.[51]

But it is also true that in later years hurricanes had far greater destructive effects, which were in direct proportion to the material advances in agriculture, ranching, and manufacturing. The insular infrastructure had expanded. Population had increased along both coasts and in the interior, new towns and settlements had been established, and the well-being of many was intimately related to the continued success of planters, ranchers, merchants, and entrepreneurs of all types. This was the human and material presence that expanded precisely along the zones that for more than a millennium were most frequently traversed by the winds of the autumnal equinox.

2. Coming into Being

Of all the Spanish possessions [Cuba] has been the most prosperous, and the port of Havana has risen, since the disasters of St. Domingo, to the rank of the first-class mart in the commercial world. A happy concurrence of political circumstances, the moderation of the government officials, and the conduct of the inhabitants, who are keen, prudent, and careful of their own interests, have preserved to Havana the continued enjoyment of a free interchange with foreign nations.

    Alexander Humboldt, The Island of Cuba *(1825)*

We passed . . . within a mile and a half of Guanajay, one of the largest of the interior towns. We noted twelve coffee estates on the road, most of them extensive; two large sugar estates, three more were in sight; two vegas of tobacco, one of ten acres, and the other of two; seven large potreros, or pastures for cattle, two of them very large . . . ; forty sitios, or . . . farms of small extent. . . . Some of the sitios had extensive fields of corn. . . . Almost every rood of the fields we passed in rapid succession was covered with some luxuriant growth. . . . And in all these directions there is high cultivation, and a vast produce prepared for the market.

    Abiel Abbot, Letters Written in the Interior of Cuba *(1829)*

How rich must be the resources of the soil, that can sustain, without exhaustion, this lavish and unceasing expenditure of its nutritious elements! How vigorous and thrifty the vegetation, that never falters nor grows old, under this incessant and prodigal demand upon its vital energies!

    Benjamin M. Norman, Rambles by Land and Water,
    or Notes of Travel in Cuba and Mexico *(1845)*

A coffee estate or plantation is a garden of beauty and is a characteristic of this climate, which must be seen to be appreciated. . . . The land is planted in regular squares of several acres in extent, each, and intersected by broad avenues of orange, palm, coconut, caimito and other ornamental trees of the tropics. The coffee plant requires to be protected partially from the sun, and for this cause shade trees are planted in their midst. Among these trees and along the walks, are planted bananas, lemons, pomegranites, oleanders, cape jasmines, roses, and heliotropes filling the air with fragrance. The coffee blossom is white as snow and so abundant that it seems as if the plants were covered with them. Fruit trees are scattered abundantly all over an estate, and it is a perfect flower garden with almost every luxury the heart could wish for.

Joseph D. Dimock, Impressions of Cuba in the Nineteenth Century *(1859)*

The news traveled fast. The distance was short, to be sure, and certainly this was a factor: a mere thirty miles across the Windward Passage separated the French colony of Saint Domingue from Cuba. But still the news traveled very fast. Such was the nature of tidings that bode ill to the practices by which privilege was transacted: information of importance to men of property and power had a way of arriving in a timely fashion.

The slaves of Saint Domingue had risen in rebellion. The French colony was ravaged by civil strife in which opposing forces routinely applied methods of scorched earth as the principal means of waging war and exacting revenge. The most prosperous plantation colony in the Western Hemisphere had collapsed: an estimated 800 sugar plantations, producing an annual average of 71,000 tons of sugar, were razed; nearly 3,000 coffee estates, yielding more than 30,000 tons of coffee annually and accounting for almost two-thirds of the world supply, ceased to produce; more than 700 cotton plantations, producing 2,800 tons of cotton, were no more.

The news of slaves in rebellion anywhere produced disquiet among holders of slaves everywhere. It could hardly be otherwise, for it was based on an understanding — even if only intuited — of the degree to which slave owners irrespective of nationality and location were implicated in each other's experiences. So it was in Cuba, and word of slave insurrection in Saint Domingue sent shock waves across the island.

But the news from Saint Domingue was not all bad. Some of the more perspicacious Cuban producers were quick to recognize windfall possibilities, despite — indeed, because of — the devastation of the French colony's productive capabilities. Slowly Saint Domingue had succumbed to civil strife until all that remained was subsistence farming for local consumption. The plantations ceased to produce and eventually disappeared; harvests failed, production plummeted, exports declined, and planters departed. The collapse of export production in Saint Domingue, most notably of sugar, coffee, cacao, and cotton, created new opportunities for Cuba.

Producers in Cuba were in an ideal position to seize the opportunities presented by the collapse of Saint Domingue. They did not hesitate. Few circumstances could have so favored the expansion of Cuban agriculture. The world supply of sugar and coffee had diminished, and all at once Cuban producers inherited new international markets, deepening world shortages, rising demand, and increasing prices.

Cuba benefited from the upheaval in Saint Domingue in other ways. Thousands of French planters and their families took flight and emigrated to Cuba, there to resettle in the interior districts of the east and across the rich agricultural zones in the western half of the island. They arrived with capital and expertise in the production of sugar and coffee, and with the determination to revive in Cuba the agricultural wealth lost in Saint Domingue.[1]

These were years, too, of successive colonial legislative measures that transformed the forms of land tenure in Cuba. Previously property ownership had been characterized by complex and confusing title patterns, whereby landholders typically did not own property but rather had use of a fractional portion. Almost all land—fields as well as forests—was owned by the Spanish monarchy. Subjects were entitled to hold and develop land, but at the pleasure of the Crown; the terms were always subject to reversal or revocation by the Court. A series of decrees between 1815 and 1819 suspended many laws obstructing private ownership and development of land, declared the freedom of fields and forests, and ratified ownership of lands by their current holders.[2]

The decrees of 1815–19 opened the way to land development, and the timing was perfect. Among the immediate beneficiaries were claimants to extensive landholdings, particularly owners of sugar plantations, coffee estates, and cattle ranches. Also profiting from these measures were the smaller property holders, including tobacco farmers, vegetable growers, ranchers, and small cultivators, who enjoyed a similar period of expansion.

The hinterlands surrounding the towns and cities developed rapidly into vast stretches of flourishing agricultural enterprises, a mixture of sugar plantations and coffee estates, orchards and groves, small vegetable farms and ranches. Traveler Benjamin Norman could hardly contain his delight at the sight of the resplendent countryside along the thirty-mile route between Havana and Güines. "The country is too beautiful, too rich in verdure, too luxuriant in fruits and flowers, and too picturesque in landscape, to be hurried over," he exulted. As Norman explained:

> Passing the suburbs of the city . . . the road breaks out into the beautiful open country, threading its narrow way through the rich plantations and thriving farms, whose vegetable treasures of every description can scarcely be paralleled on the face of the earth. The farms which supply the market of the city with their daily abundance of necessaries and luxuries occupy the foreground of this lovely picture. . . . Those who have not visited the tropics, can scarcely conceive the luxuriant and gigantic growth of their vegetable productions.

Frenchman Eugene Ney was smitten by the countryside outside the city of Matanzas. "Almost immediately," he confided to his diary, "we found ourselves in the midst of the most beautiful land in the world: mountains covered with trees, hills and valleys, fields of coffee, of mangos, of enormous palm trees, hedges of lemon trees, and bamboo forming leafy shady arches." While traveling between Havana and Güines, Spaniard Jacinto de Salas y Quiroga had a similar reaction: "Upon leaving Havana I admired from a distance the magnificent surrounding countryside. . . . I saw the richness of the vegetation, fields planted with beautiful pineapples. . . . I saw banana plants distributed everywhere, without any order, with their wide-leaves stretched out in every direction. . . . I saw the wild cocoanut trees. I saw the fields covered with that beneficial green cane that when gently swayed by the breeze its tips bend sighing sweetly." John Wurdemann was also impressed by the countryside outside Havana. "We were soon beyond the immediate neighborhood of the city, its gardens, its farms, and its hamlets," Wurdemann wrote in 1844, "and their places were supplied by extensive sugar and coffee estates, with their large potreros and woodlands. . . . The whole country was under high cultivation, forming one immense garden."[3]

These were boom years for Cuban agriculture, characterized by balanced development in key sectors of the colonial economy. The number of *fincas* (farms) expanded rapidly across the island, increasing almost fivefold from 7,580 in 1778, to 34,798 in 1827, to nearly 50,000 in 1846.[4] Production increased, and so did exports. As trade expanded, Cuba was drawn into ever-widening participation in world markets.

Much of this development centered in the western and central jurisdictions. Of the total number of fincas in 1827, fully 75 percent—26,194 out of 34,978—were located in the western and central zones.[5] Within three

TABLE 2.1. Coffee Exports, 1792–1840

Year	Arrobas
1792	7,104
1804	50,000
1808	137,148
1812	263,618
1816	370,229
1820	686,046
1826	1,773,798
1832	2,048,890
1840	2,143,574

Source: Jacobo de la Pezuela, *Diccionario geográfico, estadístico, histórico de la Isla de Cuba,* 4 vols. (Madrid, 1863–66), 1:225.

decades, the western half of the island had developed into the principal production zone for both commercial production and domestic consumption.

In some sectors agricultural development was spectacular. Coffee cultivation expanded rapidly across the island, stimulated by increasing demand and rising prices. Between 1792 and 1796 the world price of coffee doubled. Prices again increased from 2.40 pesos per quintal in 1808, to 13 pesos per quintal in 1815, to 17 pesos in 1818.[6]

Producers in Cuba responded. The number of cafetales increased from 2 in 1774, to 108 in 1802, to 586 in 1804, more than doubling to 1,315 by 1806, and almost doubling again to 2,067 by 1827, more than half of which (1,207) were located in Occidente, chiefly Pinar del Río, Havana, and Matanzas, which accounted for more than 75 percent of Cuban production. The number of coffee estates in the district of Havana increased from 60 in 1800 to 779 in 1817, first through the western zones of Havana surrounding Artemisa, then expanding southward and eastward to Güira de Melena, Alquízar, Quivicán, Santiago de las Vegas, Bejucal, Jaruco, and Madruga.[7]

The number of cafetales in Matanzas increased from 75 in 1816 to 244 by 1826. Coffee expanded into the Cienfuegos hinterland. In the space of two years between 1829 and 1831, Cienfuegos coffee exports increased from 416 arrobas to 1,320 arrobas (1 arroba = 25 pounds). Indeed, in the early decades of the nineteenth century coffee rivaled sugar for the control of land and labor.[8] Between 1792 and 1804 the value of Cuban coffee exports increased more than sevenfold, from 7,104 arrobas to 50,000 arrobas, doubling thereafter every few years (see Table 2.1). Between 1825–30 and 1836–40 production rose from about 2 million arrobas to 3.4 million arrobas annually.[9]

Coffee cultivation flourished across the western provinces. By 1820 about 80 million pesos had been invested in the cafetales of western Cuba. The Reverend Abiel Abbot estimated in 1828 that there were six coffee estates for each sugar plantation in the countryside of western Havana. In 1822 an estimated 18,800 acres were under cultivation in Alquízar: 466 acres devoted to sugar, 13,620 acres to coffee, and the balance to corn, rice, plantains, and *viandas* (root crops).[10] Expanded cultivation also meant new population centers. Guanajay increased to 23,500 residents, almost all of whom were connected in one way or another to coffee production.

This was a region very familiar to Cirilo Villaverde, who used the local landscape as the setting for his novel *Cecilia Valdés* (1839–82). "The further one traveled from Hoyo Colorado," Villaverde narrated,

> the more *cafetales* one found on one side or the other of the road, as if these were the only rural estates of any importance in that zone of the western plain, at least until 1840. We are now speaking about the famous garden of Cuba, bound within the jurisdictions of Guanajay, Güira de Melena, San Marcos, Alquízar, Ceiba del Agua, and San Antonio de los Baños. At the time, farms were not dedicated to agricultural production in the strict sense of the word, but rather to the recreation of their pleasure-seeking proprietors, as long as the price of coffee remained high.[11]

Villaverde's observation underscored one of the salient facets of the coffee estate in early-nineteenth-century Cuba. It was not simply that coffee production had obtained spectacular commercial success. What was especially noteworthy about coffee cultivation was that it engaged creole participation; Cuban-born planters early entered into commercial production and assumed an ever-larger role in the colonial political economy. "The great demand and high prices for coffee," historian Ramiro Guerra y Sánchez wrote of the expansion of coffee cultivation in Havana province early in the nineteenth century, "encouraged Cuban families, many already well-to-do or with the possibilities and the desire to become well-to-do, to develop new sources of agricultural wealth that appeared to offer great opportunity."[12] Compared to sugar, coffee production demanded comparatively less capital resources to inaugurate and operate. Land and livestock costs were lower. Slave labor requirements were less. A profitable cafetal of 200,000 coffee trees on eight *caballerías* of land, with slaves, buildings, machinery, and livestock, cost 80,000 pesos to inaugurate and operate. A comparably profitable *ingenio* (sugar mill) required 30 caballerías of land, together with a commensurate number of slaves, buildings, machinery, and livestock at a cost of 170,000 pesos.[13]

Coffee cultivation represented a self-contained world, responding to the logic of production and the calculus of profit, of course, but also to the manifest desire for social standing and patrician pleasures. Coffee often had as much to do with status as it did with production and profits. Cafetales were exquisitely designed to proclaim grace and elegance, to serve, as Leví Marrero correctly observed, as "centers of civilization and gracious living for their owners and invited guests."[14] The *casa de vivienda* (the estate's primary residence) was designed to proclaim the proposition of felicitous prosperity. This was the scene that must have greeted Ramón de Palma, who incorporated it into his novella *Una pascua en San Marcos* (1844). "The *cafetal* of Don Tadeo Amirola was one of the most beautiful of the district," Palma characterized a coffee estate in Artemisa. "This affluent gentleman had spared neither money nor work to make it into a delightful mansion fit for an Eastern prince. There pleasure not profit was what mattered. The very plants of production were subjected to the dictates of art, and each coffee plot looked like a garden." The family of Anselmo Suárez y Romero owned property in Güines, where the young writer passed much of his time. "Speaking to you frankly of how I feel," Suárez y Romero wrote in 1840, "I do not like the *ingenios*. To have seen one is to have seen them all. Nothing more than vast light-green cane fields that define the horizon, divided into squares of various size by straight boundaries (*guardarrayas*), at whose edges are not seen—as one sees in the *cafetales*—the wide tree-tops, nor the mamey, nor the honey berry, nor the avocado; nor do they exude the citron flower fragrance of the lemon and orange trees."[15]

The cafetales were magnificently landscaped and meticulously maintained; they often assumed the appearance of tropical gardens. Royal palms lined the entrance to the casa de vivienda. The *guardarrayas* between straight rows of coffee plants appeared as avenues and footpaths, demarcated by an assortment of ornamental trees of dense and expansive foliage, including acacia, poinciana, and canistel, and a wide variety of fruit tress, typically mango, mamey, avocado, and sapota, and citrus trees. Harvested fruit was variously used as a supplemental source of income or distributed locally, principally for internal consumption, which together with provision grounds provided the dietary staple of estate slaves.[16] The trees also had a vital function as a source of shade to protect young and maturing coffee

"Entrance to Cafetal.*" Reprinted from Samuel Hazard,* Cuba with Pen and Pencil *(London, 1871).*

plants against the intense sun and keeping the soil moist. No less important, trees were designed to serve as breakers, to protect the buds of the flowering coffee plants against the effects of wind.[17]

Visitors usually drew the desired inference — a combination of wonderment and enchantment. J. B. Dunlop described the cafetal Catalina outside Havana as a place "beautifully planted with Coffee trees, symmetrically arranged in rows of about 12 feet asunder, and in a state of perfect cultivation. These articles together with Negroe Provisions such as Bananas, which are planted between the rows of the Coffee fields when young, Maize, & Yams are the prevailing articles of Culture of this fertile district." Several decades later John Wurdemann traveled through the same zone and was unabashedly lyrical in his description of the cafetal. "Imagine more than three hundred acres of land planted in regular squares with evenly pruned shrubs," he wrote in 1844, "each containing about eight acres, intersected by broad alleys of palms, oranges, mangoes, and other beautiful trees; the interstices between which are planted with lemons, pomegranates, cape-jessamines, tube-rose, lilies, and various other gaudy and fragrant flowers." He, too, noted that in addition to coffee "the cultivator plants his grounds largely in maize and plantains, which he sells to sugar estates; and yams, yuca, sweet potatoes and rice, which yields well on the uplands, for his own consumption." Wurdemann added: "And when some of the flowers have given place to the ripened fruit; and the golden orange, the yellow mangoe, the lime, the lemon, the luscious caimito, the sugared zapote; the mellow alligator pear, the custard-apple, and the rose-apple, giving to the palate the flavor of otto of roses;—when all these hang on the trees in oppressive abundance, and the ground is also covered with the over-ripe, the owner of a coffee estate might safely challenge the world for a fairer garden." On first sight of a coffee plantation, traveler Xavier Marmier was elated: "The plantation! I would have mistaken it to be the residence of a prince. Imagine an avenue a quarter league in length . . . bordered right and left with a row of royal palms resembling columns of marble. That is how one reaches the *casa de vivienda*." [18]

Benjamin Norman, who traveled extensively throughout Havana province, was enchanted by the cafetal. "The low and evenly trimmed coffee plants," he wrote of a visit to one coffee estate outside Havana, "set in close and regular columns, with avenues of mangoes, palms, oranges, or pines, leading back to the cool and shady mansion of the proprietor, surrounded with its village of thatched huts laid out in a perfect square, and buried in over-shadowing trees, form a complete picture of oriental wealth and luxury." William Hulbert visited the same region several years later. "The cottage of the *cafetal*," he rhapsodized, "was an elegantly proportioned little tropical mansion, cool, dark, floored with marble, wainscoted, and furnished with rich deep-hued Indian woods. A garden filled with heavy blooms, of jasmine and roses, and the gorgeous purple Carolina, and a hundred drooping odorous flowers, made the air faint with fragrance. A dense grove of oranges trees near by, was lighted up through all its recesses by the glowing fruit." According to Hulbert:

The plantain tree . . . reaches the height of twenty feet or more, and its heavy dark green leaves nodding over the ruddy ground, make a delightful shade, a sort of cool baptistery, from which you pass into the statelier sanctuaries of the *cafetal*. There the full-leaved orange, the thrifty, dark glossy foliage of the mango, the tall elm-like aguacate, the coneshaped mamey, cover the land on both sides as far as the eye can reach. Everywhere you see the light, shrubby outlines of the coffee plant springing up beneath the taller trees. Avenues, miles in length, lead to the different

"Coffee Field." Reprinted from Samuel Hazard, Cuba with Pen and Pencil *(London, 1871).*

quarters of the estate, formed as they are of the full exuberant mango, or the branching aguacate, planted alternately with the towering royal palm, become forest aisles of surpassing beauty. The height of the palms is immense, many of them rising more than a hundred and twenty feet into the air. Overtopping thus the other trees, their sweeping noble arches do not exclude the sunlight, which pours through the intervals as through the clere-story windows of a cathedral, and illuminate the green solemn of the majestic colonnades.[19]

"In short," concluded Maturin Ballou after visiting the Buena Esperanza estate, "a coffee plantation is a perfect floral El Dorado, with every luxury . . . the heart could wish."[20]

Coffee production flourished during the early decades of the nineteenth century and developed into one of the most profitable agricultural activities in Cuba. Coffee early established a predominant position throughout the jurisdictions of Matanzas, Havana, and eastern Pinar del Río. The zone of Artemisa-Guanajay included the Angerona cafetal, with 750,000 coffee trees worked by a *dotación* (labor force) of 450 slaves; the Mariana estate, with 250,000 trees and 140 slaves; the Unidad, with 230,000 trees and 140 slaves; and the Reunión, with 450,000 trees and 300 slaves. On the Ubajai estate owned by Antonio García, 200,000 coffee trees were maintained by 110 slaves. The Uva cafetal outside Batabanó contained 70,000 trees and 30 slaves. The 300,000 trees on the Carlota estate in Madruga were capable of producing in one year a harvest worth more than $100,000.[21]

Agriculture for domestic consumption, known variously as *cultivos menores* and *agricultura de subsistencia,* also prospered. The number of small farms (*sitios* and *estancias*) increased more than threefold—from 8,224 in 1827 to 25,292 by 1846. Sitios and estancias, typically between 10 and 100 acres in size, formed agricultural belts around population centers and were dedicated mostly to the cultivation of vegetables, fruits, the raising of poultry, and the production of milk and eggs. New lands (*hatos* and *corrales*) were opened for growing livestock herds.[22]

Agricultural production of all types expanded. The value of cotton exports increased from 37,000 arrobas in 1827 to 40,000 arrobas in 1829 and to 82,000 arrobas by 1840. The number of farms dedicated to tobacco cultivation (*vegas*) grew—from 4,960 in 1811 to 5,534 in 1827—with the production of leaf climbing from 9.3 million pounds to 12.5 million pounds annually. By 1836 leaf production had nearly doubled (22.5 million pounds). Cacao cultivation expanded, principally in central Cuba; by 1827 there were 60 cacao estates (*cacahuales*) on the island, most of them located in Las Villas, mainly in Remedios (41) and Sancti-Spíritus (13).[23] Orange groves increased, as did corn production and the cultivation of such basic foodstuffs as bananas, rice, beans, wheat, vegetables, and viandas. The number of apiaries (*colmenares*) grew to nearly 1,700 in 1827 and included about 312,000 beehives (*colmenas*); nearly 1,500 apiaries and 280,000 hives were located in the central and western zones.[24] Benjamin Norman penned a vivid description of the region surrounding Alquízar and Bejucal, a zone possessing "large tracts of cultivated plantations and farms, which make this beautiful island a perfect garden," adding: "The orange and pine-apple, both of a delicious flavor, abound on all sides. Indian corn, the sweet potato, rice, and a great variety of other important edibles are extensively cultivated, giving wealth to some, and sustenance to thousands." Güines, Norman continued, "is sprinkled all over with cattle and vegetable farms, and coffee and sugar estates, of immense value, whose otherwise monotonous surface is beautifully relieved by clusters, groves, and avenues of state palms, and flowering oranges, mangos and pines, giving to the whole the aspect of a highly cultivated garden."[25]

Some of the most spectacular advances of the early nineteenth century were registered in sugar production. Cuban planters were beneficiaries of auspicious market conditions at about the time that new production technologies became generally available. Steam power was introduced in 1817 and vastly improved the efficiency of the mill. Iron rollers replaced wooden ones. Vacuum boilers were introduced during the 1830s. Within a decade, the use of the centrifuge improved the process of purifying sugar. The construction of railroad lines, beginning in the 1830s, linked an ever-larger radius of interior sugar zones with provincial ports. All the requisite capital elements for profound transformations of the Cuban economy became available within several decades.

Sugar expanded rapidly across the island. Old producers increased production and new ones initiated operations. Both the number of estates and the zones of cultivation grew. The number of sugar mills in the jurisdiction of Havana increased more than fourfold—from 70 in 1763 to 305 in 1796; by 1817 there were 625. The number of sugar estates in Güines soared from 2 in 1780 to 66 in 1846. The first sugar mill in Sagua was founded between 1810 and 1820; by the mid-1840s Sagua had 59 mills. The 26 ingenios of Trinidad in 1780 had increased to 32 by 1795. Within twenty years of the founding of Cienfuegos in 1819, 26 sugar mills were in operation; seven years later the number had almost tripled (71), and by the mid-1850s there were 102. By 1846 the total number of ingenios in Cuba had reached 1,442. Production increased in spectacular fashion, from 15,600 tons in 1790 to 28,400 tons in 1800; it almost doubled (58,000 tons) in 1809 and nearly tripled (162,000 tons) by 1841.[26]

Sugar expansion initially centered along the zones around Havana, between Guanajay on the west, Matanzas on the east, and Batabanó to the south. Production subsequently extended inland and eastward, outward onto the northern coastal plains reaching Jaruco, Cárdenas, and Sagua la Grande, thence on to Remedios and Caibarién, zones that enjoyed favorable patterns of rainfall and comparatively ready access to ports. In the 1830s cultivation penetrated farther inland, toward the central plains around Unión de Reyes, Bemba (Jovellanos), Colón, and eventually eastward into Sancti-Spíritus, Nuevitas, and Puerto Príncipe. Sugar zones also took hold along the southern coast, mainly around Cienfuegos and Trinidad.[27]

Towns and cities all across the western central provinces prospered. During the late 1820s Trinidad's good fortune was driven by the production of 56 ingenios, 35 cafetales, 460 tobacco vegas, and 148 apiaries. The total value of Trinidad exports in 1827 had surpassed 557,000 pesos, and im-

"View of Havana from Casa Blanca" (I). Reprinted from Federico Mialhe, Album pintoresco de la Isla de Cuba *(Berlin, 1853).*

ports were nearly 690,000 pesos; by 1841 these value had increased to 1.2 million pesos and 943,000 pesos respectively. The number of ingenios in Matanzas swelled from 4 in 1774 to 111 in 1827, estancias increased from 270 to 935, and from not a single cafetal in 1774 to 203 in 1827. In Matanzas from 1774 to 1827, the number of ingenios swelled from 4 to 111, estancias from 270 to 935, and from not a single cafetal to 203. In 1817 the district of Batabanó contained 13 ingenios and 13 cafetales; Remedios claimed a total of 17 sugar plantations and 73 coffee estates.[28] Thirty miles southeast of Havana the jurisdiction of Güines thrived. "It is, perhaps, the richest district in the island, and in the highest state of cultivation," concluded Benjamin Norman.[29]

The expansion of sugar was cause and effect of other changes no less far-reaching and long-lasting. Soaring sugar prices and rising land values provided incentive for the expansion of transportation facilities. Old highways and roads were improved, and new ones were constructed. By 1838 the first Cuban railroad was completed, linking Havana with Güines, followed thereafter by the construction of branch lines all through the expanding sugar zones. New rail lines made possible the opening of new production zones. Planters could extend cultivation on both sides of trunk lines through the construction of private feeder lines. Transportation costs declined. It was not only cheaper to haul sugar out, it also cost less to bring supplies in. Machines, fuel, foodstuffs, and provisions arrived in greater quantities, over longer distances, at lower cost. Indeed, within a decade virtually every major sugar-producing region in Occidente was connected to the nearest principal port.[30]

The expansion of sugar production in the nineteenth century was itself product and portent of other changes, none perhaps as dramatic as the growth in population. Over the seventy years between the censuses of 1774 and 1841, the population of Cuba increased almost sixfold, from 172,000 to more than 1 million.

Certain facets of this remarkable growth were striking. The number of residents of Havana more than doubled, from 76,000 to almost 160,000, including about 22,000 people appearing in census rolls as "transients," primarily seamen of national and foreign vessels, passengers in transit, and garrison troops. The 1841 census enumerators considered the inhabitants of the contiguous districts of Regla, Casa-Blanca, Horcón, Cerro, and Jesús del Monte as a "continuation" of the capital, thereby including another estimated 25,000 residents and raising the total population of metropolitan Havana to more than 184,000.[31]

The city of Havana was transformed. The burgeoning population crowded into the three-quarter square mile of the original city and inexorably into new residential zones beyond the old walls (*extramuros*), expanding mostly westward over a new expanse of about two square miles. "The city [is] a depot of mercantile and agricultural opulence," the Reverend Abiel Abbot wrote in 1828; "the immense extent of public buildings; the cathedral, churches, and convents; the Governor's palace, post office, and other public buildings, with the palaces of nobles and opulent gentlemen . . . ; in short, a spot wholly occupied with buildings except a very scanty portion devoted to lanes . . . proclaim Havana within the walls, one of the richest and most important spots, for the numbers of its roofs, on the face of the earth. And yet Havana within the walls, is less populous than Havana without."[32] Indeed, by 1841 nearly three-quarters of the total population of Havana—135,000 out of 184,000 inhabitants—resided outside the old walled city. New neighborhoods and residential zones arose in rapid succession, many filling with people of modest social origins; these were barrios like Salud, Guadalupe, Horcón, Jesús María, and San Lázaro. By midcentury Havana came to embrace the proposition of a metropolitan area known as Gran Habana.[33]

Population increased across the island. During the 1774–1841 intercensus

"View of Havana with Part of Extramuros." Reprinted from Federico Mialhe, Album pintoresco de la Isla de Cuba *(Berlin, 1853).*

period, notable increases were recorded in Trinidad (from 5,600 to 28,000), Sancti-Spíritus (from 8,300 to 34,000), Santa Clara (from 8,100 to 44,400), and Pinar del Río (from 2,617 to 33,400). Older port cities grew and prospered. Good times in Trinidad led to the modernization of the port facilities in Casilda in 1818. The population of Santiago de Cuba increased from 18,400 to 91,500. Matanzas was transformed from a languid port settlement into a bustling entrepôt, from a population of 3,250 in 1774 to 85,000 by 1841; its contribution to the royal coffers increased from 74 pesos in 1762 to 250,000 pesos in 1818. Whereas in the closing years of the eighteenth century Matanzas had contributed virtually nothing to the insular production of sugar, by 1827 it accounted for 25 percent of Cuba's total production. Between 1810 and 1830, sugar exports climbed from 17,900 boxes to 160,000 boxes, while the value of coffee exports soared from 8,500 arrobas to 288,000 arrobas. The total value of exports out of Matanzas between 1831 and 1840 doubled, from 2 million pesos to 4 million pesos.[34] "Matanzas, by sudden growth," commented Abiel Abbot the following year, "has become a considerable city, and is destined to be a great one. Eighteen years ago it was but a little larger than Cardenas; most of its growth has been within ten years. The country makes the town; and the fertile region in its neighbor-

TABLE 2.2. Imports and Exports, 1810–1842 (pesos)

Year	Imports	Exports
1810	15,729,528	7,903,700
1826	14,925,754	13,809,838
1830	16,171,562	15,870,968
1838	24,729,878	20,471,102
1842	24,637,527	26,684,701

Source: José Alvarez Díaz et al., *A Study on Cuba* (Coral Gables, Fla., 1965), p. 128.

hood, which is fast settling, and pouring its important staples into its bosom, will swell its population."[35]

Trade linkages expanded, which provided further stimulus to production. In 1818 Cuban ports were opened to unrestricted trade with all foreign countries, after which colonial commerce with overseas markets flourished. The value of sugar exports nearly doubled in the period from 1796–1800 to 1821–24, from an annual average of 11.4 million arrobas to 20.0 million arrobas; the value increased to 32.5 million arrobas in 1826–30 and nearly tripled (93.4 million) in 1846–50. Tobacco exports rose from 129,000 quintales (1 quintal = 100 pounds) in 1825–30 to 306,000 quintales in 1840–45. The value of beeswax exports increased from an estimated 43,000 arrobas in 1803, to 63,000 arrobas in 1827, to 290,000 arrobas by the mid-1840s. Between 1818 and 1834 Cuban foreign trade more than doubled in value, from 15.5 million pesos to 33.0 million pesos (see Table 2.2). Colonial revenues, principally in the form of taxes, tariffs, and duties, jumped from 3.4 million pesos to 8.9 million pesos.[36]

/ / / / /

Prosperity acted upon population and vice versa. The expansion of transportation facilities promoted the opening of new production zones, which, in turn, encouraged the development of the surrounding hinterland and the establishment of new towns and settlements; this, of course, promoted further expansion of transportation facilities. Between 1775 and 1840 more than fifty new towns were founded across the island. These included, in 1775–1800, San Antonio de las Vegas, Güira de Melena, San Antonio de los Baños, Morón, and Madruga; in 1800–1809, Candelaria, La Salud, Nueva Paz, Esperanza, Báez, and Manicaragua; in 1810–19, Artemisa, Cabañas, Cifuentes, Alacranes, Güines, Colón, Sagua la Grande, Manguito, Santo Domingo, Gibara, and Guantánamo; in 1820–29, Cabeza, Pedro Betancourt,

"View of Havana from Casa Blanca" (II). Reprinted from Federico Mialhe, Album pintoresco de la Isla de Cuba *(Berlin, 1853)*.

Mayajigua, San Juan de los Yeras, San José de las Lajas, Santa Cruz del Sur, San Nicolás, San Luis de los Pinos, Palma Soriano, and San Luis (Oriente); and, in 1830–39, Corralillo and Rancho Veloz.[37]

The expansion of production and population in the provincial interior acted to promote the development of new ports along the coast. Prosperity of Remedios led to the establishment of the port of Caibarién (1819); the expanding economic needs of Puerto Príncipe resulted in the founding of Nuevitas (1819). Producers in the region of Guanajay were instrumental in the opening of Mariel harbor (1820); the expansion of the local economy of Bayamo was largely responsible for the opening of the port of Manzanillo (1827). The founding of Cienfuegos (1819) was related to the expansion of sugar into virgin interior land. Occasionally, it was the other way around: the creation of a coastal settlement was instrumental in the development of the local interior economy. The founding of Bahía Honda (1779) was decisive in opening the interior to the expansion of sugar and the establishment of San Diego de Núñez. Other port towns included Cabañas (1818), Guantánamo (1822), and Cárdenas (1828).

At least as remarkable as the increase in urban populations was the stunning rise of people of color, free and slave. Between 1774 and 1841 the number of free people of color increased fivefold, from 30,800 to 152,800. Even more striking, the slave population experienced a tenfold increase, from 44,300 in 1774 to 84,600 in 1792, to 199,000 in 1817, to 436,500 in 1841. Indeed, nearly two-thirds of the total population growth between 1774 and 1841 was registered in the population of color, with the white population increasing by almost 322,000, from 96,400 to 418,300.[38]

The data on the distribution of the expanding slave population are incomplete and in places contradictory. Most slaves worked in agriculture, and on this point the available sources are unanimous. Beyond this agreement, however, a number of sharp disparities appear. One of the salient facets of the colonial economy of the early nineteenth century was the degree to which coffee cultivation competed with sugar production for land and slaves. According to a British report of 1822, nearly two-thirds of all slaves (265,000) were laboring on ingenios (155,000), followed by cafetales (54,000), sitios and estancias (36,000), and household service (20,000). But five years later the census of 1827 calculated an estimated 221,000 rural slaves (esclavos de las fincas), of whom 70,000 worked on sugar estates, 50,000 on cafetales, and the balance on sitios, estancias, tobacco vegas, and potreros. Data for 1830 provided by Ramón de la Sagra calculated a total 240,263 rural slaves, distributed in descending order among ingenios (100,000), sitios and estancias (66,000), cafetales (60,000), and tobacco vegas (14,263). One agricultural census of fincas in Occidente, taken between 1832 and 1833, listed 48,513 slaves on ingenios and 39,835 slaves on cafetales.[39] In some instances regional variations in the local economy often resulted in the deployment of more slaves to cafetales than to ingenios. In Ceiba Mocha in 1817, a larger portion of the total slave population worked the coffee estates than the sugar plantations; specifically, 1,073 out of a total 2,797 slaves labored on cafetales as compared to 972 slaves on ingenios. In Camarioca, coffee production accounted for more than 56 percent of total slave labor.[40]

/ / / / /

The early decades of the nineteenth century brought prosperity to virtually all regions of the island. The economy expanded and diversified, driven principally by favorable market conditions and improved access to international markets. Trade increased and foreign commerce developed into ever-more salient facets of Cuban well-being.[41] Land tenure forms were in transition, with the diversity of agriculture expanding even as consolidation of

TABLE 2.3. The Value of Private Property and Production, 1842

Type of Farm	Total Acreage	Percent	Total Land Value (pesos)	Production Value (pesos)
Ingenios	1,000,000	28	45,000,000	12,000,000
Cafetales	480,000	14	24,600,000	50,635,000
Sitios and estancias	759,000	22	45,610,000	48,610,000
Hatos and potreros	1,094,140	31	3,285,700	NA
Vegas	166,500	5	3,500,500	3,500,000

Source: Leví Marrero, *Cuba: Economía y sociedad*, 15 vols. (Madrid, 1972–88), 10:93.

land into larger estates gathered momentum. Certainly, sugar production was gaining ascendancy and as an economic activity accounted for an ever-larger share of real wealth, reflected mainly in the value of land and the capital invested in industrial infrastructure and slave labor. But it was also true that the ingenios coexisted with other production forms, most notably cafetales and tobacco vegas, sitios and estancias, and various types of ranches, including hatos, corrales, and potreros. In terms of area under cultivation, land value, and total capital investment, the value of production of these other land tenure forms compared favorably to that of sugar (see Table 2.3).

In fact, the agrarian economy had obtained some measure of productive equilibrium. Although the body of available data is incomplete and inconclusive, it indicates some of the salient trends during the 1830s. Bejucal, for example, had a total of 5 ingenios accounting for more than 50,000 acres, while 176 potreros held nearly 70,000 acres of land, and the combined value of production by the estancias and sitios exceeded the value of sugar.[42]

Towns and cities across the surrounding countryside in Occidente were engaged in diversified production. Güines had expanded to 16,200 inhabitants, including 7,250 whites, 7,770 slaves, and 1,270 free people of color, distributed mainly among 21 ingenios, 26 cafetales, and 843 sitios and estancias. Sugar production engaged a total labor force of 2,950, and coffee accounted for some 1,740 workers. The estimated 5,600 inhabitants of the town of Madruga were distributed among 11 sugar estates, 17 coffee plantations, and 157 farms. The population of Matanzas reached nearly 85,000, of which 27,100 were whites, 53,300 slaves, and 4,570 free people of color; approximately 29,700 worked on 161 sugar plantations, 13,330 on 175 coffee estates, and 20,950 on sitios and estancias. The town of Limonar contained 13,150 inhabitants, including 1,196 whites, 11,800 slaves, and 140 free people of color, of which 5,778 persons were employed on 30 ingenios, 5,906 on

73 cafetales, and 1,207 on 44 sitios and estancias. The town of Pendencias had 458 whites, 3,860 slaves, and 31 free people of color out of which 190 worked on 1 sugar plantation, 3,861 on 45 cafetales, and 298 on 12 sitios. In San Antonio de los Baños, the 8,631 inhabitants were distributed among 18 coffee estates and 280 estancias. The population of 3,367 whites, 9,612 slaves, and 149 free people of color in Lagunillas were distributed principally among 38 sugar estates (5,216), 40 coffee farms (2,518), and 253 sitios and estancias (2,961). The jurisdiction of Trinidad contained a population of 28,060 (10,280 whites, 11,688 slaves, and 6,092 free people of color), most of whom were distributed on 44 sugar estates (7,004), 24 coffee farms (9,905), and 826 small farms (6,611); the balance worked in the city.

Cuban economic development was thus driven by expanding agricultural production that possessed diversity and a measure of balance. Cuban producers approached the midcentury decades with reason for optimism. The island had escaped the political upheaval and civil strife by which the Spanish colonies on the mainland had obtained their independence. On the contrary, Cuba experienced the early decades of the nineteenth century in relative domestic tranquility, a status that favored sustained economic development. Creoles had opted for the security of colonialism over the uncertainty of independence. It appeared that property holders on the Ever Faithful Isle had chosen wisely.

3. A Time of Tempests

The month of October is the month that inspires the greatest terror among the inhabitants of Cuba, due to the frequency of hurricanes that lay waste to everything in their violent course, as much on land as at sea.

    Félix Erenchún, Anales de la Isla de Cuba *(1859)*

The Cuban hurricane of October 5–7, 1844, is calculated on very modest estimates to have worked during the three days of its progress . . . with an energy of 473 million horse-power.

    William M. Davis, Elementary Meteorology *(1894)*

Sad, very sad, is the picture that this island currently presents after the calamities of the year 1843 and the beginning of 1844. Then came the hurricane of October which together with the horrible drought . . . have left the countryside in such a condition that the sugar harvest will not even reach half the amount of previous years and the harvests of coffee and food will be zero, to such a point that the population in the countryside will soon suffer a hunger of frightful proportions. Think about our situation and you will be able to understand how much more there is yet for us to suffer. And only God knows if after these calamities others are yet to follow.

    Miguel de Aldama to Domingo del Monte (February 4, 1845)

The most violent and cruel hurricanes were those of October 5, 1844 and October 10, 1846, whose devastation was ever more grievous and extensive, given that they

released their full fury upon the richest zones of the island: precisely those zones en-
compassed within Pinar del Río, Sagua la Grande, and Cienfuegos, including the
full radius of Havana, Matanzas, and Cárdenas. It is impossible to recall the two
hurricanes without horror. The violence of the winds toppled buildings, uprooted
trees of all kinds whose roots had penetrated many feet into the depth of the earth,
hurled ships anchored in the bay against the shoreline, and even twisted the iron
piers to which the ships were tethered by cable. The torrential rain transformed the
low-lying areas near the coast into lakes. The shock [was] terrible.

    Jacobo de la Pezuela, Diccionario geográfico, estadístico,
    histórico de la Isla de Cuba *(1863–66)*

Future generations will read that in 1846 Nature unleashed threatened beautiful
Cuba with destruction.

    Sociedad Económica de Amigos del País, Memorias *(1846)*

It was said that *auras* had multiplied prodigiously in 1843. It was said, too,
that it was not a good sign. Much about daily life in rural Cuba was governed
by omens in the relentless search for clues by which the gods revealed their
purpose. But the matter of the auras was only partially related to decipher-
ing signs. Rather, it had to do with conventional wisdom, which, in turn, was
derived from knowledge accumulated from experience and passed on from
one generation to another. It was known that good times for buzzards meant
hard times for everything else. The increase in the flocks of auras signified
that they were eating well, which meant that other animals were not eating
so well. That was not good.

/ / / / /

It is difficult to determine how—or even if—the fact of the hurricane
figured into Cuban developmental strategies in the early nineteenth century. The perils of the storm season had become a familiar hazard, never
to be taken lightly, to be sure, but, on the other hand, always taken as a
matter of course. There was hardly much choice. This was, in the end, part
of the Cuban condition, to which the most obvious response was acquiescence. Then, too, almost five decades had passed since the last fearsome
storm had ravaged the island in 1791. Subsequent hurricanes had been confined largely to localized disturbances, to specific regions like Bayamo in
1800, Cienfuegos in 1825 and 1832, and Trinidad in 1837. Under the circumstances, it is not difficult to understand why many producers and property
owners regarded hurricanes as occurrences with which they could arrive at

a satisfactory modus vivendi. But the structure of production on which the prosperity and well-being of the island had come to depend could not have developed in ways more vulnerable to the winds of the autumnal equinox.

The winds of the 1840s began early in the decade. A rare late November storm hit the northern coast of Havana in 1841: a minor disturbance, by most accounts, causing more passing inconvenience than lasting destruction. In September 1842 the northern coast of western central Cuba was struck by a slightly more powerful, fast-moving hurricane. Strong winds and heavy rainfall caused flooding along the waterfront districts in Cárdenas, Matanzas, and Havana, with some resulting damage to anchored ships, commercial buildings, and homes along the bay fronts.[1] Both hurricanes passed as more or less unremarkable occurrences, the type of storms that most people had become accustomed to. Life continued as usual.

/ / / / /

The 1844 storm season had been comparatively quiet and seemed to be passing without even as much as a tropical depression. This was not good. Cuba had been in the throes of a dry spell all summer, and the absence of rain aroused deep anxiety among producers across the island. In late August the daily *El Faro Industrial de La Habana* worried editorially about the "severe drought that has parched the countryside."[2]

No one could recall a drought as unrelenting. Spring waters dried up. Rivers were reduced to streams; streams disappeared. Alarm spread. The crops were failing, animals both domestic and wild were dying. And the buzzards multiplied.[3]

Farmers large and small faced ruin. In Gibara, on the northeastern coast of the island, planter John Taylor searched the skies daily for any sign of rain. Daily he was disappointed. "Every evening, during the continuance of the proper season of rain," he wrote years later, "clouds gathered in the opposite direction of the wind — namely, in the south-west; distant lightning flashed in the sultry evenings, and thunders were, though barely, audible. . . . But no [rain] fell in our district." Taylor was among the many farmers who were losing their livelihood. His crops were failing. He had started with more than a hundred beehives and was reduced to eight. His livestock was dying off. "The poor pigs came home from the forest, where neither food nor water was procurable, and wandered about like ghosts, dropping off by twos and threes," he wrote. "The cattle — it was piteous to see them! Reduced to extremes, they devoured all sorts of unwholesome food." Most of all, Taylor recalled the auras: "[They] plied well their task as scavengers. . . . Wherever our eyes were directed, hundreds might be seen in circling flight, or sitting, gorged and stupefied, on the fences and trees. They seemed to have been specially multiplied for the occasion, and no doubt, were of vast utility."[4]

As early as October 2, moist breezes were first noticed on the southern coast as southeasterly winds, accompanied by unsettled seas and unstable clouds. Fifteen years later Enrique Edo recorded the portents of October 2 in Cienfuegos, a day "in which the thermometer fell considerably, to the point that indicated the imminence of a storm in this zone."[5] The moist breezes of early October 1844 were initially received with widespread rejoicing.

By the morning of Friday, October 4, the day of San Francisco de Asis, the light breezes gave way to gales and gusts, accompanied by squalls and surge, and then, finally, the full impact of the hurricane was felt. The center of the hurricane entered Cuba on the southern coast, between Batabanó and Cienfuegos. Landfall was recorded shortly before midnight.

It was a dreaded nocturnal hurricane, always associated with a special kind of terror, for the blackness of the night exacerbated the storm's cruelty. Visibility was indispensable for survival. An impenetrable darkness descended, making movement almost impossible, though relieved periodically by brilliant flashes of lightning. Confusion gave way to panic in the face of the roaring winds, torrential rains, booming thunder, and the sounds of falling buildings and the smashing of flying debris.[6]

In the course of the next ten hours, Hurricane San Francisco de Asis thundered across Cuba on a northeasterly course with sustained winds of 115 miles per hour, gusting to 150 miles per hour. The storm center exited on the northern coast at about 10:00 A.M. on Saturday, leaving in its wake a panorama of devastation that extended across the western third of the island.

The landscape of destruction stretched bleakly almost three hundred miles between Cortés and Casilda on the southern coast and between Bahía Honda and La Isabela on the northern coast. Coastal zones were devastated by the winds and the storm surge. Especially hard-hit were the ports and towns along both coasts, including Batabanó, Casilda, Bahía Honda, Havana, Matanzas, and Cárdenas, with effects felt as far east as Remedios. "All the thatched houses have been blown down," one resident reported from Batabanó, "and their dwellers are reduced to the most atrocious misery. There is not a single *sitio* with its houses left standing." A journalist from Remedios wrote that the "wind has destroyed forests and toppled trees of every kind. Not even the small plants had been spared, like yucca and yams, which have been totally uprooted."[7] Cienfuegos was ravaged again. "I am obliged to report," Francisco Zoyestino, the demoralized municipal treasurer, wrote the governor general in Havana several weeks later, "that perhaps not with the same intensity as in the western part of the island, the said hurricane has caused widespread devastation throughout this jurisdiction." A score of ships were destroyed in the harbor, docks and piers were washed away, and government buildings, commercial establishments, and private homes were destroyed, Zoyestino reported. "Not a single wooden home in the path of the winds that raged during the storm remains standing. In some zones nothing remains standing."[8]

Waves approaching ten to fifteen feet invaded Havana harbor, with devastating effect all along the bay front. Dock and port facilities were lost; warehouses and waterfront commercial establishments were demolished. The majority of the ships that had sought safety in the spacious harbor were damaged beyond repair. Indeed, the destruction in Havana harbor was itself corroboration of the power of the storm. The landlocked harbor, historically unrivaled for the security of its waters—"one of the safest, best defended, and most capacious in the world," David Turnbull had proclaimed only four years earlier—proved to be a death trap for most of the two hundred vessels that had sought safe anchorage inside the bay.[9] "Many [ships] were dismasted," commented nineteenth-century meteorologist William Redfield, "numbers were sunk, and several had overset, remaining bottom up. The southwestern shores of the harbor were strewed [sic] with wrecks, and this in a port unrivalled for its secure anchorage."[10] British naval officer Robert McClure, who happened to be in Havana that weekend, could hardly believe his eyes. "In fact," he wrote, "words cannot convey any idea." McClure described the condition of Havana harbor on Saturday morning:

> From our poop could be counted, 23 vessels, either floating bottom up, or blown high and dry on the beach, wreck and cargo floating in all directions, ships dismasted, and driving pell-mell. On the following day, I went round the harbour, and counted eighty-five vessels sunk or blown completely out of the water; one schooner actually in a field, some yards above the beach. I have heard that there are five more on the beach, near the Punta, perfectly wrecked—making a total of ninety vessels, varying in size from sixty to 300 tons.[11]

The destruction extended across the capital, within the old walled city but especially beyond the walls. The narrow, unpaved streets of old Havana, hardly able to withstand normal rains, were almost washed away.[12] Commercial establishments and private residences, government buildings, street lamps, and carriages were ruined. "Now that we have had an opportunity to move about the entire city," *El Faro Industrial de La Habana* editorialized several days later, "now that we have laid eyes on the innumerable ruins and have heard with horror accounts of a thousand disasters and seen a thousand scenes of devastation that have befallen the city in less than twelve hours, we are hard pressed to summarize the effects of a hurricane without parallel in the annals of Cuba." The editorial continued:

> The collapse of houses, fences, trees, doors, and windows began at 1 A.M. Rare indeed is the house in our extensive *intramuro* and *extramuro* population that has not sustained more or less damage. What an interminable night! To the crashing noise that resounded in the elements were joined the wailing (*ayes*) of the victims, the moaning of helplessness, the cries of misfortune, the prayers of the faithful raised to the Highest. . . . After the hurricane passed, the city presented a view of a place that had just been sacked and bombed.

Several years later William Redfield conservatively estimated the cost of the destruction to have surpassed one million pounds sterling.[13]

The devastation inland was no less catastrophic. Few towns escaped without damage. Virtually nothing remained standing in Vereda Nueva. "The villages of Sabanilla, Limonar, and Santa Ana no longer exist," reported *El Faro Industrial de La Habana*. "The town of Puentes Grandes has been left almost totally destroyed." Jaruco, Quivicán, San Cristobal, and San Antonio de los Baños sustained extensive losses. The town of Trinidad was also battered, and almost all the outlying sugar plantations received widespread damage. One report from Santiago de las Vegas provided a grim account of conditions:

> Few, very few, are the dwellings that have not suffered some damage to walls, doors, etc., and it can be said with complete certainty that every family . . . has suffered losses valued at no less than 30 pesos. The losses in the countryside are considerable. Two-thirds of all the houses have been blown down and in the course of which various families were buried alive in their own homes. The rice harvest and in general all the vegetation and a large part of the tubers have been completely lost. At least half of coco-palms, palm trees, the great ceiba trees, and fruit trees are found laying on the ground or are severely damaged. We have seen in particular things that seem incredible: mamey and zapote [trees] more than a *vara* and a half [1 vara = 33 inches] in diameter ripped up, roots and all,

at two and three *varas* from where they originally stood. Those that are still standing have been so totally stripped of leaves that it looks more like we are living in the arctic region.[14]

The damage in Matanzas was immense. The scene along the waterfront was one of desolation. The docks and piers, the warehouses and their content, and almost all the bay front structures suffered large-scale destruction. Over five thousand boxes of sugar were lost. The two rivers that forged through the city, the Yumurí and San Juan, backed up and overflowed their banks, causing major flood damage to upriver settlements and agricultural zones and ravaging the lower part of the city. "Yesterday morning," wrote one resident, "the San Juan and Yumurí rivers swelled to dimensions never before seen, sweeping aside everything in their path."[15] The inland towns of Aguacate, Madruga, and Tapaste also experienced severe damage. Outlying sugar plantations and coffee estates were wasted. "The effects of the recent hurricane are still visible in the country," the U.S. consular agent in Matanzas wrote in December, "and the crop of sugar for this year will be . . . one third less than last."[16]

The devastation to the rich agricultural zones of the hinterlands surrounding the cities was beyond belief. "We have just experienced a horrifying hurricane," wrote one farmer from Pinar del Río several days after the storm, "the results of which will subject this fertile part of the island of Cuba to new and greater damage than was experienced with the drought. The planted fields of rice, corn, yucca, plantains — everything has perished. Fences, houses, trees, forests — everything has been left destroyed."[17] Municipal treasurer Francisco Zoyestino reported horrendous conditions in the countryside surrounding Cienfuegos. "In fact," he wrote, "the destruction in the countryside (*campo*) is far worse than in the town [*villa*]":

In general there have been great losses in the more lightly constructed buildings, especially the palm-thatched *bohíos* of the countryside that could not withstand the violence of the winds. Neither could the crops and the products of the land. Not a single fruit-bearing banana plant remains standing in the entire jurisdiction; all were snapped broken and all that remains are sprouts. Crops of rice, sugar cane, and corn have been destroyed. All the sugar cane and corn stalks were snapped broken and are presently drying out. So powerful was the wind that many trees were toppled and uprooted. . . . The general loss of the agricultural products and the complete destruction of others has had a sorrowful effect on the condition of families in the countryside, creating unemployment and misery.[18]

Robert McClure described bleak conditions in the countryside surrounding Havana. "The country it is reported," he wrote, "has suffered most fearfully, the fodder for the cattle, and Indian corn is swept away, gardens laid bare, and plantations razed to the ground; the land which on Friday was most luxuriant, to-day is laid bare and desolate, not a vestige of verdure meets the eye."[19]

Saltwater mixed with rainwater, which was carried deep inland by hurricane winds, contaminated freshwater supplies and scorched plantation crops, vegetable gardens, fruit trees, and pastureland. "The rain that fell during the hurricane was salty," another observer reported, "for it mixed with water from the sea carried by the wind over great distances. . . . It was noted at a distance as far as two leagues. Many people with cisterns in their homes have noticed this condition and it is imperative that they empty and clean them of these deposits of brackish rain water . . . and wait for new rainfall," adding further, "The trees and shrubs that have remained standing all have their leaves burned, as if they had been scorched by frost. This no doubt is the result of the impact of the wind as well as the salinity of the water carried by the rain."[20]

Cafetales endured a tremendous pounding. The rich coffee-producing zones of Jaruco, Vereda Nueva, and Managua were devastated. "Everything is ruined," wrote coffee grower Vicente Valdés Peñalver; "coffee and corn have been razed. Not a single tree remains standing, for those that were not uprooted were truncated." In the south around Majana, the administrator of three cafetales described similar conditions:

> The hurricane has destroyed the workshops, groves, and fields of these estates. . . . All the thatched workshops have been blown away, the ones of masonry and tile . . . have suffered substantial damage. In some instances [it] will be necessary to demolish them for they are ruined. Only a tenth of the palms and cocoanut trees remain standing. The other trees have suffered equal damage. The *platanales* lay strewn everywhere; some coffee plants have been ripped up by their roots, others are broken and burned and all the berries are scattered all over the ground.[21]

The most productive cafetales of Artemisa, including Matilde, Rotunda, Ascensión, Mariana, Unidad, La Reunión, and Unión, were casualties of the floodwaters and winds. According to the owner of the Unión estate: "Everything is enshrouded in gloom. The devastation of the fields by the horrible hurricane has deprived the farmer of the little hope that remained after the drought. Tobacco, *boniato*, coffee plants, plantains—everything has disappeared. The woods appear burned, stripped of their leaves, with many [trees] uprooted."[22] Miguel del Aldama provided some sense of the despair that settled over the rural jurisdictions of Havana:

> [T]he frightful drought that desolated the countryside, resulting in hunger and misery for a large part of the population, have not been sufficient calamities to calm the ire of Heaven against us: today that Island of Cuba that you knew in the fullness of its natural beauty, rich with forests and magnificent gardens no longer exists: everything, everything has been razed by a ferocious hurricane that during the eighteen hours that it beat down on us delivered desolation and ruin everywhere. Its forests no longer exist; its great *ingenios* and *cafetales* have been ruined; the various plants nurtured by its soil have been uprooted. . . . The ruin has been general: the poor have lost the little they own and the rich contemplate the loss of their homes, cane fields, and gardens. . . . In sum, everything provides a picture of horrors the type of which Cuba has never before seen.[23]

The loss of life was high, especially on both coasts and along the many bay fronts of the score of harbor towns in western Cuba. Many were swept away during the initial storm surge. Others disappeared in inland floods. In the cities, particularly Havana and Matanzas, many perished in collapsing buildings. In total, an estimated five hundred people died. Countless thousands were injured.[24]

The effects of Hurricane San Francisco de Asis were experienced well beyond the western provinces. John Taylor and other planters in the region of Gibara depended on western merchants and producers for supplies vital to the local economy. Two or three times a week, ships would arrive in Gibara from Havana laden with needed provisions and supplies, but not on October 6. "[A] vessel, returning empty," Taylor recalled, "brought us the astounding news of the great hurricane, which had laid waste the entire of Havana, and the country as far as Matanzas or further, and destroyed almost every living plant." Taylor described a "dreadful calamity, *never before known* in that part of Cuba," that had cost "so many lives and ruined so many interests," adding: "In the west of the island, the hurricane was followed by tremendous floods, which equally destroyed cane, coffee, and produce already stored, and the rivers rose to a height never dreamed of. I

Tracks of the hurricanes of September 1842, October 1844, and October 1846.
Reprinted from Ivan Ray Tannehill, Hurricanes: Their Nature and History
(Princeton, 1938).

am afraid to say, from memory, at how many *thousand* tons of sugar the loss
was then estimated."[25]

Conditions in the interior jurisdictions were about to become worse. In
fact, the hurricane had wrought havoc on insular maritime traffic. Scores
of vessels engaged in the coastwise shipping of the island, and on which
outlying provincial towns and cities depended for supplies and furnishings,
were among the many ships destroyed in the harbors of Mariel, Havana,
Matanzas, Cárdenas, Batabanó, and Cienfuegos, with predictable effects.
Hard times in Gibara became harder. Taylor noted: "For three whole months
. . . my only food consisted of some . . . 'tasajo,' or jerked beef, boiled or

stewed, with a few 'frijoles,' or black-eyed peas, which, though nearly a year old and terribly riddled by weevils, were, indeed, duly prized, and I know I was in this case the envy of many less fortunate neighbors."[26]

/ / / / /

After October 1844 weather became a source of brooding preoccupation for many Cubans, especially with the approach of autumn. The hurricane season of 1845 passed uneventfully. The next year, however, some seasonal squalls in Matanzas in late September 1846 caused widespread panic. "It was with no small amount of fear that we passed the last week," declared the resident correspondent for *Diario de La Habana*, "for the weather presented threatening aspects. During three days heavy clouds and squalls plunged the population into alarm, and everyone raced about to procure emergency provisions in case of the second act of San Francisco of 1844. The week passed, and with the improvement of the weather tranquility has returned to our spirits."[27]

In Havana in early October 1846, no one was giving much thought to hurricanes. On the contrary, *habaneros* had been distracted by events of public revelry leading to Saturday, October 10, the birthday of Queen Isabel II. Loyal subjects had given themselves to daylong celebrations, including public concerts, military parades, and promenades customary on such occasions. The events of the tenth climaxed in the evening, when the most distinguished representatives of colonial high society assembled at a gala ball hosted by the Havana Philharmonic Society. Everyone who mattered was present, including Governor General Leopoldo O'Donnell, the Intendant General Conde de Villanueva, and the many men and women who represented the most socially prominent families in the capital. Guests arrived late, delayed by the driving rain and gusting winds that had started earlier in the evening. Spanish writer Miguel Rodríguez Ferrer happened to be visiting Havana that weekend and through the influence of a friend had obtained an invitation to the ball. Many years later he recalled:

It is nearly three-quarters of a league from El Cerro to the city, and the resistance of the rain, the wind, and the darkness en route was great, for it was only the bolts of lightning that illuminated the way for the coachman driving us. But finally we arrived at the Plaza . . . at the site of the dance, and taking note of the loud noise made by the wind whirling among the tree-tops before entering, we began to worry. . . . The dance started without the illustrious gathering acknowledging . . . the sounds of the wind and rain striking against the walls and windows of that magnificent location, so brilliantly illuminated and which formed such a contrast to the profound darkness that had descended upon the streets.[28]

No one could have imagined the fury that was bearing down on the capital that Saturday evening. What the assembled personages at the society ball could not have known was that at precisely that moment, approximately 1:00 A.M., on the day of San Francisco de Borja, a hurricane had made landfall on the southern coast of the island, near the port city of Batabanó, and was driving in a northerly direction. Unstable winds and unsettled waters had been noted late Saturday along both coasts, and knowledgeable observers knew that east-northeast winds signified an approaching storm. What they could not have anticipated, however, was the speed of the approaching storm and its dimensions, the intensity of the rain, and the velocity of the wind.

What also could not have been expected, especially so soon after San Francisco de Asis in 1844, was that a far more fearsome storm, with a far wider radius, would lay siege to the western half of the island for more than twelve hours, as a result of which Cuba would never be the same. Indeed, it was precisely because this eventuality was so inconceivable that early warning signs passed largely unheeded. "We heard knowledgeable men," complained the Sociedad Económica de Amigos del País some weeks later, "intelligent and experienced persons, assure us that we were no longer in danger of further storms for the remainder of this season. As a result, nothing was said about the signs days prior to the approaching hurricane. . . . No one anticipated the need for preparations until mere hours before the fatal encounter."[29] Several days after the storm planter Rafael José Madrigal wrote:

> On Saturday, around 4 in the afternoon, amid intermittent squalls and strong and sustained northeast winds, we noted low-ceiling and fast moving clouds, accompanied by plainly audible but distant rumblings. This led us to expect, at most, the change of the season, or perhaps the arrival of the first of the *nortes;* but never remotely the new hurricane that has made us shudder. It became apparent at eleven in the evening, and at that hour there was no longer any doubt of the danger by which we were surrounded.[30]

By the next morning there was no doubt in anyone's mind. Hurricane San Francisco de Borja had produced an epic disaster. "The worst storm in the memory of Havana," Inspector General Manuel Fernández de Castro affirmed several decades later. Samuel Hazard was even more categorical: "The most violent hurricane ever known upon the island." In hurricane annals, this would be known as the "Great Havana Hurricane of 1846."[31]

The incongruity of such frightful destruction at a time of festivity was noted. "What a contrast!" *Diario de la Marina* editorialized: "Yesterday everything bustle and cheer celebrating the birthday of Her Majesty. Luxurious coaches criss-crossing the streets in all directions and paying their respects at the Palace of the Government. . . . And at night, under the roof of the Philharmonic, the melodious notes of the voluptuous *danzas habaneras* resonated and obscured the roar of the hurricane that was beginning."[32]

/ / / / /

The hurricane of October 1846 extended across the western half of Cuba, from La Coloma to Casilda on the southern coast and from Bahía Honda to Caibarién on the northern coast. The storm center entered east of Batabanó in the south and moved in a northwesterly direction, exiting several miles west of Havana in the north. That is, it traversed much of the same region affected in 1844, but with a larger radius and with far greater intensity. The greatest destruction was registered between eastern Pinar del Río and western Matanzas; the storm affected areas as far east as Puerto Príncipe but devastated the regions surrounding Havana, Matanzas, Güines, Madruga, Alquízar, Cárdenas, Sagua la Grande, Trinidad, and — again — Cienfuegos. As it moved north toward the Florida Keys, the hurricane caused the death of more than six hundred people and thousands of injuries.[33]

No one could recall gales of such violence; gusts reached an estimated 190 miles per hour. The storm surge devastated coastal zones and penetrated miles inland. After the fury of the storm had passed, torrential rains continued all day Sunday and Monday and into Tuesday afternoon. Whereas Hurricane San Francisco de Asis in 1844 hit drought-stricken Cuba, Hurricane San Francisco de Borja struck after weeks of diluvial rains, with the land already saturated with water and unable to absorb any more. On October 8, two days before the hurricane made landfall, *Diario de la Marina* published a letter from a resident in Guane despairing of the relentless rains: "It is impossible for me to communicate the details concerning the lamentable effects of the rains of September. . . . It has rained without stopping a single moment for days and nights. The rivers have swollen to menacing proportions, the roads have become impassable. Tobacco farmers have lost almost everything."[34] Indeed, the destruction wrought by the hurricane in October

1846 followed widespread losses resulting from the September rains. As a resident of Paso Real de San Diego commented, "The rain, or better said, the downpour during a period of a month without pause . . . resulted in the loss of the tobacco seed beds and the spoiling of all the beds of *yuca, boniato,* and other *viandas*." [35]

It would be weeks before authorities in Havana arrived at some understanding of the magnitude of the destruction. On October 12 Governor General Leopoldo O'Donnell forwarded his grim report to Madrid. O'Donnell did not yet know the full extent of the property damage and human loss, but he feared the worst. He had lived through 1844, and this one, he knew, was much more powerful. "Another hurricane of far longer duration than the one suffered on the night of October 4, 1844 has struck and further crippled the island of Cuba," O'Donnell informed the Ministry of Ultramar. "The hurricane yesterday has exceeded the previous one in violence and duration, and its consequences will be far more lamentable." He thus prepared authorities in Madrid for the most deleterious result. "From 11 P.M. onward on the night of the 10th the storm developed," he explained, "increasing in its violence from between 7 to 10 A.M. with inconceivable fury, causing in the towns, in the country, and in the port [of Havana] immense damage." [36] O'Donnell's worst fears had, in fact, underestimated the devastation.

///// /

Havana experienced direct and prolonged battering from Hurricane San Francisco de Borja. Once again, the ships that had sought safety in the harbor found destruction instead. Thirty-foot seas drove across Havana harbor. Ships drifted in the bay, dragging their anchors behind them; some crashed into one another, sinking and overturning at the point of contact, while others were smashed against harbor constructions and blown aground, often far onto shore. "What a sight our beautiful bay presents!" exclaimed one resident five days after the hurricane had passed. "Dismasted ships, crashing against one another, foundering, destroyed, their timbers and riggings entangled with one another, crashing against the docks and other debris. The floating planks and fragments of a thousand vessels subject to the shifting impulse of the wind: rich merchandise atop the water, boxes of sugar, bales of tobacco, pieces of hemp, barrels, cases. Everything confused, everything crashing together, everything destroyed." [37] One hundred and five merchant vessels, 70 sloops, pilot boats, and a number of warships of various nationalities suffered extensive if not total damage. In addition, 111 coastwise ships were demolished, and once more insular maritime trade was disrupted, re-

Federico Mialhe, "The Hurricane of 1846 (Havana)." Courtesy of Museo Nacional de Bellas Artes, Havana. Photograph by Rodolfo Martínez García.

sulting immediately in shortages of every type in the interior provinces. "In this capital," Governor General O'Donnell reported from Havana, "the port and its bay in particular present a painful sight: all the merchant ships and coastwise vessels have suffered considerable losses — some more, some less. Many have been totally lost."[38]

What made the hurricane of 1846 so destructive in Havana and other port cities was the degree to which the breakup of ships, the collapse of warehouses, and the shattering of the docks of the Tallapiedra Pier contributed to the waterborne debris, which, in turn, was hurled against raised structures along the waterfront. One news report in *Diario de la Habana* was suggestive:

> On the day of the calamity our port was filled with trading vessels from all friendly nations. . . . And at daybreak of the mournful day of [October] 11, all that remained were their destroyed vestiges resting atop damaged piers, thrown against the walls of the city and entangled in mangroves, while thousands of packages and barrels, and boxes of sugar and tobacco, and sacks of coffee, and the shattered pieces of boats, tenders, schooners, and coasters, battered by the twin effects of the wind and the sea, floated atop the waves of the bay.[39]

It is unlikely that a single building in the capital escaped at least some damage. Walls of masonry were razed to the ground. The resplendent and newly renovated Teatro Principal was reduced to rubble. Buildings along

"Memorable Hurricane of October 11, 1846." Reprinted from José María de la Torre,
Mapa historica pintoresco moderno de la Isla de Cuba *(1853). Courtesy of Biblioteca*
Nacional José Martí, Havana.

the waterfront were demolished. The gas plant was incapacitated when the
smokestack collapsed. Churches were leveled. The roof of the cathedral was
severely damaged and the roof of the Monteserrate church was blown off.
Parish churches in Jesús del Monte and Guanabacoa were destroyed. A number of hospitals were in ruins, including the important Real Hospital de
San Lázaro. At the moment of greatest medical need, Havana found itself
with limited capacity to care for the thousands of injured habaneros. "All
my work has been lost," despaired Alfredo Saurulle, director of the Real
Hospital de San Lázaro. "The principal entrance has collapsed. . . . Various
wards and the new infirmary building have suffered much damage; all the
roofs are ruined."[40] The destruction was too extensive, concluded *Diario de
la Marina*, to have been caused by a hurricane: "The number of those of
us who believe that Havana also experienced an earthquake is considerable
and to which we attribute the ruin of several walls and houses, and not to
the wind of the hurricane."[41]

Vast areas of the urban landscape revealed themselves as mangled piles
of debris and rubble. In the jurisdiction of Guanabacoa, about 1,275 houses
were destroyed and another 1,040 were damaged. Only hours after the hurricane passed, the editor of *Diario de la Marina* went out into the city: "It
is 1 P.M. on [October] 11. . . . We have just completed an inspection of a part
of *intramuro* Havana, or more correctly half of it up to the bay. We do not
have any real idea of what happened during [the hurricane of] 1768 or in

1796, but we can affirm that neither in 1842 nor in 1844, years in which we were here, did we see anything closely resembling what we have just seen." A week after the storm, Manuel Rodríguez Ferrer walked through the capital in a state of numbed disbelief: "The streets of Havana were nothing more than a continuous field of ruins and wreckage. Its streets were almost entirely covered with debris material, wooden planks, and tiles: its gardens destroyed, the palm trees truncated or topless; the trees uprooted. Many balconies [were] at the point of imminent collapse and some were twisted and strewn all about. And the port? Here is where the desolation appeared most frightful, for the eyes of the observer took in within that circumference of water a sight of utter horror."[42] U.S. consul Robert Campbell had experienced several hurricanes before but never one of this magnitude. "The destruction in this, and the other cities heard from in the Island, of houses, crops, vessels, and of everything else," Campbell wrote from Havana on October 15, "has been most calamitous, and unparalleled in the history of the Island. Many lives have been lost in this port and city. . . . No house in the city has entirely escaped." On entering Havana harbor several days later after travel abroad, Carlos Martí was stunned. "We have returned to Havana without incident," Martí wrote to a friend on November 2, "but at the very moment of entering the harbor through El Morro, we have come to understand the terrible misfortune that this island has suffered on October 10–11. What a very strange contrast: the joy of returning to the desired port of destination and the pathetic sight of the harbor and city."[43]

/ / / / /

The destruction in the provincial interior was unimaginable and thus incalculable. Towns and cities across western Cuba suffered various degrees of damage; smaller villages and rural settlements (caseríos) disappeared altogether. Vast stretches of some of the most productive lands in the Western Hemisphere had been laid waste. Entire forests were razed or transformed into desolate stands of stumps. Where anchorage was sufficiently strong, the trees snapped; those that remained standing were stripped of their leaves.

Towns and villages across the interior hinterland of western Cuba experienced extensive and in some instances irreparable damage. That the 1846 hurricane—like the one of 1844—moved through western Cuba on a southern to northern course meant that the most powerful winds, located northeast of the center, the point where rotating winds converged with linear winds most forcefully, ravaged the most productive agricultural zones and the most densely populated regions of the island.

The northeasterly winds had begun to stir and swirl around the southern port of Batabanó in the early evening of October 10. By dawn the next day, the town was under siege as a storm surge riding the water of high tide, with huge waves rolling inland, some of them thirty feet high, crashed down on coastal structures. Within hours, all the *bohíos* and most of the tiled-roof houses had been demolished and washed away. Twenty houses remained standing. Food reserves were destroyed; fresh water supplies were spoiled by saltwater. The receding floodwaters deposited inches of mud and muck and piles of debris throughout the town.[44]

In fact, almost all port towns and cities received extensive damage. In the towns of Caimito and Rosario the warehouses and their contents, as well as the piers and wharves, were washed out to sea; not a single dwelling was left standing. All the docks and the majority of houses in Cabañas disappeared. Of the twenty-three houses in the small fishing town of Cojímar, sixteen were destroyed.[45]

Matanzas again suffered devastation. Winds started to stir on Saturday evening and continued to gather velocity through predawn Sunday morning. The full fury of the hurricane hit at early daybreak and pounded the city through the early afternoon. Almost all the ships in port were destroyed, including scores of coastwise vessels.[46] Many sank at the point of anchorage; others were driven aground. The harbor was littered with the wreckage of countless ships. Waves leaped from the rising ocean and rolled ashore in sequence, toppling buildings and flooding the lower portion of the city. Smaller wooden structures and larger stone ones, many weakened by the hurricane of 1844, collapsed on impact of the first rolling waves. Buildings and homes along the bay front, as well as communities located along the banks and inland of the Yumurí and San Juan Rivers, were washed away by the rising floodwaters. "An infinite number of houses of masonry and wood along the banks of the San Juan river have disappeared," according to one observer.[47] A small plantation house a short way up the San Juan was washed out to sea. More than forty persons perished in the initial flooding. "There is not a single street that does not bear the effects of the hurricane," reported the daily *Aurora de Matanzas*. "Wherever one looks in Matanzas and its ravaged neighborhoods, one beholds nothing but ruin."[48]

Slowly the magnitude of devastation in towns and villages of the interior became known. In Güines, all homes, public buildings, and commercial establishments were demolished, and one hundred people perished. "I am picking up the pieces of the factories that existed in this town, for all have collapsed under the force of the hurricane," Bartolomé Junqué wrote from

Güines on October 12; "not a single board remains standing. Two distilleries, a packing plant, a lumber mill, a supply warehouse, in a word: everything, everything, everything — all that remain are empty lots."[49] In Pinar del Río, death and destruction came mostly from flooding, as the rapid accumulation of torrential rains on the southern mountain slopes bloated the rivers and small water courses, causing flash floods against which local communities were defenseless.

Not a single home escaped damage in the towns of Bejucal, San Antonio de los Baños, Santiago de las Vegas, and Mariel. The houses that remained standing were roofless. "Almost all the houses of the poor have been reduced to wreckage," a local official reported from Bejucal. Of the nearly 80 houses in San Antonio, 70 were destroyed. Almost 75 houses met the same fate in Alquízar. A similar report arrived from Santiago de las Vegas: "Only four houses are left standing, for all the rest have been totally destroyed." Nueva Paz lost 110 houses; Madruga, 100. In Managua only 5 homes survived, while in Quivicán the 8 homes that remained standing suffered extensive damage; only 32 of the 82 houses in Jibacoa withstood the storm.[50]

In some places it was worse. Located at the confluence of the Guanabo River and its tributary Chuchón Creek, the town of Guanabo was all but washed away by floodwaters, leaving most of its residents homeless. "In this *pueblo*," wrote the *Diario de La Habana* correspondent from Guanabo, "there exists only one house; all the others have been destroyed." Some villages and settlements ceased to exist altogether. The *caseríos* of Mantilla, La Chorrera, and Paula vanished. The caserío of Bayate (Candelaria), located between the San Juan de Contreras and Bayate Rivers, was washed away. And there were others. The vast majority of houses and shops in Cayajabos, Wajay, Candelaria, and Aguacate collapsed. "Alquízar, in the jurisdiction of San Antonio," wrote Diego Fernández Herrera on October 17, "as well as Güira de Melena and Vereda Nueva, can be considered as practically erased from the territorial map."[51] Similar reports arrived from Guatao ("This town no longer exists; all its houses have been destroyed, including the church, which was considered one of the most solid of all the rural churches"), Quemado ("This town has been almost totally destroyed"), and San Antonio de los Baños ("Only four houses remain standing, for all the rest have been completely destroyed").[52]

/ / / / /

Throughout the small agricultural villages and farming hamlets of the hinterland, on the small sitios and estancias and across the large ingenios and cafetales, on the orchards and groves, on tobacco vegas and caseríos, from family farms to slave provision grounds, the destruction was staggering. The fields were ravaged. In a matter of twelve hours landscapes were reshaped. In some regions, the face of the countryside was completely changed. Vast stretches of land had been stripped of all identifying vegetation, trees disappeared, fences were washed away, and markers of all kinds vanished. In some instances, proprietors found it impossible to locate the old boundaries of their respective estates. The trunks of uprooted palm trees carried by floodwaters served as battering rams, leveling fields of sugarcane, plantain, and corn — smashing, toppling, and dragging away almost everything in their path. Mills, warehouses, processing and packing plants, stables, and storage facilities all suffered permanent damage. Bridges were washed away, as were country stores and the inventories on which numerous families depended. One report from Palacio was representative of conditions across the countryside: "The shops of this town, which number five, do not have bread.... There is neither jerked beef nor codfish, which is what is typically consumed in these parts. There is not a single onion or garlic available in the entire town."[53]

Rural bohíos and slave barracones, farmhouses and plantation casas de vivienda, as well as stables, chicken coops, and pigeon houses (palomares), were razed. Entire herds of livestock perished. Stocks of goats, pigs, mules, horses, and cattle were washed away. Most chickens disappeared. Tens of thousands of beehives vanished.

The magnitude of the destruction was inconceivable. The countryside was strewn with fallen trees and downed crops. In places trees and bushes had been completely defoliated, appearing to many as winter in the tropics. Acres of trees were stripped of their leaves. In some regions, not one fruit tree was left standing. Crops of rice, corn, and yucca were laid waste. "The countryside appears scorched," Governor General Leopoldo O'Donnell reported grimly.[54] Across the farmlands and grazing fields of rural Cuba the scene was one of flooding, mud, debris, wreckage, and misery.

For a large portion of the rural population, life had been disrupted and would never be the same. Entire villages were flattened. Roads were impassable for days and weeks after the hurricane. "In this district," declared a resident of Bauta, "there is not a single farm large or small that has not suffered substantial damage to the buildings and fields, in such a manner that the countryside appears as if it has been devastated by a fire."[55] Similar conditions were observed in Quivicán. "All the sitieros of this zone," wrote

Joaquín Cotilla on October 13, "are found today living in the open, like birds perched under the branches of trees that remain, for the majority of the houses have collapsed and disappeared. They are without any immediate hope of finding shelter. The sight breaks one's heart with pain and we can hardly hold the pen in our hand as we describe such horrible and frightful scenes."[56]

Few could believe their eyes. On October 17 Diego Fernández Herrera wrote: "We weep and are consumed by our tears . . . as desolation and death assault us from all sides. . . . We see Nature converted to wreckage, ruin, and bloody and mutilated cadavers." He continued:

> The unforgettable hurricane of San Francisco de Asis . . . was frightful but the one of San Francisco de Borja . . . after a duration of more than 20 hours, was doubly formidable. . . . The first traveled low; it burned sugar and coffee fields, scorched pasturage land, toppled forests, fruit trees and palm trees, brought down houses, and smashed hundreds of ships against the coast. . . . The second completed the work of destruction [la obra de destrucción]: it traveled all night high, shearing the robust pine trees and flexible palm trees in half. It toppled the tallest trees and the highest buildings and swept away the strongest tiled roofs, leaving almost all buildings exposed to the entry of the torrential rains, soaking all the fruits stored in warehouses, ruining harvested coffee, and dissolving stored sugar.[57]

Almost all crops suffered. The small subsistence crops, the fruits, vegetables, and viandas on which the rural population depended, were lost. Avocado trees were stripped of their fruit. Many were uprooted and others were so badly damaged that it would be years before they recovered their fruit-bearing capacity. Indeed, twice in as many years the loss of fruit on trees was almost complete. The citrus crop and mangoes were lost. Pineapple fields were flooded. Almost all the platanales were destroyed. The *Aurora de Matanzas* was succinct: "All the *plátanos* have disappeared."[58] Farmers lost reserves of seeds and seedling beds, maturing crops, work animals, stocks of domestic animals, and tools and equipment. Most were left without the means to replace what they had lost. "Provisions are scarce," reported a resident of Macuriges, "and soon we will not have even one kernel of corn."[59] José Bruzón lost almost all the animals on his potrero, including cows, mules, horses, and chickens. A resident of San Diego provided a sorrowful account of local conditions:

This hurricane is worse than the one of October 4, 1844, for on that occasion we had gathered [a] sufficient quantity of corn, the result of a bountiful harvest that year, that allowed us for months to make up for the scarcity of *plátanos* and *viandas* caused by that storm. But this year, we had not even gathered the seed for the corn that we planted as a result of the continual rains of the previous ten months. All our plants have spoiled. We can not even begin to imagine what the future will bring. The banana plants, loaded with abundant fruit, are lost, having been uprooted by the violence of the wind; similarly, the yuca plants have been ripped up by their roots and the vast part of the rice harvest has been lost.[60]

Diego Fernández Herrera surveyed the damage in Alquízar, Güira de Melena, and Vereda Nueva and described grim conditions. "The storm of 1844 reduced the harvests by three-quarters of what should have been produced," he wrote on October 17, 1846. "The cane fields, the coffee plants, and other fruit trees were left in damaged condition [after 1844] and made for a futile harvest in 1845. But in 1846, recovery seemed within reach, for the coffee had recuperated and sugar was superabundant. Tobacco had revived and yucca was especially fertile. Only corn remained scarce, and this was partially offset by the expansion of plantains that provided sustenance for the poor. . . . Now nothing remains."[61] A visitor to the town of Sierra Morena along the northern coast noted that "entire cane fields lay flattened, not a single banana plant is left standing, and all that remains of some mills are scattered tiles. Never before have I seen it rain for so long with such force and without cessation, between Saturday and Monday it was a deluge, so that the land everywhere appears as a flowing lake."[62]

Large numbers of tobacco vegas across the jurisdictions of Pinar del Río and Havana were destroyed. Almost all the seeds for the next year's crop were lost, as well as a large part of the previous year's inventory. The harvest of 1846 was almost a total loss. None of the 76,000 tobacco plants on one vega in Govea survived. Vast expanses of tobacco seedbeds were lost, delivering a body blow to prospects for the following year. Coming in the aftermath of the 1844 hurricane, these developments threatened scores of family farms with extinction. Nearly two months would be lost in planting new seedbeds and transplanting the young plants to the vegas. Instead of completing the planting in early November, as was the custom, farmers would be delayed until late December or early January. Rarely was the quality of late-season crops of tobacco as good as early ones. The seedling beds around

Artemisa, Alquízar, and San Antonio de los Baños were all destroyed. Thousands of bales of harvested tobacco stored in warehouses suffered extensive water damage. Entire tobacco inventories were lost. Dwelling houses, tobacco barns, and storage facilities were demolished.

Sugar also suffered widespread damage. Cane fields were devastated by the force of the wind. Local surveys of the damage across the zones of the western interior painted a somber picture, indeed. Cane was twisted at the base, split open, and frequently uprooted. Significant acreage of sugarcane was flattened in the fields, intertwined, and lying in every direction. It was difficult if not impossible to strip the cane of its leaves while it was lying flat, adding cost and time to what could be salvaged of the harvest. Considerable sucrose content was lost in damaged cane. Twice in two years, the harvest was delayed due to damage to the sugar mills. Between 1844 and 1845 total Cuban production declined by more than 45 percent, from 183,000 tons to 85,000. Production in the jurisdiction of Havana dropped by nearly 50 percent, from 96,000 tons to 47,000.[63] In most instances, however, unless the sugarcane was washed out of the ground by floodwaters, damage was not permanent, for the cane resumed normal growth the following year.

Some of the most serious damage was to buildings and equipment. Almost all the mills in the affected region suffered losses. Several small mills disappeared. Chimney towers were damaged, buildings were deroofed, and machinery was destroyed. Some mills were not able to repair the damage and lost the season. Others lost everything. All that remained standing on the ingenio San Francisco de Paula in Güira de Melena was a purging house, but without a roof. A resident from Sabanilla reported that "everywhere one looks one sees only horrible sights of destruction. The cane fields, whose lush growth this year raised expectation of an abundant harvest, lie strewn with mangled cane stalks. . . . All the mills that were not constructed as a huge fortress have collapsed." Visiting what remained of the Buen Amigo sugar estate in Matanzas days after the 1846 hurricane, a reporter for *El Faro Industrial de La Habana* struggled to describe the indescribable:

> I do not think that a more destructive hurricane has ever been seen. This looks like Judgment Day. The houses collapsed one after the other. It looks like the end of the world. The slaves sought refuge in the *casa de vivienda* because all the *bohíos* were blown down. They arrived clasping each other two by two so that wind would not blow them away. . . . Ay! If you could see this *ingenio* you would be horrified. Everything has come crashing down. It used to be so beautiful, and everything has dis-

appeared in less than one day. Everywhere all that can be seen are ruins. Virtually all the factories collapsed. The house of the *ingenio* is partially ruined; the crushers are completely destroyed, the boiling facility and the purging house are partially ruined. The *cañaverales* are totally lost: all the cane lies flat strewn across the field. It is a pity to see the product of so much work destroyed. Such a magnificent harvest was promised, such wonderful hopes dashed, for there will be no harvest. Everything has been lost.[64]

The coffee estates were pounded. Indeed, the effects of the two hurricanes were widespread and long-lasting. "The reports that are beginning to arrive from the countryside are very grim," announced the *Aurora de Matanzas* on October 13. "The *cafetales* have been particularly hard hit by the hurricane, with the crop approaching maturity: the plants have been overturned from which it will be impossible to pick the berries. These farms had only recently begun to recover from the disaster of 1844. Just when their owners had developed renewed hope a new calamity again acted to reduce producers to a lamentable condition."[65]

All the cafetales around Hoyo Colorado reported major destruction: flooded fields, uprooted trees, overturned coffee plants, and shattered buildings. The cafetal Payares reported most of its fields under water and the majority of the trees uprooted or destroyed. The mill of cafetal Marcial collapsed. The coffee estates in Quivicán were in ruins. All that survived of the cafetal Bella Arsenia was the casa de vivienda and the mill. The San Pablo estate was inundated by the floodwaters of the Santa Bárbara River, which washed away all dwellings and the mill and destroyed the crops of coffee, rice, and corn. Reports from Las Cangrejeras outside Havana indicated that the cafetales owned by the Marquesa de Cárdenas de Monte Hermoso "have been reduced to total destruction, the coffee fields are devastated and all the plants uprooted, the *platanales* have been overturned, and the workshops are in ruin. The picture is one of major desolation." Not far away, at the cafetal Delicias, virtually all the platanales, fruit trees, coffee plants, were laid waste and the buildings collapsed. Coffee estates around Artemisa, Consolación del Sur, and San Diego de los Baños suffered wind damage, uprooting the majority of coffee trees in central Pinar del Río. Damage was extensive in the region of Palmira, Cruces, and Camarones. "On my farm," wrote Domingo Landín from Camarones, "[the hurricane] has not left a single plant upright; what it did not uproot it smashed. On my lovely *platanales*, not even a sprout can be seen; the coffee plants, the trees, and the berries are strewn all over the ground. In my beautiful *batey* not [a] single work shop remains."[66] The cafetales Ascensión and Mariana owned by Miguel Chapotín in Artemisa lost tens of thousands of coffee plants, a well, and the curing building. In sum, forty cafetales around Artemisa sustained damage estimated at more than 100,000 pesos.[67] Conditions in Ceiba Mocha were typical of the devastation. Nearly all dwellings had collapsed. "The majority of homes in all the *sitios*," reported the *Aurora de Matanzas*, "have been destroyed. . . . The *ingenios* and *cafetales* have suffered much, with entire stocks of banana plants overturned and fruit trees uprooted, leaving the coffee plants stripped clean, for all the berries have fallen. Warehouses, coffee mills, and plants everywhere have suffered extensive damage." Within a week of the 1846 hurricane, *El Faro Industrial de La Habana* reached a somber conclusion: "The *cafetales* have been the hardest hit by the hurricane. Fully-mature plants have been razed, and it is probable that the majority will be permanently lost."[68]

Harvested coffee was similarly destroyed. Stored coffee inventories were ruined when the roofs of storage facilities were blown off and torrential rains entered. Coffee in the drying sheds (*secaderos*), typically of light construction, was carried away by winds and flood currents. The deroofing of warehouses wracked stored coffee sacks ready for shipment.

By the end of October 1846, Governor General Leopoldo O'Donnell had gathered sufficient information to make a detailed report to Madrid on the devastation wrought by what was already being called a "historic hurricane." O'Donnell hardly knew where to start:

> The cultivated fields, of vegetables and *viandas*, are generally the sites that have been completely destroyed everywhere in the countryside. In addition to those losses, are the losses of domestic animals, particularly fowl and cattle, that all perished. Also destroyed are the many houses of lumber and thatched roofs [*casas de maderas y guano*], losses that will weigh particularly heavy on the needy. The well-to-do [*los pudientes*], that is, the great property owners, have also suffered great losses. . . . The paralysis that this disaster has caused to business, to buying and selling, and to commercial transactions of all types is without doubt another lamentable result of the hurricane. The losses caused generally to shipping, and specifically with regard to the merchant vessels, in large part affecting foreign trade, are grave. The destruction of smaller ships, especially those engaged in coast-wise trade, is the damage that affects us most directly.[69]

It was difficult for the many people who had lived through the destructive fury of San Francisco de Borja to look at the gathering of clouds without a mixture of fear and foreboding. "Today, still," commented one Havana resident weeks after the hurricane, "upon the mere appearance of clouds, the eyes turn upward at the sight of the darkening sky and the soul despairs, fearful that the Almighty might once again discharge his ire against us."[70]

4. When Winds Disturb the Surface

Two hurricanes in the space of two years, and of mounting fury, have left morale so utterly dispirited that upon the slightest gust of wind we are terrified by the possibility of a third repetition of this horrific and desolating weather.

Desiderio Herrera, Memoria sobre los huracanes en la Isla de Cuba *(1847)*

The ruin that this town experienced as a result of the floods and the devastating winds . . . was so vast that the pen trembles, memory loses its natural power to recall, and thought is devoid of ideas when sitting down to write about what happened during those wretched times.

Manuel de Garay y Echeverría, Historia descriptiva de la villa de San Antonio de los Baños y su jurisdicción *(1859)*

The calamity to which we have all been witness has reduced the once opulent and rich city [of Havana] to the saddest and most wretched condition that the human imagination can conceive.

Cabildo de La Habana *(October 13, 1846)*

I am on my cafetal San Jose! I no longer see the forests or the numerous palm trees. Nothing of the banana plants. All the coffee trees have been obliterated. The ripened fruit is enveloped in muck and weed. Three giant ceiba trees have been shattered into a thousand pieces scattered among the coffee trees, destroying them by the sheer weight of their thick branches. . . . An indescribable stupor seizes my faculties at that moment. I stop my horse and brace myself so as not to fall off my saddle.

Diego Fernández Herrera (October 17, 1846)

I have heard a good deal of what occurred during the last hurricane. One spot was pointed out to me . . . where stood a little peasant farm. The whole family were assembled in the house, twelve in number. The tempest shook the dwelling; the father admonished them all to pray; they threw themselves on their knees around him; he stood upright in the middle of the room, and prayed in the name of all. The tempest tore open a hole in the roof, and in the same moment overturned the house, leaving the father standing upright, but burying his wife, his children, and servants. Not a single one escaped excepting himself.

Fredrika Bremer, The Homes of the New World:
Impressions of America *(1853)*

What appeared at any given point as random desolation was actually part of a vast expanse of destruction stretching across the western half of the island: ravaged towns, ruined fields, and communities in disarray. No sector of the colonial economy escaped disruption, and no sector was afflicted more than agriculture. Virtually all crops suffered extensive and in some instances irreversible damage. A pall of despair descended over the countryside. "It is painful," one observer commented from the hinterland, "to cast a view over the vast and previously luxuriant fields of sugar cane, coffee trees, and *plátanos*. It appears as if the destructive hand of the weather set out purposefully to ruin everything that might be of value to us. God willing these difficult times will be followed by happier occasions, for without them and a protective hand the agricultural richness of this valuable island will disappear."[1]

From large plantations to small family fincas, from commercial production to slave provision grounds, farmers, ranchers, beekeepers, rural workers — all endured losses. Reports from the interior countryside shared a tone of disbelief. Rich agricultural zones were no more. Huge stretches of productive land were stripped of all vegetation, cultivated fields were defoliated, forests were razed. The countryside was a mangle of scalded vegetation. The winds had lifted salt spray miles inland, searing all vegetation like a swift-moving prairie fire. "An acquaintance," John Taylor related of 1844, "who then returned from Havana, said the only comparison he could think of was, that the effect appeared as if in that one night a quantity of boiling water had been suddenly poured over every green plant."[2]

TABLE 4.1. Production of Frutos Menores, 1827 and 1846 (millions of pounds)

Crop	1827	1846
Corn	324	17
Viandas	733*	520*
Beans	3	2

Sources: Cuba, Capitanía General, *Cuadro estadístico de la Siempre Fiel Isla de Cuba, correspondiente al año de 1827* (Havana, 1829), n.p., and *Cuadro estadístico de la Siempre Fiel Isla de Cuba, correspondiente al año de 1846* (Havana, 1847), pp. 42, 153.

*Includes plantains.

The devastation two years later was depicted in strikingly similar terms. "There is not a single finca, large or small," declared a resident of Bauta, "that has not suffered damage to its workshops or its plantings, to such an extent that the countryside appears as if it has been devastated by a fire." From Güines, it was reported that "the destruction in the countryside has been widespread; the majority of the houses of the *potreros, sitios,* and *vegas* have disappeared and the *ingenios* and *cafetales* have suffered substantial damage."[3]

Agricultural production of virtually every type plunged into an immediate decline. Citrus groves and orchards were stripped of fruits: in places, successive rows of trees were snapped. Cornfields and platanales were especially vulnerable to the winds; the plants buckled and broke. Across the countryside, banana plants under commercial cultivation as well as the countless thousands intended for local subsistence were leveled. The value of cotton exports plummeted from 80,000 arrobas in 1840 to 339 arrobas by 1850 (1 arroba = 25 pounds). The colmenares that had numbered nearly 2,000 in 1827 were reduced by half by 1862. "Apiculture is presently found in the most deplorable state of abandonment," pronounced one observer in 1865.[4] Production of the population's most basic food staples, including corn, viandas, plantains, and beans, was obstructed. The data, though incomplete, suggest that production between 1827 and 1846 decreased while the population, both free and slave, increased (see Table 4.1).

What made the October hurricanes of 1844 and 1846 so devastating was that they struck just as crops were nearing maturity, on the eve of preparations for harvesting and milling. The coffee crop, which matured in September and October, was ready for harvest as the peak of the hurricane season approached. In October tobacco farmers transplanted the mature seedlings from the nursery seedbeds planted in August to open fields, where they reached maturity within three months. October was also the month when the ingenios prepared for the sugar harvest.

The magnitude of disruption of the cafetales was incalculable and in many instances permanent. Planters who had survived the drought of 1844 and the rains of 1846 faced a new round of adversities. Two successive hurricanes had plunged these producers into a crisis from which many never recovered. Coffee trees were stripped of their berries and foliage. On many cafetales the coffee trees themselves were damaged. "The hurricane has razed everything," despaired one coffee grower in Artemisa in mid-October 1846, "and in my opinion was more powerful and more destructive than the one in 1844. Trees and mills that the latter respected have been toppled. The coffee trees have been denuded of their fruit and as a result the entire harvest has been lost. There was no harvest in 1844. Nor in 1845. This year we had hopes, for the trees were loaded with berries. . . . All is lost." [5]

Coffee estates across Occidente lay in ruins. Plants ripened on the eve of the harvest were ravaged. "The hurricane has damaged the *cafetales* most," the correspondent of the *Diario de La Habana* reported within days of the 1846 storm; "mature berries have been strewn all over the ground, where the majority will be lost, leaving almost nothing of value to be gathered." [6]

Millions of coffee trees were completely uprooted. The number of trees declined by almost half, from about 405 million in the 1830s to 264 million by the 1850s. [7] No less devastating for the coffee growers was the destruction of the dense foliage that protected the maturing coffee plants. Shade trees were shattered and splintered, others were uprooted. "When I asked for trees," wrote poet William Cullen Bryant while visiting Cuba three years later,

> I was referred to the hurricanes which have recently ravaged the island. One of these swept over Cuba in 1844, uprooting the palms and the orange groves, and laying prostrate the avenues of trees on the coffee plantations. The Paseo Isabel, a public promenade, between the walls of Havana and the streets of the new town, was formerly over-canopied with lofty and spreading trees, which this tempest levelled to the ground; it has now been planted with rows of young trees, which yield a meagre shade. In 1846 came another hurricane, still more terrific, destroying much of the beauty which the first had spared. [8]

Moreover, both storms occurred at a time when coffee production in Brazil was increasing and the world price of coffee was decreasing. Between 1820 and 1840 Brazilian coffee exports rose from 64 million pounds to 137.3 million pounds. In fact, by midcentury Brazil produced one-half of the world's coffee.[9] The prospects of recovery for coffee producers in Cuba were bleak indeed.

The results were immediate. Thousands of cafetales across western Cuba were unable to resume production. In Vereda Nueva, the combined effects of two hurricanes delivered body blows to local agriculture. Local producers had hardly had time to recover from the effects of 1844 when the hurricane of 1846 hit. Almost all coffee trees were toppled. Saltwater spray carried inland some thirty kilometers by gale-force winds ruined crops of every type. San Francisco de Borja proved fatal for Vereda Nueva, for the damage was irreversible. Coffee production never recovered.[10]

Production across Occidente plummeted. Many growers lacked the resources to tide them over the three to five years required to bring new trees into production. The storms had not only ruined the coffee harvests of 1844 and 1846 but also had destroyed the accumulated inventories of previous harvests. Much of the capital equipment, including processing buildings and mills, was lost. By midcentury most coffee estates around Alquízar, Artemisa, and Cuzco hovered at the brink of total ruin. Planters lived precariously off what *frutos menores* (fruits and vegetables) they were able to produce and sell, forestalling foreclosure but in the end unable to overcome the combined effects of the destruction of property at home and the decline of markets abroad.[11] "Our situation is terrible," declared one coffee planter near Artemisa after the 1846 hurricane. "We are without a corn harvest, now even without rice, without palm trees for the [feeding of] pigs; we have nothing other than land and slaves. Only those planters who have ample resources will be able to maintain their estates for several years until they produce again." The owner of the cafetal Arcadia struggled to recover from the effects of 1846 but floundered and eventually failed. At the end, the estate lacked even the resources to maintain the dotación.[12] The two cafetales owned by the Marquesa de Cárdenas de Monte-Hermosa in Las Cangrejaras, reported one resident in mid-October 1846, "have been totally destroyed, their fields of coffee plants uprooted and devastated, the *platanales* razed, and the shops in debris. They offer a painful sight of extensive desolation."[13] The once prosperous cafetal Carlota in Limonar was no more. In late October a local planter wrote: "The hurricane toppled six buildings, among them the coffee mill and the stable, both of which had been rebuilt in the aftermath of the hurricane of 1844. Sad is the state of those of us who live in this small part of the island, for we find ourselves in the most grievous condition. . . . On September 4, 1842 a storm resulted in losses, but the hurricanes of 1844 and 1846 have left our *fincas* in the most lamentable condition."[14]

Without available capital and lacking collateral other than slaves for loans, coffee growers across Occidente failed to recover from the destruction at a time of expanding international competition and declining world prices. Some estates resumed production but in a condition of decline and were barely able to make ends meet. In the weeks and months following the 1846 hurricane, advertisements announcing the sale of coffee estates appeared in the Havana press with increasing frequency.[15] Based on his tour of San Antonio in 1849, William Cullen Bryant provided poignant testimony to the decline of what had been once the resplendent world of the cafetal: "Here and there was an abandoned coffee plantation, where cattle were browsing among the half perished shrubs and broken rows of trees, and the neglected hedges of the wild pine, *piña raton*, as the Cubans call it, were interrupted with broad gaps." At one estate, Bryant recounted,

> We passed up to the house through what had been an avenue of palms, but was now two rows of trees at very unequal distances, with here and there a sickly orange-tree. On each side grew the coffee shrubs, hung with flowers of snowy white, but unpruned and full of dry and leafless twigs. . . . The *mayoral* . . . received us with great courtesy. . . . "These coffee estates," said he, "are already ruined, and the planters are abandoning them as fast as they can; in four years more there will not be a single coffee plantation on the island."[16]

Ten years after Hurricane San Francisco de Borja, traveler Carlton Rogers could not conceal his disappointment at the "dilapidated appearance" of the cafetal he visited outside Güines. "This estate was not in a very prosperous condition," Rogers lamented,

> and did not quite come up to my expectations. I had heard such glowing descriptions of these plantations, that I expected to witness a scene of unsurpassed natural beauty; to revel amid such wealth of fruit, foliage, and flowers, that I would almost imagine myself in a terrestrial paradise. . . . The disastrous hurricanes which occasionally visit this island, damaging and destroying many of the coffee estates, . . . have materially diminished its cultivation. . . . I could imagine that in its prosperous days . . . it must indeed have been a beautiful sight.[17]

Coffee production declined from an annual average of 72 million pounds in the late 1820s, to 42.5 million pounds during 1841–45, to 18.5 million

TABLE 4.2. Production of Coffee, 1827, 1846, and 1862 (thousands of pounds)

Jurisdiction	1827	1846	1862
Vuelta Abajo	10	3,473	1,775
Havana	46,253	13,533	3,880
Matanzas	7,903	9,386	1,072
Las Villas	3,193	615	665
Puerto Príncipe	125	33	—
Oriente	14,545	15,526	11,129
Total	72,029	42,566	18,521

Source: Leví Marrero, *Cuba: Economía y sociedad*, 15 vols. (Madrid, 1972–88), 11:132.

pounds in the early 1860s. Regional variations were even more striking. Production in the jurisdiction of Havana dropped from 46.2 million pounds in 1827, to 13.5 million pounds in 1846, to 3.8 million pounds in 1862—a decline of more than 80 percent in less than three decades (see Table 4.2). In mid-1847 the U.S. consular agent in Matanzas wrote of the "rapid decline of the coffee trade, formerly the first article of . . . production, but now scarcely constituting an item of export."[18] Overall coffee exports between 1840 and 1858 fell by almost 90 percent, from approximately 50 million pounds in 1840, to 14 million pounds in 1845, to 4.5 million pounds by 1858.[19]

These developments foreshadowed other changes. The cafetales were disappearing: the 2,067 operating in 1827 were reduced to 1,670 in 1846 and to less than 1,220 in 1852. By 1862 only 782 cafetales were functioning—a loss of nearly 50 percent of the total number of coffee estates.[20] The total capital invested in coffee production dwindled from 86 million pesos in 1831 to 45 million in 1852.[21] No less important, the amount of land dedicated to coffee production as well as the percentage of total land engaged in production also fell markedly. In 1842 coffee estates had accounted for an estimated 480,000 acres, approximately 14 percent of the total. By 1852, within the space of ten years, this amount had declined to 333,700 acres, approximately 5 percent of the total land in use.[22]

/ / / / /

Aggregate numbers told only part of the story, however. In some zones, the collapse of coffee production was complete. Most of the 649 cafetales operating in the jurisdiction of Havana and its thirty-two rural partidos had disappeared by 1862. So too did the 23 coffee estates in Guanajay. Of the 203 coffee estates in the region of Matanzas in 1827, only 30 survived in 1862; in the same period the number of cafetales in Trinidad dropped from

35 to 9. In Santiago de las Vegas, 255 cafetales were reduced to 7. Between 1846 and 1861 three-quarters of the coffee plantations in Bejucal—66 out of 88—disappeared. Only 3 of the 75 coffee estates in Remedios continued to operate. During this period 111 of the 123 estates in Cárdenas ceased to function. Between 1846 and 1859 the 50 cafetales of Artemisa declined by exactly half. Of the 86 coffee plantations in Güines in 1846, only 19 were operating in 1862. Between 1847 and 1858 the 206 cafetales in San Antonio de los Baños were reduced to 84.[23] Historian Ramiro Guerra y Sánchez provided a detailed chronicle of the fate of José de Jesús Valdés, owner of the Jesús Nazareno cafetal near Batabanó, who having only barely recovered from the 1844 hurricane was struck again in 1846. Guerra y Sánchez wrote: "Together with the terrible losses occasioned by the hurricanes and the low price of sugar . . . Don José de Jesús Valdés did not have the means to reconstruct the estate. Four years later, with the *cafetal* definitively defunct, Don José de Jesús died. . . . Thousands of beautiful estates, destroyed and ruined during the last six years of the disastrous decade of 1840–1850, shared the same fate, never again to be revived as *cafetales*." In 1853 Jesús Nazareno was sold and its operations soon shifted to the cultivation of sugarcane.[24] Not far away, and not many years later, Fredrika Bremer visited the cafetal Concordia and could only imagine the prosperity "which prevailed in the flourishing times of this coffee plantation." Hardly anything remained:

> The depreciation of coffee as an article of commerce, and two hurricanes in succession, have changed the state of things in this part of the island. In the last which occurred, in the year 1848 [*sic*], the house . . . was leveled to the ground, and books and pictures, which have since been dug out, were drenched and destroyed by salt water, which during the hurricane was driven upon the island. It is said that the ground is still sick from this dreadful tempest, and that the trees and plants have not yet recovered their former vigor. Many large trees, and among these a magnificent ceiba, lie still in the pasture meadows, prostrate on the ground.[25]

The total number of people, both free and slave, engaged in or dependent on coffee production also fell dramatically. Between the intercensus years of 1846 and 1862 the number of persons working coffee in Matanzas dropped by more than 70 percent, from 6,497 to 1,805. In Cárdenas the decline was nearly 80 percent, from 5,541 to 1,266. (See Table 4.3.) A history of Alquízar published in 1859 provided a first-person narrative of the hard times that accompanied the decline of the cafetales: "This town in the recent past

TABLE 4.3. The Population of Cafetales and Ingenios, 1846 and 1862

	Cafetales		Ingenios	
Jurisdiction	1846	1862	1846	1862
Matanzas	6,497	1,805	21,780	25,523
Cárdenas	5,541	1,266	28,172	24,415
Mariel	9,475	1,168	12,482	12,305
Güines	4,591	962	8,386	18,130
Santiago de las Vegas	1,204	884	462	829

Sources: Cuba, Capitanía General, *Cuadro estadístico de la Siempre Fiel Isla de Cuba, correspondiente al años de 1846* (Havana, 1847), n.p., and *Noticias estadísticas de la Isla de Cuba en 1862* (Havana, 1864), n.p.

was so happy as a result of its prosperous wealth. . . . But everything has changed, everything has disappeared with the low price of coffee and the dismantling of the large number of coffee estates which have not been able to maintain their solvency. Of the [previously] large number of estates, only the *cafetales* Buen Concepción, Fortuna, Casualidad, and a small number of others have survived."[26]

A far-reaching transformation was in full swing. The implications of the decline of coffee production reverberated across the political economy of mid-nineteenth-century Cuba and must be considered as one of the signal developments of colonial production systems. The structural equilibrium that had characterized the Cuban economy earlier in the century fell into disarray.

Two trends developed simultaneously. In the zones southeast of Havana, principally around Güines, Madruga, San Nicolás, and Nuevo Paz, and west and southwest of Havana, around Mariel, Cabañas, Guanajay, Artemisa, and Alquízar, many former coffee estates were converted to estancias and potreros and contributed to the commercialization of frutos menores and livestock.[27] After the mid-1840s new farms cultivated crops and raised animals (*crianza*) for food. Other agricultural forms also seemed to have benefited from the demise of coffee in Occidente. In the zones of Alquízar and San Marcos, demolished cafetales were converted into potreros and sitios.[28] In 1860 Ramón de la Sagra wrote of the abandonment of coffee cultivation in Cuba, resulting in the transformation of "the elegant and charming *fincas* of S. Marcos, Alquízar, and Artemisa into pitiful *potreros*."[29] In all, the number of potreros increased from 1,467 in 1846 to 5,727 in 1862; during the same period the number of estancias rose from 12,286 to 22,500.[30]

More commonly, however, former coffee estates moved into sugar production. In the middle decades of the nineteenth century, the scale slowly tilted against diversified agriculture and in favor of sugar. The process had already begun, of course, at the turn of the century with the decline of sugar production in Saint Domingue. But the expansion of sugar specifically at the expense of coffee began in earnest in the 1840s. The once prosperous cafetal Angerona near Artemisa moved directly from coffee into sugar. Traveling outside Artemisa in 1843, John Wurdemann recorded in his journal visiting "a large field of cane, planted on an abandoned coffee estate."[31] Almost all the cafetales of Nueva Paz and Güira de Melena had shifted to sugar by midcentury. An 1847 study examining conditions in the former coffee zones in the jurisdiction of Mariel commented on the recent emergence of "what could be called new *ingenios*." Years later, Elisha Atkins reminisced about his early life along the southern coast between Cienfuegos and Trinidad, where the Atkins family subsequently established its vast sugar holdings. One after another, Atkins recalled, the ruined cafetales began to cultivate sugarcane "as planters one by one saw the advantage in it. . . . Thus it was that sugar became the great staple of the island." Of one sugar estate outside Matanzas that he saw in 1849, William Cullen Bryant observed: "The house stands on an eminence, once embowered in trees which the hurricanes have leveled, overlooking a broad valley, where palms were scattered in every direction; for the estate had formerly been a coffee plantation." The Adriana ingenio, Richard Henry Dana learned ten years later while visiting Matanzas, had formerly been the Laberinto cafetal. Dana wrote:

> The successive disastrous hurricanes of 1843 and 1845 [*sic*], destroyed many and damaged most of the coffee estates . . . are commonly said to have put an end to the coffee plantations. . . . The damaged plantations were not restored as coffee estates, but were laid down to sugar-cane; and gradually, first in the western and northern parts, and daily extending easterly and southerly over the entire island, the exquisite cafetals have been prostrated and dismantled, the groves of shade and fruit trees cut down, the avenues and footpaths ploughed up, and denuded land laid down to wastes of sugar-cane.[32]

At about the same time, John Taylor wrote that "all the [coffee] estate having been converted, in the district of Holguin, into sugar plantations before I arrived there, and a great majority of the remaining ones to the westward were cleared away by the hurricane of 1844."[33]

///// /

In the mid-nineteenth century, as Cuba took enormous strides toward a deepened dependence on sugar, many of the enduring features of the colonial economy assumed permanent form. This development had far-reaching implications for production modalities, labor organization, and colonial demography. The preeminence of sugar, to be sure, developed early and in some zones advanced further and faster than in others. Describing conditions in Trinidad in 1840, *fiscal* Francisco Letamendi wrote: "I believe it impossible for the country to make rapid progress in prosperity, especially in regard to the population of whites, for the existing wealth is connected to the owners of the *ingenio*. Having fixed the boundaries on all the land, they have created a fiefdom out of the entire jurisdiction." Letamendi added: "Thus it can be said that there is no other agriculture other than that of those estates, where only what is necessary for the owners is planted, and since they are the ones who determine what is planted they do not leave the poor with any recourse, no matter how industrious they may be. They do not rent even 3 inches (*un palmo*) of land, so that the people are left with a great need for land."[34]

But it is also true that the process by which sugar became dominant in western Cuba was not completed until the mid-nineteenth century, as other crops, which had previously competed with sugar for land and labor, began to falter and fail. In the years that followed, vast tracts of land moved directly into sugar production. "The planters find it more profitable to convert their coffee into sugar plantations," observed the Reverend L. Leonidas Allen in 1852.[35] The process seems to have been completed within twenty-five years. "The 'cafetales,' or coffee plantations," pronounced H. W. Bates of the Royal Geographical Society in 1878, "were formerly the most considerable culture in Cuba, but they have long been almost everywhere superseded by those of the sugar cane."[36]

In the next decade the zones of sugar production expanded and the number of sugar mills increased, in what Laird Bergad has characterized as "a wave of ingenio construction in the 1840s and 1850s." Twenty years after Hurricane San Francisco de Borja, Henry Latham marveled at the "great expanse of sugar cane" on a plantation in San Nicolás south of Havana. As he explained, "Coffee used to be grown formerly on this plantation; and the mill for separating the berries from the husk, and the great platforms of smooth plaster upon which the coffee is spread to dry in the sun, were still remaining, all in order." About the same time W. M. L. Jay observed that "[t]he coffee-culture . . . is fast declining in Cuba," explaining: "Year by year . . . these lovely gardens and groves are cleared, and transformed, as far as the nature of the ground will admit, into a vast monotony of sun-steeped cane-fields. For the cane loves sun, not shade, and wherever it appears, the trees fall,—except in the few palm-avenues which are retained for boundaries and roadways, and the shade trees of the *casa de vivienda*."[37]

Regional economic differentiation acquired sharper relief across the island. As production systems in Occidente expanded around large-scale, slave-based sugar production, the agrarian systems of Oriente developed around smaller estates. The demise of coffee production in the western provinces contributed to the rise of smaller cafetales in the east. Some coffee estates continued to function around Remedios and Trinidad, but in the main coffee production shifted dramatically to Oriente, mostly in the areas of Santiago de Cuba and Guantánamo. Whereas the number of coffee estates in Oriente represented approximately one-third the total number in 1827 (725 out of 2,067), by 1862 Oriente accounted for more than half the total (426 out of 782). In 1827 Oriente had accounted for approximately 20 percent of total insular coffee production (14.5 million pounds out of 72 million); by 1862 *oriental* production represented more than 60 percent of the total (11.1 million out of 18.5 million pounds).[38]

/ / / / /

Tobacco production suffered short-term adversity but soon recovered; indeed, it eventually emerged as another long-term beneficiary of the devastation wrought by the hurricanes of the 1840s. The drought and storm of 1844 and the rains and storm of 1846 had disrupted production. Tobacco exports in 1844 were 25 percent less than in 1843, and cigar exports declined nearly 40 percent.[39] Over the longer run, however, tobacco benefited from the demise of the cafetales, particularly in the western region of Vuelta Abajo. As early as the 1820s, a number of marginal cafetales in Vuelta Abajo had started to hedge their production strategies in response to erratic international coffee prices by expanding into tobacco. "Since coffee has been depressed in price," the Reverend Abiel Abbot observed in 1828, "planters have sent small lots of hands to cultivate vegas, or tobacco patches; and have found it profitable."[40]

The outcome reinforced the dominant position of the ingenio and the vega at the expense of the cafetal. In some instances, estates were partitioned into small units and resumed production as tobacco vegas. In other cases, producers converted defunct coffee estates into large vegas, reallocating slave labor to tobacco production. Increasingly, too, the vega in Occidente was the beneficiary of slave labor previously employed in the cafetal. For a time — if only briefly — large-scale slave labor was applied to tobacco production. Producers had previously worked the vegas with less than 10 slaves. By midcentury, the tobacco vegas had expanded and in the process enlarged the labor force to about 25 to 30 slaves. Indeed, in the jurisdiction of Pinar del Río, the total number of people engaged in tobacco production nearly doubled during the intercensus years of 1846 and 1862, from 32,248 to 58,039.[41]

After midcentury the number of vegas also increased, almost doubling from 5,534 in 1827 to 9,102 in 1846; by 1862 there were 11,541. The growth of tobacco farms was noteworthy in Occidente. Between 1846 and 1862, the number of vegas in the western jurisdiction registered a 40 percent increase, from 3,990 to 6,381.[42]

Production gains were stunning. Between 1846 and 1862 total insular output expanded from 168,094 bales of tobacco to 305,626 bales. In Occidente, the rise from 59,434 bales to 134,710 bales was even more significant. The Santa Isabel vega near San Juan, with a labor force of 110 slaves, increased production from 6.6 million pounds of tobacco in 1845 to 8.8 million pounds in 1846 and 9.3 million pounds in 1847.[43]

The value of tobacco exports rose from 298,000 arrobas in 1845 to 364,000 arrobas in 1850 and 480,000 arrobas in 1855. "The increase in the cultivation of tobacco," Ramón de la Sagra wrote at midcentury, "is dated from the decadence of the cultivation of coffee, promoted by the purchase of land from the neighboring *cafetales* in the regions of Vuelta Abajo, whose owners began to designate part of their complement of slaves [*dotación*] to the cultivation of tobacco."[44]

At about this time, too, many owners of tobacco vegas made the transition from farmer to manufacturer. In fact, among the cigar factories, many of which were founded during the 1840s, were names that would dominate the industry in the years to come. Jaime Partagás, owner of several vegas in Vuelta Abajo, established the Partagás factory in 1844. Other enterprises established in that decade included the H. Upmann factory, La Reforma, and La Corona. In 1845 Ramón Allones opened La Eminencia. In the same year, symbolically perhaps, El Huracán was founded.[45]

Property values were in flux, mostly rising, as the combined effects of tropical hurricanes and global markets reverberated across the colonial po-

TABLE 4.4. The Value of Private Property, 1852

Type of Farm	Total Area (acres)	Percent	Total Land Value (pesos)
Ingenios	1,406,000	20	64,900,000
Cafetales	333,666	5	15,030,000
Sitios and estancias	1,263,335	18	75,876,000
Hatos and potreros	3,905,357	55	27,527,000
Vegas	152,914	2	3,214,000

Source: Leví Marrero, *Cuba: Economía y sociedad,* 15 vols. (Madrid, 1972–88), 10:92.

litical economy. The changing land tenure patterns and property values in the aftermath of the turbulent 1840s stood in sharp relief in 1852 (see Table 4.4).

/ / / / /

Sugar production experienced immediate but only short-lived reversals. Countless acres of cane fields, many of which were ready for harvest, were flattened in 1844 and again in 1846. Between 1844 and 1845 total sugar production was reduced by more than half, from 208,506 metric tons to 98,437 metric tons.[46] Exports declined in the years immediately following the 1844 hurricane. "In 1844," commented one U.S. trade magazine in 1849, "a long drought was followed by a hurricane, which was felt in its effects for two years, as the crop of 1845, which was exported in 1846, suffered from these terrible visitations of 1844."[47]

Sugar harvests soon returned to prehurricane levels, and indeed surpassed the volume of previous crops. But damages to the physical plant and equipment were far more complicated and often irreparable. News reports from across the sugar zones referred to collapsed chimneys in mills, destroyed buildings, and damaged equipment. The *casa de purga* of the ingenio Torrontegui was demolished. At the ingenio owned by Juan Antonio Cordero in Havana, the boiler plant worth more than 12,000 pesos was a total loss.[48] Hundreds of thousands of pesos had been invested in the construction of elaborate industrial plants, including mills, machinery, railroad lines, and storage facilities, often in the form of loans secured against the earnings of future crops.

The fate of planters thus affected is not always clear. Some sugar producers were ruined by the destruction visited on their properties. Damaged fields (*cañaverales*) could generally recover from one year to the next, although the loss of the harvest of any one year signified substantial impairment. More serious, however, was the loss of life among slaves and destruction of the industrial plant. Planters had invested huge amounts of capital in labor and manufacturing, neither of which could be easily replaced. For producers heavily in debt, a destructive hurricane could have dire consequences. In Nicolás Heredia's novel *Leonela* (1893), planter Carlos Mendoza was ruined by a hurricane: "The hurricane delivered the fatal blow [*el golpe de muerte*]," the narrator comments, and Mendoza explains his financial condition to his son: "Our businesses are lost. I owe I don't know how much to Foronda and Company; 10,000 *pesos* to Don Cosme Arencibia. . . . You have already seen what has happened to the *ingenio* and understand my situation. The estate can still be productive if it can grind; but the problem is to get it to grind. The immediate problem is Don Cosme, to whom I have given a note that is due now. I don't have a cent to pay the interest, much less the principal, and worst of all is that I need more money."[49]

The available evidence is only suggestive, but it may indeed indicate long-term results of the hurricane-related devastation. The fields of cane may have recovered in a comparatively brief period, but this was not true of the industrial plant. Not all planters possessed the means to return to the manufacture of sugar. Numerous factors help explain the decline in the number of mills at midcentury, including consolidations and business failures related to other causes. The 1846 census identifies the existence of 1,442 mills (ingenios and *trapiches*) across the island. Subsequent census reports indicate a decline in the number of mills. Ramón de la Sagra and Carlos Rebello fixed the total number in 1860 at 1,365. Jacobo de la Pezuela identified even fewer mills in 1861, calculating the number to be 1,167.[50]

/ / / / /

Sugar production recovered in short order and, indeed, soon emerged as the principal beneficiary of the midcentury hurricanes. A new source of slave labor, previously engaged in coffee production, became generally available to sugar growers and thereby enabled planters to expand the zones of cultivation and increase the levels of production. The availability of a new, internal supply of slaves was especially important, for it coincided with declining importation of African slaves. The abolition of the slave trade first by Denmark in 1804, followed by England in 1808, and successively by the United States, Sweden, Holland, and France added to mounting international pressure on Spain to suppress the slave trade in its Caribbean colonies. The British, in particular, pursued an aggressive policy of opposition to the slave trade and registered notable achievements in intercepting slave vessels and disrupting the movement of African cargoes.[51]

The suppression of the legal slave trade had the net effect of increasing the cost of doing business. The years of cheap and plentiful supplies of slaves were coming to an end. In 1835, under intense British diplomatic pressure, Queen Isabel II acceded to the suppression of the slave trade in all Spanish realms, an agreement backed by the presence of British war vessels along Cuban coasts. According to historian Arthur Corwin, Great Britain made its greatest inroads against the slave trade between 1840 and 1848.[52]

These were portentous developments in Cuba and, set against the larger context of the hurricanes of 1844 and 1846, had far-reaching implications. The available data do indeed suggest that the number of slaves introduced into Cuba declined dramatically during the mid-nineteenth century (see Table 4.5). Between 1836 and 1840 annual slave imports averaged slightly more than 19,000, but during the five-year period 1841–45, that figure dropped to 17,700. In 1846–50 the average rate plummeted to slightly more than 3,000 annually—roughly 15 percent of the average a decade earlier. By the closing years of the 1840s, slave imports had dwindled to the lowest levels since the previous century.

What makes these statistics significant is a matter of timing. The decline of slave imports occurred at precisely the moment that Cuban sugar production was entering a dynamic phase of expansion. New industrial technologies were becoming available to Cuban planters, promising greater production capabilities and improved transportation efficiency. Producers seized every opportunity. Between 1846 and 1854 they imported more than $3 million worth of sugar equipment.[53] In 1851 traveler Edward Sullivan wrote with wonderment of technological developments on the island:

> [T]he Creoles of Cuba, scorning the anti-improving spirit of the inhabitants of old Spain, who seem to consider it of more consequence to spend time than to save it, and who view with horror any of the innovations of this progressive age, seize upon every new adaptation of steam and improved machinery for the manufacture of sugar with the greatest eagerness; and the introduction of any improvement on one estate is speedily followed by its adoption over the whole island; and risk and expense are disregarded in real Yankee style, when the objects to be gained are a saving of time and an increased production.[54]

The railroad had early captured the Cuban imagination. The Real Sociedad Económica de La Habana was unabashedly euphoric. "Like a conquer-

TABLE 4.5. Estimated Number of Slaves Imported to Cuba Annually, 1836–1850

Year	Number of Slaves	Year	Number of Slaves
1836	20,200	1844	10,000
1837	20,900	1845	2,600
1838	21,000	1846	1,000
1839	19,900	1847	1,700
1840	13,700	1848	2,000
1841	11,600	1849	7,400
1842	4,100	1850	3,300
1843	7,100		

Source: David Eltis, "The Nineteenth-Century Transatlantic Slave Trade: An Annual Time Series of Imports in the Americas Broken Down by Region," *Hispanic American Historical Review* 67 (February 1987): 122–23.

ing army that introduces with its sovereignty civilization and wealth to a savage country," the Sociedad exulted in 1848, "[the railroad] lays down its tracks, establishes its presence near vast forests and fertile but undeveloped land, and the lonely countryside is transformed into an object of industry."[55]

The first railroad between Havana and Bejucal, completed in 1837, was extended to Güines the following year and set the stage for the rapid expansion of sugar cultivation across the rural interior. By 1845 branch lines reached Batabanó and San Antonio de los Baños. The Matanzas-Guanábana line had been inaugurated in 1843, with rail extensions to Sabanilla installed two years later. At about the same time, rail connections between the northern port of Cárdenas and Bemba (Jovellanos) and Navajas in the south were completed. In 1851 Cienfuegos established rail links with Palmira that extended to Cruces two years later.[56]

Across the island producers celebrated the promise of the railroad. The possibilities seemed unlimited. The opening of the interior permitted simultaneously the expansion of old production zones and the creation of new ones. Sugar production was on the brink of spectacular development.

But the timing was not good. Even as the railroads opened the interior to development, British war vessels closed the coast to slave imports. "Something has us a little concerned," Francisco Diago told his commercial agent in New York as early as 1841, conveying the prevailing mood of Cuban planters, "and that is that the Spanish government is disposed to take effective measures for the purpose of halting the introduction of slaves from Africa. . . . [Such] effort . . . will be felt by some like me who have been unable yet to fill the *dotación* of blacks. Once the [slave] trade is suppressed [planters] will have to pay $1000 for each black when we pay now $400." The Socie-dad Económica de La Habana immediately understood the implications of these developments. "If the ease of penetrating even the most remote re-gions allows for the development of lands today virgin and unproductive," it observed in 1849, "so much the better for the Island of Cuba. . . . The procurement of labor (*brazos*), regrettably, will not be as easy to obtain as one might wish." [57]

But there was more. The 1830s and 1840s were also years of of deepen-ing tensions in Cuba, of unrest and uncertainty among colonial producers. Chattel slavery was under assault from another source from within: that is, the very slaves on whom colonial prosperity depended. Slave uprisings on individual plantations increased all through Occidente. In 1835 slaves on the Magdalena sugar estate in Matanzas destroyed property and fled. In the same year, a slave uprising on several cafetales near Aguacate resulted in the death of two overseers and several white farmhands. Insurrections in the late 1830s were reported on estates in Havana, Trinidad, and Cienfue-gos.[58] In January 1843, 200 slaves of the ingenio Triángulo near Matanzas rebelled, killing the *mayoral*. Two months later 250 slaves of the *ingenio* Al-cancía near Cárdenas revolted. In November 1843 a more formidable rebel-lion broke out on the Triunvirato plantation in Sabanilla and subsequently spread to the neighboring Acana estate, then to Concepción, San Lorenzo, Merced, San Miguel, San Rafael, and Jesús María. Within days, Sabanilla was the site of full-scale military operations between an estimated 300 slaves and Spanish infantry and cavalry units.[59]

The outcome was never in doubt, but the extent of destruction and espe-cially the magnitude of the rebellion took planters and political authori-ties by surprise. The repression that followed was swift but failed to calm a brooding disquiet that had taken hold among representatives of the planter class. Incidents previously dismissed as unconnected individual acts of slave insubordination and disobedience now assumed an ominous pattern. They had ceased to be uncommon. They were different, too. "The blacks on this occasion," Domingo del Monte reflected on Triunvirato, "were not content with burning the cane fields and taking flight into the mountains, as they have customarily done in similar situations. Rather, they killed six whites and made their way to neighboring estates with the intention of inciting to rebellion the *dotaciones* of slaves and proclaiming liberty for the black race. It was then necessary to understand that these repeated uprisings had an origin and a character different from all the previous ones." [60]

The more thoughtful planters did not fail to divine the signs. "We here are doing well," wrote José Luis Alfonso from Havana in December 1843, "despite the fact of being somewhat alarmed by the state of exaltation in which all the slave laborers [*negradas*] on the estates find themselves. . . . The increase of their resolve, a greater tendency to rebel and contend forcibly for their rights, is noticeable daily." This was a sobering assessment, especially coming from a planter and the nephew of the owner of Triunvirato. Alfonso was entirely lucid on the problem facing the planter class. He continued: "Fortunately our estates are tranquil up to the present moment. But, should we be surprised that men—slaves—would rise and fight for their liberty? Planters now seeking security ask for the deployment of military units in the countryside. . . . What imbeciles they are! Concerned about their own security they think only in the killing and punishment of those poor wretches. They do not consider how ineffective bayonets are when used against those who fight for such a just cause." [61]

Only a few months had passed when, in early 1844, planters were again jolted by news that authorities claimed to have uncovered a far-flung slave conspiracy. The response was immediate. The ensuing repression of slaves suspected of complicity in La Escalera conspiracy developed into what historian Robert Paquette has characterized as a "reign of terror." Untold hundreds of slaves were tortured, imprisoned, and executed merely on suspicion of sympathizing with the alleged plot. "A horrible conspiracy of blacks," wrote sugar planter Miguel del Aldama in March 1844, "in which, without exception, all slaves and ex-slaves [*libertos*] of the island are implicated, was at the critical moment of erupting when the government began to apprehend suspects. The large part of the *negradas* of more than 200 estates (including ours) are in prison." [62]

But not even Miguel de Aldama was prepared for the savagery of the repression that followed. "The prisons are filled with black leaders of the conspiracy," Aldama despaired, and continued:

The manner of confession or, more correctly, of making them confess, is truly savage. They apply the whip without distinction to class, free or slave, rich or poor. The inquisitorial flogging makes them confess to the horrible conspiracy that was on the verge of breaking out. A number of them have succumbed to the brutality of the punishment. Others have died of spasms or of gangrene of wounds. One man received face down 1,600 lashes, in the manner which our plantation overseers are accustomed to administering whippings. Whoever is not horrified by such deeds is our enemy and must be treated accordingly. . . . I believe that the blood that has been shed in such a vile manner will ask for revenge. You thus see in all the cities blacks restive and haughty to such a point that I am afraid that driven by despair they will give a cry [*grito*] that will fill us with sorrow and misery.[63]

The appalling level of mortality long associated with slavery in Cuba — the result principally of disease and illness, overwork, and suicide — merely increased the demand for slave labor at precisely the time when new slave imports were on a precipitous decline. In fact, the death rate was so high that the plantation labor force could not be maintained without a constant influx of new slaves. Although estimates vary, there appears to be a general agreement that mortality rates on Cuban sugar estates averaged between 10 and 12 percent annually. On some ingenios mortality rates reached as high as 15 to 18 percent.[64]

These circumstances struck body blows to prevailing production strategies. Production on the Alejandra sugar estate in Güines was in decline, David Turnbull learned during his visit in the late 1830s, a condition he ascribed "to a deficiency of labour." Turnbull drew the obvious inference. "The dilapidation had arisen in the ordinary course of nature," he concluded, "no fresh Bozals having been purchased to supply the place of those who had been carried off by that stern law of mortality which so rapidly and ruthlessly cuts down the gangs of negro labourers on the sugar estates of this country."[65] As disquiet deepened among Cuban planters over the future supply of African slaves, sugar producers turned to alternative sources of labor, most notably the importation of Chinese contract workers. Ramón de la Sagra dates the arrival of the first 600 Chinese laborers to Cuba in 1847. In less than twenty years, the estimated number of Chinese workers on the island approached 125,000.[66]

The effects of the declining slave trade in the 1840s, together with the high slave mortality and the deaths associated with La Escalera, shed light on one of the stunning population collapses of nineteenth-century Cuba (see Table 4.6). A comparison of the census data between 1841 and 1846 reveals a loss of almost 26 percent of the total slave population, a decline from 436,495 to 323,759 slaves. More than 80 percent of this loss (93,461 out of 112,736) was registered in Occidente.

It may well be, of course, that the census figures are incorrect or perhaps were even deliberately falsified. Colonial authorities had every reason to manipulate data in reporting what would have constituted illegal slave imports at a time of mounting international pressure against slave trafficking. On

TABLE 4.6. The Slave Population by Jurisdiction, 1841 and 1846

Jurisdiction	1841	1846
Occidente	321,274	227,813
Centro	50,156	46,985
Oriente	65,065	48,961
Total	436,495	323,759

Sources: Cuba, Capitanía General, *Resumen del censo de población de la Isla de Cuba a fin del año de 1841* (Havana, 1842), p. 56, and *Cuadro estadístico de la Siempre Fiel Isla de Cuba, correspondiente al año de 1846* (Havana, 1847), n.p.

the other hand, the census figures are not entirely inconsistent with available data on high mortality rates in sugar production at a time when slaves could be readily or cheaply replaced. Deaths associated with the repression in the aftermath of La Escalera as well as the midcentury hurricanes and disease further contributed to the drop in the slave population.[67]

These developments were occurring simultaneously with the possibility of expanding Cuban sugar exports on the international market, most notably to Great Britain. Between 1846 and 1848 Great Britain was engaged in the revocation of a series of protective tariffs against foreign sugar, thereby opening up new market opportunities to Cuban producers. By the terms of the Sugar Duties Act of 1846, England abolished protective tariffs in favor of free trade, mandating the gradual abolition of duties on foreign sugar imports over the next four years.

The value of slaves thus increased markedly at midcentury, due in part to the reduced supply of slave imports, in part to the increased price of sugar on the world market, and in part to the demands created by the expansion of sugar production. In other words, even as land became available for the expansion of sugarcane cultivation, as new technologies were developed to increase production, and as new markets appeared and prices increased, the supply of slave labor declined. As could be expected, the dramatic decline in the availability of slaves was accompanied by an increase in their value. The scarcity of slaves was experienced almost immediately. "The lack of workers is beginning to be felt," Miguel de Aldama commented tersely as early as January 1845.[68]

The ruin of coffee producers coincided with the marked shortages of slave labor. It thus appears that slaves were among the most valuable possessions of coffee growers devastated by the hurricanes of 1844 and 1846. The inexorable logic of the law of supply and demand was carried to its inevitable conclusion. Slaves on cafetales valued at 300 pesos in the 1820s were sold for as much as 900 pesos in the 1840s. Slaves possessing specialized skills, including carpenters, masons, boiler makers, and machinists — classified as "los negros de primera clase" — were often sold for more than 1,000 pesos each. Joseph Dimock reported even higher prices while traveling in Cuba during the 1850s. "An able bodied male slave is now valued at an average of $1200 to $1500," he recorded in his diary, "and some good house servants are held at over $2000." Alternatively, many coffee planters arranged lease contracts charging between 15 to 20 pesos monthly for the services of their slaves.[69] A study of the jurisdiction of Mariel (which included Guanajay, Cabañas, Guayabal, Puerto de Güira, Cayababos, Seiba del Agua, and Quiebra Hacha), completed in 1847, documented the effects of the collapse of the local coffee economy: "The degree to which [coffee] production has declined is well known. Hard times extend to all regions. Known, too, is the fact that [a] considerable number of *cafetales* have been converted to *potreros* and that all or the large part of the *dotaciones* of the *cafetales* have been applied to more lucrative industries. These are found in critical and lamentable circumstances and are suffering a great necessity of *brazos*. They are in most urgent need of attention by the most efficacious and direct means."[70] Whereas some coffee estates rented or sold slaves, others parceled their land out for rent. The San Lorenzo cafetal managed to avoid total failure during the late 1840s and early 1850s by combining income generated from rental property and living off the sale of subsistence crops and livestock raised by slaves.[71]

After the mid-1840s sugar planters found a new supply of slaves from among the failing coffee estates. On this point, Miguel de Aldama was clear. "There are now neither slave-dealers (*negreros*) nor ships engaged in the slave traffic," Aldama wrote Domingo del Monte in September 1845, "... and we now clearly see that the defunct coffee estates can supply for some time to come the laborers that are needed."[72] In January 1849 the British commissary judge in Havana informed London of the large-scale reallocation of slaves occurring in Cuba: "[T]hough lately a larger demand for slave labour had arisen, on account of the higher price of sugar, yet this demand [has] been met by a supply of negroes from abandoned coffee plantations, to the number then estimated of about 30,000. . . . This supply I should think sufficient for the necessities of some years to come." Historian Manuel Moreno Fraginals has calculated that as many as 50,000 slaves over an unspecified span of time were transferred from cafetales to ingenios.[73]

Put another way, at least twice the total number of slaves imported be-

TABLE 4.7. Distribution of Slaves by Production Sector, 1827, 1841, and 1862

Sector	1827		1841		1862	
	N	%	N	%	N	%
Cafetales	50,000	17.4	60,000	13.6	25,942	7.0
Ingenios	70,000	24.4	100,000	22.6	172,671	46.9
Fincas	100,000*	34.8	66,000	14.9	71,926	19.5
Vegas	NA	NA	14,263	3.2	17,675	4.9
Urban	67,000	23.4	202,196	45.7	75,977	20.6
Total	287,000		442,459		368,366**	

Sources: Cuba, Capitanía General, *Cuadro estadístico de la Siempre Fiel Isla de Cuba, correspondiente al año de 1827* (Havana, 1829), p. 26, and *Noticias estadísticas de la Isla de Cuba en 1862* (Havana, 1864), n.p.; Instituto de Historia de Cuba, *Historia de Cuba: La Colonia: Evolución socioeconómico y formación nacional, de los orígenes hasta 1867* (Havana, 1994), p. 403.
*Includes *vegas*.
**Includes 4,175 slaves listed as distributed "*en otros establecimientos*."

tween 1845 and 1850 were transferred to sugar from internal sources, thereby making the sustained expansion of sugar production possible. Commenting on the impact of the British Duties Act during his visit to Cuba, Robert Baird declared:

> It is a fact well known and universally admitted in Havanna [*sic*] that . . . the price of slaves immediately rose greatly; and such was the demand occasioned by the increase of sugar cultivation in the island, that slaves formerly considered so old, infirm, and superannuated, as to be exempted from working were again put to work; and some were drafted from the lighter work of the caffetal [*sic*], or coffee plantations, on to the heavier labour of the sugar estates: and these consequences arose solely from the fact that the slavers were unable to supply the demand with sufficient rapidity, being prevented by the vigilance of the British and French cruising squadrons.[74]

In August 1845 Miguel de Aldama was optimistic about the prospects for a bountiful harvest. "Here there is really nothing new," he wrote to Domingo del Monte in Paris, "except the magnificent spring that we have had which appears will permit in large part recovery from the calamities we suffered last year, with the monstrous drought and the no less terrible hurricane. The crops promise to be abundant, so much so that we have been obliged to rent 50 blacks for the sugar harvest."[75] British merchant Jacob Omnium, of the London mercantile house of Omnium, Dibs, and Rhino, who visited Havana

TABLE 4.8. Land Usage by Jurisdiction, 1827, 1846, and 1862

Jurisdiction	Ingenios			Cafetales		
	1827	1846	1862	1827	1846	1862
Occidente	449	735	1,253	1,207	1,012	356
Centro*	246	404	135	78		
Oriente	305	303	268	725	580	426
Total	1,000	1,442	1,521	2,067	1,670	782

Sources: Cuba, Capitanía General, *Cuadro estadístico de la Siempre Fiel Isla de Cuba, correspondiente al año de 1827* (Havana, 1829), n.p., *Cuadro Estadístico de la Siempre Fiel Isla de Cuba, correspondiente al año de 1846* (Havana, 1847), n.p., and *Noticias estadísticas de la Isla de Cuba en 1862* (Havana, 1864), n.p.

*The 1862 census was based on territorial reorganization in which the jurisdiction of Centro was not used.

in 1847, provided a vivid chronicle of the changes overtaking Cuban sugar production at midcentury:

> I spent the beginning of [1847] in Cuba, with a view of ascertaining the preparations which were being made in that island to meet the opening of our markets. To an Englishman coming up from Grenada and Jamaica contrast between the paralyzed and decayed aspect of trade in those colonies, and the spirit and activity which [the duty] measures had infused into that of the Havannah [*sic*], was most disheartening. The town was illuminated when I landed in consequence of the news of high prices from England. Three splendid trains of De Rosne's machinery costing 40,000 dollars each, had just arrived from France, and were in process of erection; steam-engines and engineers were coming over daily from America; new estates were forming; coffee plantations were being broken up, and their feeble gangs of old people and children, who had hitherto been selected for that light work, were formed into task gangs, and hired out by the month to the new *ingenios*, then in full drive.[76]

Only two years later, Governor General Federico Roncali paid tribute to the success of expanded sugar exports: "[S]ugar exports have increased . . . as a result of the participation of more laborers. . . . Without the allocation of slaves from the *cafetales* to the *ingenios* and without the arrival of any [new] slaves, the Island, rather than the admirable prosperity which it has enjoyed these years, would have declined noticeably."[77]

The number of African slaves engaged in coffee production—both in terms of absolute numbers and as a percentage of the total—decreased in

	Vegas			Potreros			Sitios/Estancias	
1827	1846	1862	1827	1846	1862	1827	1846	1862
2,561	3,990	6,381	8,284	1,467	5,727	2,561	12,286	22,500
1,390	967	1,672	2,579	3,173	6,678			
1,583	4,145	5,160	188	342	468	2,490	6,328	12,046
5,534	9,102	11,541	10,144	4,388	6,195	8,224	25,292	34,546

the years that followed, as cafetales successively continued to fail (see Table 4.7). "Coffee, which previously competed with sugar in production and profits," observed Spanish economist Mariano Torrente in 1852, "presently finds itself in the most extreme state of decline, so that many of these estates have been dismantled, designating their lands to *estancias* or *potreros*, for which few slaves are needed and among whom can be the more enfeebled, and transferring the most robust [slaves] to the opening of new sugar *ingenios*."[78]

Sugar production soared. Harvests increased at astonishing increments, from 162,000 tons in 1841 to 264,000 tons ten years later. By the mid-1850s, annual production was approaching the 400,000-ton mark. On the eve of the Ten Years War (1868–78), Cuba had produced 750,000 tons of sugar.[79]

/////

These were critical years of transition and transformation. In 1827 sugar had represented 26 percent of the total value of colonial production. By 1860 this proportion had climbed to 61 percent. During the same period, the total value of tobacco rose from 6.5 percent to 15 percent. At the provincial level, the increases were often stunning. In Havana, sugar accounted for nearly 70 percent of total value. In Matanzas, it was 90 percent.[80]

Commercial agriculture was slowly displacing subsistence production (see Table 4.8). A number of factors were responsible, to be sure. Certainly, the expansion of overseas markets provided a powerful impulse for increasing production for export. International price fluctuations also favored the expansion of sugar and tobacco even as they impeded the resumption of coffee production. Moreover, colonial fiscal policies, trade regulations, and tariff structures all tended to support production for export over production for consumption.[81]

But it is also true that the effects of the hurricanes of 1844 and 1846 loomed large in the subsequent transformation of land tenure forms and development strategies. Not all producers suffered equally — or permanently — from these storms. Indeed, over the long run there were some clear beneficiaries of these calamities. Sugar was aided at a particularly critical moment in its development.[82]

Export patterns during the late 1840s underscore the transformation of the colonial economy. Sugar exports increased from 160 tons in 1840, to 200 tons in 1850, to 477 tons in 1860. Over the same period, the percentage exported to the United States increased from 26 percent (42,000 out of 160,000 tons) to 42.5 percent (85,000 out of 200,000 tons) to 62 percent (296,000 out of 477,000 tons). Between 1840 and 1860 the proportion of sugar as a percentage of total exports increased from 60 percent to 74 percent. During these years, too, the value of tobacco leaf exports rose from 210,800 arrobas in 1840, to 364,000 arrobas in 1850, to 601,200 arrobas in 1859. All the while, the value of coffee exports declined from 2.1 million arrobas in 1840 to 520,134 arrobas in 1850 and 239,000 arrobas in 1859.[83] As we know now, the die was cast.

5. Bending to the Force of the Wind

I have been bent by the wind, not once but twice. Nothing remains of my modest home: nothing outside, nothing inside. For days I have wandered the streets like a beggar, my only possessions [being] the tattered clothing I have on. Is this to be my fate?

    Eugenia de la Concepción to Governor General Leopoldo O'Donnell
    (November 11, 1846)

My house is one of those that suffered the greatest damage, for most of it has totally collapsed. Everywhere it was penetrated by the horrendous elements of the sea, and subjected to the pounding of the waves. Everything was lost. All the furniture and clothing I owned is gone. I am reduced to poverty and find myself without any prospects of employment.

    Isidro Quillez to Gobierno Superior Civil (January 27, 1847)

I do not know what will become of us if Divine Providence does not intervene in our behalf.

    Resident of Macuriges (October 14, 1846)

Nothing is more gratifying to the heart after moments of anguish and in circumstances of having suffered a public calamity than to see the efforts of an enlightened and beneficent government in alleviating the suffering of victims, if not by lifting them entirely out of the unfortunate circumstances which have befallen upon them, then at least in mitigating their affliction and avoiding the prolongation of their despair.

      Diario de La Habana *(October 14, 1846)*

Nothing has ever happened that has caused such universal desolation. No one house in the island is exempt from danger. Very few buildings are left standing on the estates. . . . It is as yet impossible to make any accurate calculation of the number of souls who have perished in this dreadful calamity. Whites and blacks together, it is imagined to exceed some thousands, but fortunately few people of consequence are among the number.

      Robert H. Schomburgk, The History of Barbados: Compromising a Geographical and Statistical Description of the Island *(1848)*

The winds came down particularly hard on the poor: the men and women, white and black, the young and old, former slaves and itinerant laborers, the mass of humanity that had concentrated in the cities, the multitude of peasants and other rural inhabitants who toiled in the countryside, and the many tens of thousands of slaves distributed across the great plantation estates of the island—in sum, the vast numbers for whom hardship seemed to beget hardship and whose circumstance of subsistence made them especially susceptible to adversity. This is not to suggest that misfortune singled them out, but rather that when it did find them the results were disastrous. People who lived with little had little to lose, of course, but when they did lose it they lost it all.

These were the people most vulnerable to the hazards of a hurricane, who lived in more or less permanent proximity to the edge, over which they were plunged by the winds of the storm. They inhabited fragile dwellings, constructed with the simplest of materials, typically wooden planks and porous roof tiles in the city and palm tree boards and thatched roofs in the countryside, often without internal reinforcement and rarely connected to a foundation.

For people of humble means and circumstances, urban dwellers as well as country folk, hurricanes were catastrophic occurrences. Residential patterns no less than building materials reflected the social configurations that organized urban life in the nineteenth-century colony. That the pattern of greatest devastation closely paralleled the social delineations by which Havana barrios were differentiated came as a surprise to no one. In the end, hurricanes served at least as much to reveal misfortune as they did to create it.

The storms also produced hardship for the well-to-do, of course. Indeed, it was not uncommon for families of means to plunge hopelessly into debt, from which many never recovered, subsequently to disappear from both public view and social prominence and in time to pass into the quiet obscurity most commonly reserved for almost everyone else.

Nevertheless, the dominant representation of hurricanes as disaster implied magnitude and mass, which of course implicated the most vulnerable. In ways that were direct and immediate, the proposition of disaster was largely a function of the social system that had taken form during the early decades of nineteenth-century Cuba. Adversity was visited especially on Cubans of modest means who, by virtue of the material circumstances that circumscribed their daily lives, lacked the resources with which to protect themselves against the force of nature. Such families were at greater risk of calamity than affluent households. Vulnerability to the hurricane was itself a function of the material determinants around which social hierarchies in nineteenth-century Cuba were arranged. "Disaster" under these circumstances was thus one more manifestation of the terms by which resources were allocated and distributed within the colonial political economy. Families living close to or at the threshold of adversity had a far shorter distance to travel to succumb to indigence.[1]

Because disaster involved numbers on such a scale, moreover, the disruption and dislocation caused by hurricanes raised corollary issues of social control and political order. As the population increased, indeed as the base of the social pyramid expanded in exponential proportions to the apex, "disaster" implied a range of political possibilities. The midcentury hurricanes occurred at a decisive point in the demographic development of colonial Cuba. These were decades of rapid growth, as the population increased by almost 75 percent, from 272,000 in 1792 to more than one million by 1841. Towns and cities filled with ever more inhabitants, and nowhere perhaps more dramatically than in metropolitan Havana. Slavery expanded even as the condition of slaves deteriorated. By 1841, too, the size of the population of color—free (153,000) and slave (437,000) combined—had overtaken the population of whites (418,000).[2]

Colonialism in nineteenth-century Cuba derived its ultimate raison d'être among diverse sectors of privileged creoles for its capacity to oversee social order and underwrite economic prosperity. Hurricanes had a way of shattering the rhythm of the routine on which society and economy were predicated and at the same time interrupting the daily order by which colonial structures institutionalized power relationships. Indeed, it was precisely through this routine that the assumptions of colonial authority gained currency and in the end sustained the relationships by which the very logic of social stratification obtained comprehension and compliance. Hurricanes disrupted the colonial routine, thereby rendering inoperative the basis by which a large segment of the population negotiated the terms of livelihood and well-being. These circumstances had the potential to erode an array of fixed political structures sustained by tradition and to which voluntary acquiescence had been rendered as a matter of course, not necessarily as a matter of conscience. The prospect of vast numbers of people, having lost the little they owned and hence with little left to lose, driven by despair to seek amelioration of their condition, perhaps immediately by looting and sacking or worse, or over the longer term by questioning the usefulness of colonial authority, threatened to challenge the rationale of Spanish administration.

/ / / / /

The hurricanes of 1844 and 1846 delivered staggering losses to households in Havana, especially the extramuro communities, where tens of thousands of families had taken up residence, many in crowded, fragile dwellings, in barrios that had expanded without plan or policy but rather in response to need, often spontaneously. Dwellings were constructed with whatever building materials happened to be available, the principal requirement being that they were inexpensive. The social distinctions between intramuro and extramuro had been fixed in 1776, when colonial authorities called a moratorium on all future construction of homes of wood and thatched roofs inside the walled city, effectively banishing the families of modest means to the barrios of extramuro Havana. Indeed, by 1827 census enumerators reported that the intramuro city contained 3,671 houses—"all of masonry" [*todas de piedra*]; extramuro Havana had 7,968 homes—"of various types of materials" [*de varias clases de materiales*].[3]

In fact, even buildings of the heaviest construction material, structures of masonry and stone, often did not escape the fury of the midcentury storms. Several homes along the intramuro waterfront collapsed during the initial storm surge in 1846; others, not fully recovered from the hurricane of 1844, sustained serious damage from the constant pounding of wind-driven rain and buckled under at their foundations, which were undermined by the torrents of water that rushed through high-velocity floodways formed by the narrow streets of Havana. By one count, 23 houses collapsed and another 308 experienced varying degrees of damage.[4] Some of the most fashionable mansions in the Havana suburb of El Cerro reported substantial losses. The magnificent Aldama Palace, completed in 1845, suffered extensive damage during the hurricane of 1846, including the collapse of an iron balcony. Some years later Fredrika Bremer, while visiting El Cerro, came upon one estate "much neglected . . . since a terrible hurricane in 1848 [sic], which entirely destroyed the house, of which merely a ruin now remains, and injured many trees and statues."[5]

The storms wrought havoc in extramuro Havana. Dwellings of wood and other light construction materials, of course, never had a chance. Roofs were blown off, walls collapsed, and windows and doors were blown out, leaving water, mud, and muck to overwhelm the interior. The exact number of homes that caved in will probably never be known. Not all were demolished, to be sure, but because they remained standing did not mean that they were habitable. "It appears unnecessary to say," one observer wrote in the hours immediately following the 1846 storm, "that the *extramuro barrios* . . . are in calamity, for in some places the fragile homes were punished not only by the terrible winds and the constant heavy rain, but were also subjected to the lashing waves of the turbulent sea."[6] According to one estimate, of the 786 houses destroyed in the capital, 763 were located in extramuro Havana; of the nearly 2,340 homes damaged, 2,029 were extramuro dwellings.[7]

The barrios of Jesús María and San Lázaro were devastated. San Lázaro, on the north, paralleled the ocean side of Havana; Jesús María was located on the bay front. Both districts, moreover, had historical and topographical peculiarities that made them especially vulnerable to hurricanes. San Lázaro, built on low-lying land, was difficult to drain, so that in the course of ordinary rains, the streets turned into muddy quagmires. At the same time, the floors of many of the wooden houses were below street level and hence always susceptible to water runoff. The barrio was also the site of huge pits in which was deposited the garbage of Havana, making for hazardous health conditions under the best of circumstances. Jesús María had been constructed atop filled-in mangrove swamps and frequently was subjected to flooding during high tides. The narrow streets, which were uneven and unpaved, almost always transformed into mud flats during the rainy season. In this zone, wrote physician Julio LeRiverend some years later, "live a thousand poor families, whose numerous members find themselves stacked up and compressed against one another like bundles of wheat on the threshing-floor." In San Lázaro and Jesús María, LeRiverend added, were found "the wretched poor, who by virtue of necessity are obliged to lived in these dwellings . . . , where they breathe continually an air polluted by their own effluvium and that of their animals, like mules, pigs, and chickens, with which they shared their dwellings." [8]

Hard times for San Lázaro began with Hurricane Santa Rosalía of 1842. "Several houses . . . have been ruined," reported *El Faro Industrial de La Habana* in early September. "In no other part of our population has the damage of the hurricane been as substantial as in San Lázaro. Since most of the houses . . . are constructed of wood and fragile materials, the pounding of the ocean and driving force of the wind and rain resulted in more damage than anywhere else." [9]

The barrios that experienced substantial damage during the moderate storm of 1842 were devastated by the hurricanes of 1844 and 1846. Both San Lázaro and Jesús María were exposed to direct pounding of the storm surge. "Of all the *barrios*," the *El Faro Industrial de La Habana* reported in 1844, "the one to have suffered the greatest is San Lázaro. The vast majority of the houses on the street parallel to the ocean are almost completely ruined. After San Lázaro, it is [the barrio of] Jesús María." The day after the 1846 hurricane, but before reports of damage could be confirmed, *Diario de la Marina* speculated on conditions in extramuro Havana. "Some idea can be had of what has occurred," the paper editorialized, "if we consider that the iron balcony of the grand new house of Sr. Aldama has collapsed. What then can one imagine of the condition [of] the *barrio* Jesús María; what of the population of San Lázaro? We are horrified to imagine. What about the countryside? May Heaven have pity on us!" [10]

In fact, almost all the barrios of extramuro Havana suffered extensive damage, especially the poor and working-class neighborhoods of the outer city. In 1846 an estimated 460 homes in San Lázaro and 420 dwellings in Jesús María were damaged or destroyed. Other hard-hit extramuro barrios included Chávez (450), Peñalver (275), and Horcón (240). Families across extramuro Havana, as well as individual boarders and renters, found themselves without shelter, reduced instantly to indigence. "Thousands of families," the *ayuntamiento* of Havana reported, "wander aimlessly in search of a place of refuge in which to shelter themselves and in which to give thanks to the Almighty for having spared them of the death that threatened the entire city for so many hours." [11]

Information on the social composition of the extramuro barrios is scanty and scattered and must necessarily be used with circumspection. What does stand in sharp relief, however, are the color lines; indeed, it is through a

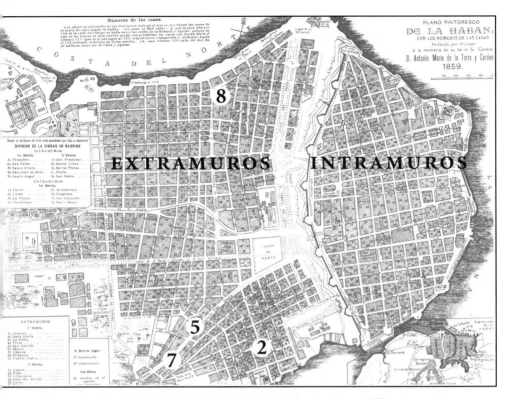

Havana in 1859, showing the division of the capital by the city wall. Barrios (identified by number on the map) most affected by hurricanes were Jesús María (2), Cerro (5), Chavez (7), and San Lázaro (8). Julius Bien and Co. Photo. Lit., 1859.

careful reading of the racial categories devised in nineteenth-century Cuba that some of the salient facets of the social landscape of extramuro Havana reveal themselves. A large percentage of people of color had concentrated outside the walls of the old city. Almost 60 percent of the population of extramuro Havana consisted of people of color, both free and slave. The numbers varied from barrio to barrio, but in almost every instance, blacks and mulattos, free and slave, constituted a decisive majority. In San Lázaro and Jesús María, people of color made up 54 percent of the population; in Peñalver, blacks and mulattoes comprised 65 percent.[12]

Large sectors of these extramuro poor became homeless and penniless, unable even to imagine how to pick up the pieces and put their lives back together. Many families lost not only their homes but also the contents of their homes. The familiar terms of daily life thus crumbled for thousands of households. The routine by which everyday behavior was scripted was instantly disrupted and no longer relevant. At the same time, the material combinations by which people represented themselves to the world—the means to arrange their personal appearance, the tools to ply their trades—in short, all those things they used to make a living, to provide for aging parents and growing children, to experience occasional joy and a measure of happiness had disappeared. Gone were their personal belongings, articles of clothing, furniture, foodstuffs and kitchen staples, memorabilia, and odds and ends accumulated over a lifetime by which place and purpose in life were often measured. Some families had supplemented their earnings through backyard gardening and raising small farm animals. These, too, were lost. The editorial comments by the *Diario de la Marina* after the 1846 hurricane were telling: "The devastation in the *extramuro* was extensive, [but] in terms of value it was not as great as the destruction in the *intramuro*." [13] The measure of value always seemed to favor the well-to-do.

Again and again survivors told of collapsing houses, of personal possessions lost, of loved ones dead, of lives in disarray. In all, an estimated three hundred habaneros lost their lives during the twelve hours of the 1846 storm. Some disappeared during the early storm surge, others perished inside collapsing buildings, and still others drowned in the accompanying floods.[14] In San Lázaro and Jesús María, floodwaters filled the streets and washed away all but the most solid constructions. "Those poor people," commented the correspondent of *Diario de La Habana* a day after the storm, "they came out of their houses into water waist-high in search of refuge on higher ground free of flooding." [15]

The experience of calamity, however, was only the beginning. All affected households faced the daunting task of rebuilding and recovery in an environment of ruin. The magnitude of the devastation in 1844 and 1846 created shortages of every type, including most immediately food supplies and clothing, but also the materials necessary for rebuilding, including wood, nails, and tiles. Invariably residents were forced to forage for building materials, most commonly obtaining those salvaged from other buildings and improvising the construction of new dwellings, no less fragile than the previous ones and, of course, equally vulnerable to the effects of the next storm to descend.

Many Cubans who had been barely able to make ends meet, surviving each day by sheer will and wile, now plunged into abject poverty. Households that lost everything were faced with the task of replacing clothing, household wares, and entire homes, often without funds or jobs.

/ / / / /

It would be difficult to imagine the magnitude of the hardships that befell thousands of households between 1844 and 1846 without the graphic first-person accounts of hurricane survivors. The archival records of the Gobierno Superior Civil, in Havana, the authority charged with oversight responsibility for relief and reconstruction, are filled with petitions and appeals for assistance, some written by the supplicants themselves but mostly in the form of transcriptions prepared by scribes and forwarded to the office of the governor general for review and action. Indeed, these narratives described exactly how the lives of ordinary residents were disrupted by the hurricanes and indicate the material losses experienced by extramuro households.

The act of petition had other implications. The process was one of formalized supplication through which residents in Havana appealed for public subsidies to get through a time of bewildering losses. But it was also an occasion for families on hard times to make sense of their misfortune, to take measure of conditions, and to set out in narrative form the nature of the losses and reflect on strategies for recovery. The occasion further provided the opportunity for people to consider their linkages to the authorities by whom they were governed. The popular imagination thus articulated collective expectations and at the same time advanced a usable definition of the responsibility of colonial administration for the common good. The procedure of sanctioned supplication provided an institutional means by which to expand the public presence of colonial administration. Authorities assumed the task of relief, whereupon residents also ascribed to the colonial officialdom the function of public assistance.

People from all walks of life gave aggregate expression to conditions in extramuro Havana in the form of a narrative on the plight of the poor. In the process, they contributed to shaping a constituency that had claims on colonial administration. A new colonial covenant was in the making, as thousands of families in Havana, displaced or otherwise disabled after 1844 and 1846, made known their expectation of public assistance to obtain food, shelter, and the resources needed to rebuild their homes, as well as to secure some means of livelihood.

Material losses accurately reflected colonial stratification and indeed were themselves the result of vulnerabilities derived from material conditions specifically associated with class, gender, and age. How and to whom "disaster" struck was, in fact, largely shaped by the very social determinants around which colonial society was organized. Extramuro resident Francisco

Cardozo sent Governor General O'Donnell a poignant description of his situation:

> Prior to the most recent and unforgettable hurricane, I owned a small wooden house where I resided with my wife and daughters. In the aftermath of that deplorable event, my house was totally destroyed, and I was left with my family wandering the streets [*vagando por las calles*] without any place in which to find shelter, without any clothing to cover our bodies, for we lost everything. But the worst of my condition is the lack of employment, for I have no opportunity to work. . . . With the help of some friends who are as poor and needy as I am, I have been able to build with available debris a small lean-to of bark and palm leaves that does not protect against the rigor of the seasons. . . . I have not been able to find a single resource with which to alleviate the bad luck that punishes my family.[16]

But having a job did not necessarily ensure recovery. "I lost my chest of drawers with all the clothing belonging to my husband and me," Isabel Landín explained, "as well as all the other furniture and kitchen ware we owned. Under these sorrowful circumstances, we are without any means whatsoever to replace our only possessions recently destroyed. Although I am married, my husband is engaged in the hard work on the docks and his meager earnings do not even begin to cover the barest of our most urgent necessities." José de Sogo wrote that "the hurricane destroyed everything in the wretched little house in which I lived with my wife and six children, leaving us in a condition of horrific misery."[17]

The loss of their most personal belongings—those things on which people relied to mediate the commonplace encounters of everyday life— meant facing the world at large with a much reduced capacity to control the terms of self-presentation. "I have lost everything," Miguel Sánchez despaired from San Lázaro. "How do I make my way? With what do I rebuild my life?"[18] The loss of clothing produced a special type of angst, a vulnerability and a heightened awareness of the relationship between self-presentation and self-preservation. Clothing was, after all, the most basic means by which to arrange the public terms of selfhood as entrée into the larger world. "Due to the horrifying hurricane we suffered last year," Francisca de Silva recounted, "I lost all my furniture and all my clothing, leaving me in the most lamentable state of nakedness [*desnudez*], without being able to go out into the street by day, all due to a lack of resources [*recursos*]." Manuel and Rosalía de Zayas described their condition as one of "a complete state of the naked poor," while Ramon López complained that he found himself "reduced to living off public charity, for I do not have even clothing to put on my back." Juana Sánchez was in a similar position. At age sixty-five, she wrote, she was a widow, "with a daughter, who is also a widow, and a grandson. We are all in the most miserable of conditions, having been reduced by these difficulties to a condition of complete nudity [*absoluta desnudez*] as a result of the ferocious hurricane blowing away the little clothing that had covered our bodies."[19]

Lost personal property often included the means to earn a living. "The hurricane reduced the house I inhabited, my only property, to total rubble," Juanita Oliver despaired, "and similarly destroyed all my furniture and clothing. As a result I find myself in a condition of utter indigence, and without the resources to remedy my situation."[20] Antonio Sánchez had previously earned a living wage by cooking at home for others. On October 11, he lost his home as well as all his pots and pans and cooking utensils. Seamstress Blasa del Val, a widow with two small children, in addition to her home, the family's clothing, household furnishings, lost all her sewing material. "Without having any other means of subsistence," she explained to the governor general, "I have no way of supporting myself and my children."[21]

Nowhere perhaps were the effects of the hurricanes more acute than among the extramuro households headed by women and the aged. Widows, especially those with dependent children, found themselves in particularly desperate straits. "I have suffered the misfortune of losing all my clothing and part of my furniture," wrote Josefa López, a widow with three small children, "and cannot return to my damaged house and lack the means of obtaining another home." Juana Domínguez occupied a demolished house with seven young children, she explained, "without having and without being able to obtain any means whatsoever to repair my home. Because of the condition of my house, I am forced to live on the streets." Widow María del Carmen Verna, who was gravely ill at the time of the 1846 hurricane, had much to be concerned about: "Not only was my house totally destroyed but I also lost a son in the full vigor of his youth [and] upon whom I based my expectations of support and assistance in my old age." Eugenia Rivero had suffered through both hurricanes. As she recounted, "I had hardly recovered from the losses and damages of the storm that befell us in 1844 . . . when the horrendous hurricane of 1846 arrived to destroy all my hopes." Elena Herrera despaired that she had "no place of shelter when night arrived and therefore I must constantly wander [*andar vagando*] among neighbors," while María Saavedra told of the weight of responsibility she bore, "for my small children and I are without any aid other than what I receive from Above. The hurricane . . . destroyed the source of consolation in my life: the little house in which we lived, where I gathered my children to cry with them over my being a widow and their being orphans. Now I do not even have that." Three months after the 1846 hurricane Ramona González related that the storm had "destroyed the small house upon which I had counted to live and to meet my needs. I have been left without a place of refuge, abandoned, to such an extreme that for some days I have had nothing to eat." The passing of two years had brought no relief to Apolonia María de Miranda Fernández. "During the terrible hurricane experienced by this city in 1846," she wrote, "and in the previous one, I suffered losses of such magnitude that I was left subject to a thousand necessities, none of which I have been yet able to resolve." [22]

The storms were especially hard on the many residents of advanced age who already faced adversity and infirmity. Eighty-year-old María Josefa Romo was a case in point. "I lived alone in a small wooden house," she explained, "without anyone who could assist me in any way, for I have no relatives in this city. In the midst of this poverty, if that is what one could call this miserable life that I have had to endure for so long, came the hurricane to destroy all my hopes." Romo's house was reduced to wind-strewn debris: "The fury of the hurricane scattered the tiles in such a form that not a single one remains. Household furnishings were ruined by the flooding of salt water that rained upon us. I lost food, clothing, and my patio garden." Caridad Romero explained her position in sorrowful terms three months after the hurricane: "In addition to being dismally poor, I find myself at an age far too advanced . . . to allow me even to contemplate a subsistence by wandering the streets begging for alms. I can count on no one for help. In fact, I often think it would be more desirable to end my days than remain in this circumstance of calamity, for the illnesses that I suffer are chronic and serve only to increase my woes and make it more difficult to put up with my miserable life." Ninety-three-year-old Gabriela Torres reported that the entire roof of her home had been destroyed and the doors and windows blown out. "Only the most dire of necessities could possibly compel me to stay in that house," she affirmed. Josefa Montero Gutiérrez described herself as of an "octogenarian age, a widow, and, of course, without father or mother and without a son who can help me. All I have is two daughters, both of whom themselves live in conditions of severe poverty. I am utterly destitute and obliged to live on the street." [23]

/////

In the countryside, the rendering of disaster similarly reflected the dominant social hierarchies of the nineteenth century. Particularly afflicted were the rural poor—those households that had few possessions and lacked access to the means for immediate relief and long-term recovery. The rains continued for days after the 1846 hurricane had passed, adding still more damage and despair to weather-battered communities. "The storm has ended," wrote one resident of the Havana countryside as late as October 23, "but the fierce rains continue upon our de-roofed houses, filled with our foodstuff and furniture. We are even unable to take advantage of the fallen fruits and destroyed palms . . . for they will rot before we can re-roof our homes."[24]

Hurricanes were especially debilitating for the countless thousands of small farmers, ranchers, rural workers, itinerant laborers, and slaves on the caseríos and small farms and in the isolated towns and villages all across the western jurisdictions. Commercial producers and subsistence farmers alike plunged into a crisis from which many of them never recovered. Their losses signified not only the demise of agriculture but also the decline of employment. In the weeks, months, and years following the hurricanes of 1844 and 1846, hunger and indigence propelled countless rural dwellers toward towns and cities, especially Havana, in search of relief.[25]

The degree to which adversity played havoc on the poor in both the cities and in the countryside was acknowledged if not always understood in commentaries of the time; indeed, such commentaries often provide graphic if unwitting testimony to the variety of ways that Cubans of modest means experienced hurricanes. The report of the lieutenant governor of Matanzas in October 1844 referred specifically to the condition of working-class neighborhoods: "The pitiful sight that this city presents, particularly the barrios in which the mass of working-class families [*familias proletarias*] live, and the details that reach me from the district captains [*capitanes de partidos*] concerning the utter hopelessness in which entire settlements have been reduced move everyone to compassion. Conditions of misery and the desolation of the countryside promise a bleak future for the poor workers."[26]

One contemporary history of San Antonio de los Baños noted that the hurricane of 1844 had resulted in an "extraordinary scarcity of foodstuffs, *viandas*, greens and various other agricultural products and vital necessities to the poor in particular." The condition of the poor in October 1846 was the subject of a report from Cabañas. "The plantains and *viandas*," wrote the observer, "the principal sustenance in the countryside, and in particular of the poor, has disappeared entirely. Because the corn harvest was so meager, the poor now must face a grim existence in the months to come. While some dwellings suffered only the loss of doors and windows, the thatched houses [*casas de guano*], which are those belonging to the poor, have collapsed or are in uninhabitable conditions and their previous occupants now find themselves living in the open. . . . The destruction experienced in the countryside is incalculable."[27] Almost two weeks after the hurricane, conditions in Güines continued to be desperate. "The scarcity of resources in this town, as well as all the *pueblos* in the immediate area," wrote one Güines resident, "[results in] a lack of assistance to attend to the needs of the injured and those indigent families who, in addition to having lost the pitiful huts [*chozas*] that sheltered them, now lack absolutely all aid to underwrite their subsistence." There was perhaps something slightly more than symbolic in one press account in 1844 indicating that of the total seventy-two houses in Quivicán, only two remained standing: one belonging to the parish priest and the other belonging to the captain of the partido.[28] The church and state always seemed to survive hard times.

/ / / / /

The midcentury hurricanes also had far-reaching effects on tens of thousands of slaves. The census of 1841 indicated that 85 percent of all slaves in Cuba (371,430 out of 436,500) were distributed throughout those zones that experienced the greatest devastation in 1844 and 1846.[29] With their living conditions simultaneously execrable and exposed, slaves suffered the full brunt of the storms. Slave quarters, typically wooden barracks (*barracones*) or clusters of bohíos, were among the first buildings to collapse. Slaves also had no direct access to food supplies, principally with the loss of domestic fowl and small livestock and the destruction of provision grounds, which generally experienced the same fate as almost all agriculture in Occidente. "The rich fruit harvests that previously filled the baskets of the *hacendados*, and provided sustenance to the merchant, the artisan, and the day-laborer," wrote an observer from San Antonio de los Baños a week after the storm, "no longer exist. There is no corn or *viandas* with which to maintain the *dotaciones* and less to feed the poor. The future presents a frightful picture."[30]

The loss of subsistence crops, especially the platanales, had grave implications. The plantain had become one of the chief products of provision grounds and a staple of the slave diet, but it was also among the most vulnerable to hurricane winds. A storm in 1796 had resulted in extensive damage to local food production in Occidente, most notably, the Junta de Fomento reported to the Crown, "the lack of plantains and grains that constituted the principal food for blacks on the sugar *ingenios*." Thirty years later the Reverend Abiel Abbot observed during a visit to San Antonio that the plantain "probably constitutes three fourths of the subsistence of the black population of the island."[31]

The effects of two successive hurricanes on the banana groves were devastating. It was difficult to imagine that a single platanal survived intact anywhere in the stricken zones. "*Plátanos* have disappeared," reported the correspondent of *Diario de La Habana* from Matanzas.[32]

Devastation of slave agriculture was a portentous development. Provision grounds served as slave subsistence farming, based on free time and borrowed land, which permitted slaves to cultivate ancillary land both to supplement their diet and to sell surplus crops commercially for cash.

The number of slaves who perished in Cuba during and in the immediate aftermath of the midcentury hurricanes is unknown, but the loss of life and personal belongings must be presumed to have been significant. Accounts of hurricanes in other plantation economies in the West Indies are suggestive. British planter Alexander Campbell described to the House of Commons in 1790 the grim consequences of such storms: "All of the Islands of the West Indies are subject to hurricanes, . . . by which provisions are destroyed, from July to November, and these happening at a season when there is no shipping in the country and the distance from this country being too great to send for a supply of provisions to feed the slaves with, they are often obliged to eat the ground provisions and corn before they are fully ripe, which often occasions fluxes and great mortality among them."[33] The Reverend George Wilson Bridges described the aftermath of the 1780 hurricane in Jamaica in similar terms: "Such a violation of nature could not but be felt severely in every part of the island," he commented. "The mortality, especially amongst the negroes, was, for some time, constant and visible; and the gloomy apprehension of the inhabitants expected almost the failure of the population. Yet the numbers that were left still exceeded the measure of subsistence, for vegetation had perished." Hector M'Neill, who happened to be in Jamaica when the 1780 hurricane struck, subsequently insisted that the devastation of property was small when compared to the grief visited upon slaves. "It is the total destruction of those provisions," he wrote in an open letter to slave owners, "which constitutes the support and existence of your Negroes — it is the inability, and impossibility of procuring other provisions in time to keep them alive — it is your sick without a hospital — your infirm without shelter; and it is the misery of beholding hundreds of wretched beings wasting around you, clamouring for food, and imploring that assistance which you cannot bestow." Between 15,000 and 20,000 slaves — out of a total of 256,000 — were believed to have perished in Jamaica during the storm of 1780. A second hurricane in the same year resulted in the death of 3,000 to 4,000 slaves in Barbados. Lowell Ragatz estimated that more than 15,000 slaves perished from starvation or disease after the West Indian hurricane of 1785.[34]

The information available for Cuba is fragmentary and incomplete. Newspaper stories and official reports rarely made more than passing reference to the condition of slaves during and after hurricanes. Death and injury of slaves were usually perceived as misfortunes befalling the slave owner, included among the other material losses suffered by the planter. "Poor *hacendado* Don Juan Hernández . . . whose *barracón* collapsed resulting in the death of two slaves," the *Diario de La Habana* reported.[35]

But the fragmentary accounts of the death of slaves that have survived provide some, if limited, insight into the effects of hurricanes. In October 1844 *El Faro Industrial de La Habana* reported the death of three slaves on the Lagunilla estate. After the 1846 hurricane, the same paper wrote of "the collapse . . . of several *bohíos* of slaves, some slaves suffering injuries" on the cafetal Ascensión and "10 injured blacks on the *cafetal* Mariana." Two slaves on the cafetal owned by Susana Benítez perished. In another instance, the infirmary of the Alejandra estate in Güines in which the dotación had taken shelter collapsed, causing the death of 56 slaves and serious injury to 26 others. Edward Garriott's study of the 1846 hurricane refers to the nearby Providencia estate, where "only a very few of the negroes escaped death." In Havana, the dotación assigned to urban labor projects under the supervision of the Junta de Fomento suffered 5 deaths and another 30 injuries when the *barracón* in San Francisco de Paula collapsed. In one official announcement of burials dated October 12 in the Cementerio General of Havana, 12 slaves were identified by name and owner as having died as a result of the hurricane.[36]

The midcentury hurricanes also disrupted the rhythm of production and weakened the capacity of the plantation system to sustain the social control around which the daily regimen of slavery depended. Such circumstances presented auspicious conditions for flight. The available evidence suggests that agricultural slaves often seized the opportunity provided by the confusion to flee from estates and plantations. Notices of runaway slaves in the classified section "Prófugo de esclavos," published in *Diario de la Marina* and *El Faro Industrial de La Habana,* increased in the aftermath of hurricanes.[37]

As a precautionary measure, colonial authorities deployed additional police and soldiers to maintain public order. There were, in fact, few recorded incidents of lawlessness, and these were mostly in the form of sporadic looting. Nevertheless, creoles and government authorities alike, particularly in the aftermath of La Escalera, were markedly sensitive to matters of public order when blacks were involved. Planter Miguel de Aldama mentioned alarm in Havana around the time of the hurricane of October 1844, as talk of an uprising of blacks spread in the capital. "From six to ten in the morning it was horrible," Aldama wrote of the hurricane. "The population was extremely fearful for there was not a house that was safe and rumors were circulating [that] the blacks had begun to plunder. This had some basis in fact but since the hurricane had so utterly terrorized everyone, people seemed disposed to create phantasmas and fear where there was no reason for alarm." Aldama did note in passing, however, that there was indeed "a subversive cry [*grito suversivo*] of some 50 blacks in [the barrio of] Jesús María and some robberies in the Plaza del Vapor. All were taken prisoner by a squad of lancers and order was not disturbed." Similarly, in the aftermath of the hurricane of October 1846, *El Faro Industrial de La Habana* reported the dispatch of military units into barrios in both intramuro and extramuro Havana. Eight infantry platoons, two mounted artillery squadrons, and four units of the King's Lancers were sent out on patrol "for the purpose," announced Brigadier Juan Herrera Dávila, "of avoiding whatever disorders might arise under such afflicted circumstances."[38] In provincial towns, too, military units assumed policing duties. In Güines, infantry units patrolled by day and cavalry squads in the evening—measures taken, the *jefe de partido* explained, "not only so that residents would be able to recover the remains of their household possessions but also to preserve the order that has been scrupulously maintained."[39]

/ / / / /

The larger consequences of the midcentury hurricanes, and indeed the enduring impact of the attending disruption, had less to do with the immediate hardship to the slave population, either in the city or in the countryside, than with the new logic of production modalities that was gaining widespread currency. The destruction wrought by the hurricanes added momentum to forces already making their presence felt and thereby contributed to transformations of the colonial political economy.

The reallocation of the dotaciones from the cafetales to the ingenios in the aftermath of collapsing coffee production had direct and far-reaching implications for slaves. The labor regimen on the sugar plantation was very different from work on the coffee estate. By all contemporary accounts, working conditions and living arrangements on the cafetales were considerably less repressive, less ruthless, and less remorseless than on the ingenios. The relationship between masters and slaves was less harsh and far less adversarial on the coffee estates, where slaves enjoyed greater material comforts, a better diet, and superior housing. On cafetales, slaves enjoyed more space, both public and private, and, at least as important, greater control over their own time with which to pursue the development of autonomous personal relationships and entrepreneurial undertakings. The Angerona coffee estate maintained a retail store where slaves bought goods with money earned on their own time. It was also common for slave birthrates to exceed mortality rates on the coffee estates, but almost never on the sugar plantations. Whereas mortality rates on the ingenios often reached as high as 18 percent, they rarely surpassed 5 percent on the cafetales. Between the 1820s and 1840s, the dotación of Angerona was sustained by natural growth.[40] "I could not," observed Robert Baird during his travels in Cuba, "although I diligently inquired, hear of any [sugar] estate on which the number of labourers was kept up by births on the estate itself. Indeed, the idea of making the slave population supply itself is the last thing that seems to enter a Cuban's mind."[41]

Coffee estates offered a greater opportunity for independent farming; they permitted slaves to cultivate provision grounds and tend livestock herds both as a means of individual subsistence and as a source of commercial remuneration. "Great quantities of corn are raised among the coffee trees," observed the Reverend Abiel Abbot in 1828. "The negroes increase the variety of their food by the product of *their own* land. They raise malanga, the top for salad, the bottom for a change from plantain."[42]

The labor regimen of daily life, moreover, was radically different. No friend of slavery in any form, David Turnbull nevertheless drew sharp distinctions between the cafetal and the ingenio. He observed: "When a *cafetal* is once formed the care and protection of the trees, the gathering of the fruit, and its removal to the barbecue . . . make when added together, an amount of labour which is not to be compared with the toil of digging the cane holes, weeding the young plants, cutting down the canes, carrying the tops to the stables, and the canes themselves to the mill preparatory to the process of grinding." Turnbull concluded: "The natural consequence inevitably follows, that while the sugar-making slave, beginning his labours at sixteen or eighteen years of age, has certainly on an average not more than ten years to live, the coffee-picking slave may fairly reckon on twenty-five or thirty years, without ever having endured the same severity of toil or same intensity of suffering." Visiting the cafetal Angerona outside Artemisa in 1828, the Reverend Abiel Abbot noted that the "proprietor carefully avoids overworking his negroes. . . . In the winter he gives them a recess from labor at noon of an hour and a half, and in summer of three hours, and no night work is permitted on the estate. The best comment on these humane arrangements is, that a more healthy, muscular, active set of negroes, as many have remarked, is not to be found on the island." [43]

Anselmo Suárez y Romero spent a great deal of time on his family finca in Güines, a rich agricultural zone noteworthy for its many coffee estates and sugar plantations. Suárez y Romero made no secret of his abhorrence of slavery on the ingenios, making this point of view the centerpiece of his novel *Francisco*.[44] "I have lived inside the *ingenios*," he wrote to a friend in 1838, "I have known them from the time I was a child, and after having seen them with greater clarity of vision I nearly burst into tears at seeing so much iniquity, so much inhumanity, and so much cruelty." At the same time, however, Suárez y Romero's description of slave life on the cafetal was almost lyrical. "The gathering of coffee on the *cafetales*," he wrote two years later, "is a very easy operation, more of a distraction than a bother to the blacks, something that is even done by the slave children [*criollitos*] playing; . . . coffee is gathered for a while and then they go to sleep." Suárez y Romero drew the comparison to sugar explicitly: "But in the *ingenio* . . . the tasks are very different. The blacks are up before sunrise, and have neither the beautiful *guardarrayas* nor the delightful trees, or fragrant gardens in which to work in the shade." [45]

These views were corroborated by foreign travelers. It is probable that John Wurdemann overstated the case when he observed in 1844 that the Carlota coffee estate "was managed with a due care to the comfort and health of the negroes." But he came a little closer to the mark in his fuller description:

> The negro cottages were also arranged with much good taste, being composed of separate houses, built on each side of the spacious yard, which, with their general kitchen, and large, airy hospital, all neatly whitewashed, presented the appearance of a thriving little village. [The owner] witnesses no overtasked labor of his slaves. Well fed, with sufficient time

allowed them for rest and the care of their own live stock of fowls and hogs, compared to the destitute of even our northern states, they are happier; and many are enabled to save enough money to purchase their freedom, which is not infrequently done.[46]

Wurdemann's passing remarks have a larger significance. Almost twenty years earlier, Reverend Abbot had also taken note of living arrangements for slaves on the Angerona coffee estate. "The bohea [sic], or square of negro huts," Abbot observed, "is judiciously arranged on a hill, fifteen or twenty rods east from the principal building of the batey. Two families are accommodated under one roof, and a space of a few yards is left between each two buildings, fenced by a high open picket. In this manner the negro huts enclose a large square. . . . When the plantation becomes as populous as the proprietor hopes it will, this square will be a little negro city, with streets running at right angles."[47]

Nineteenth-century commentaries have been supported by historical judgments. Ramiro Guerra y Sánchez described slave labor on the Jesús Nazareno coffee estate at length:

> Work on the cafetal was relatively lenient [suave] and agreeable [agradable]. To keep the coffee field clean did not require great effort. Nor did harvesting the berries demand hard work. . . . Similarly, the tasks were not of equal intensity during the entire year. As a result, the slaves of Jesús Nazareno could be employed not only in the cultivation of products for their own subsistence—a practice common to all cafetales—cultivation in which the work was not comparable to difficulty of work on the potreros and sugar mills. But slaves of the cafetal were also used in work to landscape and beautify the estate proper.

Economist Gerardo Brown Castillo characterized coffee planters as a social class that "constituted a type of rural patriciate," adding: "Their direct contact with blacks implied relations that softened the interaction between masters and slaves, something that was later lost when sugar absorbed the majority of these slaves in the aftermath of the ruin of the coffee industry." Historian Gloria García Rodríguez also drew a distinction between the labor regimen on ingenios and cafetales, suggesting that "the latter was more lenient and the dotación enjoyed the entire night to rest and sleep, which greatly contributed to higher fertility rates, fitness, and health."[48]

The nature of internal operations of the cafetal, moreover, was markedly different from the ingenio. Richard Dana commented extensively during his travels through Matanzas and Havana on the changes wrought in the transition from coffee to sugar—all for the worse, he concluded. "The sugar plantation is . . . not the home of the pride and affections of the planter's family," Dana observed. "It is not a coveted, indeed, hardly a desirable residence." Further:

Such [planter] families as would like to remain on these plantations, are driven off for want of neighboring society. Thus the estates, largely abandoned by the families of the planter, suffer the evils of absenteeism, while the owners live in the suburbs of Havana and Matanzas, and in Fifth Avenue of New York. The slave system loses its patriarchal character. The master is not the head of a great family, its judge, its governor, its physician, its priest and its father. . . . Middlemen, in the shape of administradores, stand between the owner and the slaves. The slave is little else than [an] item of labor raised or bought.[49]

The daily life of the slaves thus transferred from coffee estates to sugar plantations deteriorated radically. Their new conditions were wretched, and they worked under remorseless exploitation. Slaves who previously had lived in communities of bohíos now inhabited crowded barracones. Indeed, slave dwellings had long been a subject of colonial commentary. As late as 1837, Francisco de Paula Serrano directly addressed conditions in slave quarters in a treatise on agriculture. Influenced by his long association with coffee production, Paula Serrano declared: "The dotación should be accorded good housing. I would say not in those barracones fortified like a prison. . . . The owner would then have a moral force, the most powerful, the most appropriate for the supervision of this class of men, to stimulate them to work. The comforts and the advantages that are promised by the progress of the owners also allow them to entertain the possibilities of improvement in the condition of life in all aspects."[50]

A number of planters defended existing living arrangements as both cost-effective and secure. The Marqués de Campo Florido asserted that "the indefatigable vigilance that [I] have established day and night on my fincas has preserved order and never have I had any altercation. . . . [Male] slaves live in union with their women in the bohíos, where they have their children and obtain respite from their toils." Campo Florido noted that the slaves had become accustomed to the bohíos, which they cherished "like a sacred property [una propiedad inviolable] [and] in which they gathered everything that they legally acquired through work they do in their own behalf on their own time."[51] According to José Montalvo y Castillo, the owner of several estates in the jurisdiction of Havana, the system of bohíos was not only a more felicitous living arrangement but also a means of control. "The only source of relief for [the] African slave is his *choza*, family, and liberty and independence in the early hours of the evening," Montalvo y Castillo explained. "His livestock, his provision grounds [*conucos*], [and] his projects are at the heart of his existence. His temperament suggests the way to control him, for the yoke of slavery will never succeed against those who enjoy a certain liberty." Montalvo y Castillo feared that the system of barracones would lead to resentment and, at the same time, act as a "point of concentration . . . in which to concert plots among discontented people," adding: "It is good to divide them to better govern them." [52]

Conditions were changing, however. The transition from bohíos to barracones itself suggested larger changes that were transforming the regimen of plantation labor. The incorporation of increasing numbers of slaves into ingenios and their subsequent deployment into barracks-style dwellings responded specifically to the need for more vigilance and greater social control over the dotaciones at a time of deteriorating working conditions. Joseph Gurney described a visit to one barracón in the early 1840s outside Havana that was "built to contain one thousand negroes." [53] There life was far more regimented, far more disciplined. Six-day workweeks, fourteen- to sixteen-hour workdays, or more, often for months at a time, were common. While traveling through Havana province in the late 1840s, Richard Madden learned that during the harvest slaves were allowed to sleep about four hours a day. At the Ariadne sugar estate in 1853, Fredrika Bremer observed that slaves "worked . . . with much more severity, because here they are allowed only four and a half hours out of the four-and-twenty for rest." [54] Jacob Omnium provided a vivid description of the sugar harvest at midcentury:

> It was crop time. The mills went round night and day. On every estate (I scarcely hope to be believed when I state the fact) every slave was worked under the whip 18 hours out of the 24, and, in the boiling houses, from 5 [A.M.] to 6 P.M., and from 11 o'clock [A.M.] to midnight, when half the people were concluding their 18 hours' work; the sound of the hellish lash was incessant; indeed, was necessary to keep the overtasked wretches awake. The six hours during which they rested were spent in the barracoon [*sic*],—a strong, foul, close sty, where they wallowed without distinction of age or sex. [55]

What is striking about the midcentury transformation of the slave labor system on Cuban plantations—specifically, the transfer of tens of thousands of slaves from cafetales to ingenios—is the coincidence of increased slave rebellions during these years. The degree to which slave discontent deepened as a function of the transfer from coffee estates to sugar plantations and, of course, the attending deterioration of the moral and material condition of daily life must be considered as striking and therefore of central importance to an understanding of mid-nineteenth-century Cuba.

The available evidence is fragmentary but suggestive. The mass transfer of slaves during the 1840s appears to have contributed to increased tensions across the plantations in Occidente: on the cafetales as slaves learned of the impending transfer, either through sale or lease, and on the ingenios as slaves responded to a new and harsher labor system. Indeed, incidents of insubordination and insurrection increased markedly on coffee estates throughout Occidente, many of them apparently related to the transfer of slaves from cafetales to ingenios.[56]

/ / / / /

From one end of western Cuba to the other, communities in the countryside and in the cities struggled to comprehend the fate that had befallen them. The midcentury hurricanes had devastated the most productive agricultural zones of the island, those with a disproportionately high concentration of population and wealth, that is, the very social and economic foundations of the colonial system. The livelihood and material well-being of almost everyone in the western half of the island—from the colonial bourgeoisie to itinerant day laborers, to merchants and peasants, on the ingenios, cafetales, and vegas, in the capital and provincial ports—depended in varying degrees on the maintenance of an orderly production system, expanding exports, and access to imports derived from reliable maritime traffic and efficient overland transportation.

In fact, colonial authorities could not respond adequately to the full range and diverse forms of the needs occasioned by the hurricanes of 1844 and 1846. Part of the problem was the sheer magnitude of devastation and destitution. It was difficult to comprehend what could not be imagined. Never before had Cuba experienced such destruction, in large measure because never before had there been so much to destroy. Indeed, the magnitude of the crisis was itself a manifestation of developments decades in the making, the result of profound transformations in the colonial economy to which old political structures had become increasingly inappropriate if not completely irrelevant.

Cuba had become a different place in the course of the early nineteenth century. The population had increased nearly tenfold. Towns and cities had expanded in size and numbers. Between 1827 and 1846 the cultivated fields on which Cuban prosperity depended had nearly doubled, from about 12.7 million acres to 21.8 million. The value of agricultural production had climbed from 429 million pesos to 756 million pesos. Technological advances had transformed production modes, railroad lines had lengthened, new sugar mills had multiplied, and port facilities had modernized.[57]

In fact, almost everything had changed except the premises and policies by which Spain administered the colony. Increasingly Spanish colonial administration was becoming incongruous if not incompatible with Cuban needs. The metropolis possessed neither the means nor perhaps the motive to accommodate the changes transforming life in the colony.

These were also years of deepening discontent among growing sectors of Cuba's planter class. In bowing to British pressure to end the slave trade, Spain appeared to have arrayed itself against Cuban interests.[58] The suppression of the legal slave trade drove planters from the open market to illicit trade, where risks were commensurately higher, demands on diminishing supply correspondingly greater, and prices inevitably steeper. This was nuisance enough, to be sure, yet it did not alone threaten the system whose survival was one of the principal motives for creole support of Spanish rule. But the proscription of the slave trade, many feared, portended the end of slavery altogether. After the 1830s, when Britain halted slavery in its Caribbean territories, Cuban concerns assumed a new gravity as England stepped up its demands for abolition. Alarm spread in Cuba, for few believed that Spain possessed the will or the wherewithal to resist British pressure.

Not all Cubans were reconciled to this eventuality. Indeed, some contemplated a third alternative to the uncertainty of independence and the unreliability of colonialism: annexation to the United States. Annexation promised a marvelously simple and sensible solution to many of the planters' most pressing problems. In the short run, union with the United States promised to guarantee the survival of slavery and the salvation of the plantation economy. Slavery was flourishing and expanding in the United States, something from which slaveholding Cubans derived comfort and confidence. By joining the North American system, Cuba obtained at one and the same time sanction and security for local slave institutions. Further, union with the United States offered Cuban planters the opportunity to participate in the flourishing internal slave trade without risk and at competitive prices. The outbreak of slave rebellions on the island in the early 1840s, moreover, raised questions about Spain's capacity to guarantee social control over the growing population of color. Annexation thus promised not only the salvation of slavery but also security from the slaves themselves. Finally, many Cuban planters had developed an abiding admiration for North American political institutions, where democratic ideals seemed to coexist congenially with slave institutions. "It is an irrefutable fact," wrote annexationist Domingo del Monte in 1838, "that the United States of America . . . [has] since its founding enjoyed the greatest political liberty, and they still have slaves."[59]

Annexation also promised to resolve some of the more anomalous features of the mid-nineteenth-century colonial political economy. Across Cuba, buyers and sellers, consumers and producers had developed a considerable stake in trade with the United States. Certainly union would simplify Cuban commercial relationships. Annexation seemed a wholly logical political outgrowth of deepening economic ties. At a time when almost 50 percent of Cuban trade depended on access to North American markets and manufactures, few Cuban producers could fail to appreciate the advantages of annexation. Union promised to eliminate the onerous system of Spanish taxation on foreign imports and U.S. tariffs on Cuban products, both of which would increase profits on exports and reduce prices on imports. Slavery would survive, markets would expand, tariffs and discriminatory duties would disappear.

/ / / / /

Annexationist sentiment waned in the years that followed, due in part to the fact that increasing demands for slaves were met from internal sources, but more to the declining interest in the United States. This did not mean that Cuban discontent with Spanish administration diminished, of course. In fact, the midcentury hurricanes revealed still one more facet of colonial administration in which colonial policies were deficient and went against Cuban interests. It was difficult for Spanish authorities to deal with circumstances for which they had no readily available remedy—neither appropriate administrative structures nor adequate material resources. They were thus overwhelmed by the magnitude of the disruption and, especially, by the extent of human and material losses. It was not simply that local officials lacked sufficient resources for immediate relief. They also lacked the means to distribute the resources they did possess. More important, however, the Spanish were hampered by the larger institutional constraints from which the logic of colonial administration derived its central purpose.

Colonial authorities faced two separate but related problems. The first was the need to immediately assist the thousands of families without food, without shelter, and without means of subsistence; to tend to the injured; and to clear away the accumulated debris as the first step toward recovery. Successive hurricanes in 1844 and 1846 had depleted food supplies across Occidente, both existing inventories of foodstuffs and the plantings on which future food supplies depended. Famine was the next specter to loom over scores of communities in the days and weeks after the storms.[60]

Government officials appealed for voluntary donations and subscriptions, drawing on the resources and goodwill of both official and private contributors. In 1844 and again in 1846, Governor General Leopoldo O'Donnell appointed a Junta de Socorro to oversee government relief efforts and to distribute food and supplies. Colonial agencies coordinated subscriptions raised from private sources, usually with considerable public ceremony and official announcements. Donations were made by prominent citizens, including representatives of well-to-do families, local merchants, and prominent religious, military, and civic leaders—among them the archbishop of Havana, the Conde de Villanueva, the Conde and Condesa de Fernandina, and the Banco Español. Funds were raised by Spanish military units stationed in Havana, including the Royal Corps of Engineers, the King's Lancer Regiment, and the officers and chief of the Havana Militia Regiment. In 1844 funds were donated by the Spanish queen, the queen mother, and various government ministries such as Ultramar, War, Trade, Justice, and Treasury.[61] In addition, Governor General O'Donnell charged local civic leaders, property owners, and church officials with responsibility for raising relief funds in the affected zones.[62]

Shopkeepers, merchants, and planters made contributions of other kinds. Retailer Pablo Bustillo in Limonar donated at no cost his inventory of foodstuffs to needy residents. In Quivicán, farmers distributed meat supplies from their own livestock. In Matanzas, a number of planters offered the labor of a total of two hundred slaves, including carpenters and masons, as well as work animals, to aid in local reconstruction projects.[63]

Some relief came in the form of charitable donations distributed by various church agencies across the island. Local churches expanded their asylum facilities to provide places for orphans. A number of Catholic *colegios*, including the Colegio de Nuestra Señora del Monserrate in Colón, opened class enrollments to provide education at no cost to families victimized by the hurricanes.[64] Catholic authorities also played an important role in bolstering colonial morale by celebrating life in the midst of ruin and desolation. Within a week of the 1846 hurricane, a special mass was celebrated at the Cathedral of Havana "to offer a *Te Deum* to the Almighty for having saved our lives"; all civil, military, and ecclesiastical authorities were enjoined to attend. Similarly, in early November 1846 a church in Cienfuegos organized a special mass of thanksgiving, which served, too, as an occasion to appeal for donations for the storm victims. The onset of the hurricane season of 1847, especially as October approached, produced a brooding disquiet in the capital; the public was calmed, the ayuntamiento of Havana noted, by appeals to "the only power that is superior to the fury of the elements."[65]

Programs for long-term recovery involved the development of public works projects. Such projects created employment opportunities at a time when both the work and wages needed for recovery were in high demand but short supply. State-sponsored construction projects also contributed to recovery by repairing damaged infrastructure, including port facilities, bridges, roads, and docks, as well as public buildings such as schools, hospitals, prisons, and government buildings.[66]

/ / / / /

In the end, however, distress was only partially relieved through the allocation of resources at hand. Over the longer run, government authorities understood the importance of developing strategies for recovery, including the replacement or reconstruction of capital stock and the repair of damaged infrastructure. For this, Cuban officials needed new, readily accessible sources of supplies and provisions, most of which could be procured only from abroad.

Spain was all but useless as a source of supplies, in part because it lacked sufficient resources and in part because the distance between Spain and Cuba made fast delivery of needed provisions all but impossible. Spain was weeks away. Indeed, it was nearly six weeks before authorities in Madrid had even learned of the hurricane of September 1842. In 1844 Spain did not receive word of the devastation that occurred on October 4–5 for two months.[67] It is unclear when the Court in Madrid learned of the calamity of October 10–11, 1846. However, on December 31, ten weeks later, Governor General O'Donnell discovered that the Spanish Court was still uninformed about conditions in Cuba and wrote indignantly to complain about "the delay in the arrival of the important [October 12] communication."[68]

Authorities in Havana were thus left to their own devices to develop appropriate strategies for recovery, to revive production, and to reconstruct destroyed infrastructure. In the days and weeks that followed the 1846 hurricane, they adopted a series of measures to provide immediate relief and long-term recovery. Price controls were set in place. In response to reports of price gouging and profiteering, the ayuntamiento of Havana denounced "the alteration of prices in the aftermath of the calamity by speculators to the grave prejudice of their neighbors." The city council unanimously approved a resolution "prohibiting for a period of two months any increase in the price of bread, jerked beef, codfish, lard, salt, rice, charcoal, bricks, tiles, wood, and nails, all items of primary necessities, higher than charged on the day before the hurricane." It appealed to O'Donnell to impose an interim moratorium on civil judicial proceedings pertaining to foreclosures and outstanding debts as a way to protect debtors in the aftermath of the hurricane. The ayuntamiento also called for reconstruction projects that included the large-scale importation of equipment, building materials, and provisions. In an effort to lower the cost of foreign imports for local consumers, it urged colonial authorities "to suspend all tariffs and permit duty-free all foreign imports for a period deemed appropriate of all items of primary necessity, such as rice, lard, salted meat, jerked beef, codfish, flour, salt, wood, nails, and bricks . . . , all of which will contribute to facilitating a quick recovery from our present misfortune." [69]

Under the circumstances, the inexorable logic of geography prevailed. Obliged by necessity to obtain emergency supplies of food and provisions from the nearest source, authorities turned to the United States. In fact, only North American producers, merchants, and shippers were in a position to provide Cuba with the food supplies and provisions in the quantity needed and at the speed required.

The *audiencia* of Havana enacted most of the resolutions adopted by the ayuntamiento but balked at the proposed moratorium on collection of outstanding debts. "The relief this measure seeks," the audiencia responded, "benefits only debtors, and this benefit cannot be dispensed without inflicting proportional harm on creditors. It would appear thus that the hurricane did damage only to the former and miraculously left the latter unharmed. And if this is not the case, if the calamity was the same for one and the other, then a remedy should be found that will provide relief equally for all, and not one that favors one class with substantial prejudice to the other." The audiencia concluded: "The storm with all its violence would not be capable of causing a minimum part of the evils that will necessarily result from such an imprudent measure, and its adoption will be tantamount of inflicting upon the Island a far greater calamity than those produced by hurricanes." [70]

The governor general acted quickly—"precipitously," officials in Spain later charged. O'Donnell adopted several recommendations made by the audiencia of Havana, most notably the suspension of prevailing tariff schedules for North American imports. Cuba opened local ports to U.S. merchant vessels for duty-free importation of food supplies, provisions, and all types of furnishings.[71] Codfish imports, a staple of the slave diet, increased from 11.8 million pounds in 1844 to 13.6 million in 1845 and to 14.1 million in 1846. Imports generally registered notable increases in the years following both hurricanes, from 25 million pesos in 1844 to 28 million in 1845 and from 22.6 million pesos in 1846 to 32.4 million 1847.[72]

Food supplies from the United States increased in response to the urgency of Cuban needs. Foreign flour imports, almost entirely North American in origin, soared from 6,700 barrels in 1846 to 43,500 barrels in 1847, with a slight decrease in imports of Spanish flour, from 128,900 barrels to 125,000 barrels.[73] "The commerce of the United States," one U.S. trade magazine commented in 1845, "reaped the benefit of the increase . . . [and] is to be accounted for by the fact that, in order to supply the deficiency occasioned by the protracted drought which took place in 1844, extra quantities of American produce, such as rice, corn, corn-meal, etc., were of necessity imported. . . . The increase of 1844 is laid to the extra imports from the United States to supply the wants occasioned by the drought and hurricane."[74]

These developments had long-term consequences. The devastation wrought by the midcentury hurricanes served to further expand the volume and variety of commerce between Cuba and the United States. The moral was not lost on those for whom these developments mattered. The decline of domestic food supplies obliged colonial authorities to increase food imports in an already import-dependent economy, adding a new dimension to the logic of the island's commercial connection with the United States.

But as often was the case in colonial relationships, the practical was not always possible or even preferable. Strategies devised in Havana often infringed on the prerogatives of the metropolis, including authority over trade regulations, administration of customs schedules, and collection of colonial receipts. In the end, the commercial modifications enacted in Havana required the approval of authorities in Madrid. Strategies developed locally to aid the displaced and the destitute were hampered by bureaucratic and self-serving constraints. So narrowly did Spanish officials define metropolitan interests that they opposed concession to Cuban needs at a time of crisis. In 1844 the emergency measures enacted in Havana were rejected in Madrid. The suspension of the ordinary customs fees levied on foreign imports in the aftermath of the 1844 hurricane was condemned by both the Court and members of the Spanish parliament [*cortes*]. Madrid nullified all measures that reduced or otherwise restricted the capacity of the royal exchequer to draw on colonial receipts. Access to colonial revenues, principally in the form of taxes, tariffs, and duties, was the time-honored prerogative of empire, one that Spain availed itself of frequently and that it was loath to relinquish or otherwise share with insular authorities—under any circumstances. "I have given the queen a full account of the contents of the letters of Your Excellency . . . in which you describe the hurricane experienced on October 4–5 in that capital and the immediate surrounding areas," the minister of Ultramar informed the intendant of Havana on December 29. "The measure of [October] 7 in which absolute exemption from duties is given to the importation of boards, beams, lintels, tiles, shingles, and all types of materials for factories and buildings, and the same exemption from tariffs given to beans, potatoes and rice, and . . . a reduction of duties granted on the consumption of the meats as part of the same measure, and the other dispositions have not met with the approval of Her Majesty. She thereby orders a return of all things to the state in which they were found prior to the aforementioned hurricane." On the same day, a royal order officially disapproved the measures adopted in Havana.[75]

Spanish policies deepened the emerging estrangement between Cuba and Spain. The high cost of recovery was being passed on to Cuban consumers through taxes and duties on vital foreign imports, with the Spanish royal exchequer emerging as the principal beneficiary of Cuban woes. Residents grew increasingly impatient and openly critical of a government that appeared indifferent to their plight. Miguel de Aldama could hardly contain his indignation. "I suppose you have read about the discussions in the Spanish *cortes*," Aldama wrote Domingo del Monte in March 1845,

> agitated by the exceptions conceded to the commerce of this island as a result of the hurricane of last October. . . . Although I have not been able to read them, from what I have heard here and there I deduce that they have lost all shame to talk about this island, and within a very short time we shall be obliged to consider as a very special favor of the mother country [*la madre patria*] permission to baptize ourselves and learn to read. I would not be surprised if we were declared minors, what the Laws of the Indies did to the indigenous people, for in the end the Metropolis has displayed more affection for the Indians in the old days than they show to the legitimate creole sons of Spaniards.[76]

Slowly the breach between the colony and the metropolis widened and deepened.

6. Between the Storms

A Cuban hurricane is a drama between two celebrations. The first one is locking ourselves up to await its arrival. And the second is to go out and see what happened.
Bohemia *(November 9, 1952)*

My grandmother sought to drive away hurricanes by making crosses with ashes. When the bad weather was near, she went out with a bucket full of ashes collected from the stove and spread them in the four corners of the house, threw fistfuls of ashes into the air, and made crosses in the passageway and near the principal roof supports of the house. This was the way she sought to appease the forces of nature.
Reinaldo Arenas, Antes que anochezca: Autobiografía *(1992)*

Acisclo Aroca . . . hadn't time to take anything with him, even less to secure the windows or to gather up what loose things remained here and there. . . . [H]e would have preferred a thousand times more to disappear with his possessions than to face what he was seeing. Nevertheless, at the crucial moment he didn't believe so much destruction was possible. He thought of his life, and that it was better to run the risk of some adequately reparable destruction than to lose the only thing that couldn't be replaced. Never had the idea of a similar devastation passed through his mind, that in one night what had taken him so many years to construct had been demolished.
Edgardo Sanabria Santaliz, "After the Hurricane" *(1995)*

The country was left a disaster. There were losses of every type. But not withstanding those calamities, we did not lose faith or confidence . . . because after the water and the wind pass, the sun always comes out again.
    Daisy Rubiera Castillo, Reyita, sencillamente *(1996)*

The hurricane has done its thing; now it is time for us to do ours.
    Fidel Castro, after Hurricane Flora *(October 1963)*

The storms passed, of course, and always things returned to normal. But they were rarely the same: not immediately, not in the years to come, sometimes not ever. Hurricanes insinuated themselves into the calculus of nation, frequently in ways that were direct and immediately apparent, other times in forms that were imperceptible and undetected until many years later. Often as happenstance, at a vital conjuncture of historical circumstances, the roaring winds of the autumnal equinox swept across the island, acting to rearrange the physiognomy of the local economy and alter the course of human events. Certainly this was the case with the hurricanes of the 1840s. At a key moment in the development of Cuban production strategies, as sugar was poised to assert its preeminent position in the island economy, the impact of the mid-nineteenth-century storms was decisive. The transfer of thousands of slaves from defunct coffee estates to sugar plantations, during a time of dwindling imports of new African slaves, even as new technologies improved production capacities and new trade arrangements expanded access to international markets, played an important part in lifting sugar production into a preeminent position from which it would never be dislodged.

The devastation wrought by natural forces of this magnitude invited meditations on larger meanings, in which there was a tendency to render the hurricane as an instrument of divine purpose. Fr. Bartolomé de las Casas proclaimed that the sixteenth-century hurricanes were God's punishment of the Spanish for their mistreatment of the Indians. Some interpreted the destruction of the coffee estates in the mid-nineteenth century as the result of divine displeasure over the state of slavery on the island. Fredrika Bremer met a repentant owner of one ruined cafetal in Matanzas. "The plantation . . . had a very forlorn appearance," Bremer observed, "in consequence of the last two [hurricanes], which came in rapid succession, and left it in perfect desolation; besides which the cholera had carried off a great portion of the negro slaves." The owner contemplated his fate with remorse, she wrote: " 'The Lord punishes our sins, punishes our sins!' said the owner of the plantation, with an expression half of levity, half of repentance and acknowledgment of the justice of the punishment."[1]

/ / / / /

Hurricanes continued to shape socioeconomic developments in Cuba all through the latter half of the nineteenth century. In the decades that followed the storms of the 1840s, Cuba was subject to repeated devastation with far-reaching consequences. Another powerful storm hit central Cuba in August 1856. In the following year, the first meteorological observatory in the Caribbean was established in Havana under Jesuit administration at the College of Belén dedicated to weather forecasting and specifically to the study of hurricanes.[2]

Other hurricanes followed, including October storms in 1865, 1870, 1876, and 1882. In September 1888 an especially destructive hurricane swept across western Cuba with sustained winds of 115 miles per hour, resulting in the death of more than six hundred people. In the early twentieth century a number of hurricanes caused varying degrees of havoc and destruction across the island, including the storms of October 1904, October 1910, and September 1919, as well as the two killer hurricanes of 1926 and 1932.[3]

It is important to stress, too, that hurricane-related destruction in Cuba occurred within a larger social context, which is to say that as often as not something else was going on that gave the consequences of the hurricane a particular political or economic resonance. What made the hurricanes of the 1840s momentous for coffee production, independent of the actual material losses, was that the devastation occurred at a time of increasing international competition, decreasing world prices, and declining slave imports. Under the circumstances, there was no incentive to revive production, even if planters had the desire or the means to do so.

Hurricanes often acted as a catalyst for change, directly by rearranging the material circumstances in which nineteenth-century communities functioned and indirectly by serving as the larger context in which the boundaries of economic possibilities were reconfigured. Hurricanes intruded during the wars of independence (1868–98), affecting communications and transportation, influencing tactical decisions, and playing a role in strategic considerations. On September 30, 1873, Carlos Manuel de Céspedes brooded over a lingering storm that had hampered Cuban operations. "The horrific hurricane continues," Céspedes confided to his diary:

It has not stopped raining. All the *ranchos* are inundated. On mine a spring has burst and now has been converted into a dam. The mail cannot go out because all the streams are deep and we imagine the same of the rivers. . . . I have had to stay put in my hammock all day in order to protect myself from the rain that with the wind enters on all sides of my *rancho*. The horses are suffering a great deal as a result of the water and the lack of food . . . that is difficult to find because of the bad weather and swelling waters.[4]

In October 1895, as the Cuban Liberation Army prepared to invade the western provinces on the eve of a vital phase of the war for independence (1895–98), a powerful storm battered western Havana and the eastern half of Pinar del Río. Although it is impossible to determine the extent to which this disturbance may have contributed to the success of the invasion, the possibilities are suggestive. On October 30, from Havana, Ricardo Delgado wrote to the insurgent leadership: "Imagine . . . that a storm has recently destroyed the [tobacco] crop, and the tobacco farmers have neither seeds nor the means to obtain them simply because there are none. These poor men find themselves today in the most desperate situation. They have nothing to do, nothing to eat, and would give themselves with a song in their heart [*con un canto en el pecho*] if they could come over and join our ranks."[5] Two months later, the invading army under General Antonio Maceo crossed into Pinar del Río.

The implications of successive hurricanes of the 1890s, which added to the general devastation of the island, reached deeply into the twentieth century. In September 1894 a storm ravaged eastern Cuba and razed the banana plantations around Baracoa. Hurricanes struck Las Villas province in October 1895 and September 1896, causing extensive damage in Cienfuegos. A year later another storm hit western Cuba. In October 1898 a hurricane swept across the full length of the island and wreaked havoc on Camagüey and Las Villas. A year after that, a potent storm struck the northeastern coast of Oriente province and, coming in the wake of the 1894 hurricane and almost four years of insurrection, all but completely destroyed the *platanales* on which the local economy had depended. Many local banana producers immediately went bankrupt. Vast tracts of land subsequently resumed production, but of sugarcane under the new ownership of the United Fruit Company. One more step had been taken to deepen Cuba's dependency on sugar exports.

///// /

The hurricanes of the 1840s had other implications for the longer term. Cuba was in transition during the nineteenth century, and the changes and the sources of change were often connected. They had to be, given the effects of distant market forces on the island and the way technology transformed production systems, which, in turn, influenced labor organization and social structures.

The experience of hurricanes was part of this process. Circumstances of adversity were the means by which the social consensus and sentimental associations central to the emerging notion of nation obtained a special resonance. That hurricanes inflicted recurring devastation to all parts of the island meant that the experience was shared as a nationwide phenomenon. The nineteenth-century hurricanes in particular, against the larger landscape of demographic developments and political disquiet, helped develop the community solidarity that gave aggregate expression to the shared experiences of nation.

Care of the homeless and hungry, the displaced and injured was undertaken by friends and family in city and countryside alike. Responses to the disruptions of daily life were addressed collectively, through kinship systems interacting within larger community networks. This practice no doubt was already in place before the hurricanes, but it assumed a new prominence and, indeed, a new purpose in light of the ensuing devastation and gave form to new contingent relationships by which communities recovered and acquired a sense of self.

The hurricane was thus transformed into a social experience, at once a source of community solidarity and the means by which shared elements of a common past were forged: the hardship of adversity, to be sure, but also an occasion to celebrate collective triumph. People who previously may have had little contact with one another were thrown together in a common endeavor of survival and recovery, thereby establishing the precedents for collective action independent of established formal organizations. At least as important as structural readjustments occasioned by the hurricanes of 1844 and 1846, and certainly as long lasting, were the social transformations concurrent with and derived from the disarray associated with the storms.

The ideal of a national community did not originate solely from abstract notions or sentimental attachments. Much was forged out of actual experiences that became a familiar shared history: the stuff of memory of the past as a source for the future. The observations of Russell Dynes on the social consequences of disasters have relevance to nineteenth-century Cuba. Dynes suggests that disasters contribute in important ways to the forging of community solidarity, whereby the "consequence of a disaster event . . . is in the direction of the creation of community, not its disorganization, because . . . a consensus on the priority of values within a community emerges; a set of norms which encourages and reinforces community members to act in an altruistic fashion develops." Dynes adds:

> When people are engaged in similar activities and subject to the same or similar events, this similarity of preoccupation generates topics for conversation and creates bonds of mutual understanding. Such similarity then provides the basis upon which organization may develop. For those living close together, facing a common problem may bring about the development of organization. The result of struggling with a common problem which stimulates joint action may actually result in a locality's becoming more closely knit than it was before.[6]

These circumstances thus contributed to the development of behaviors and attitudes that acted to redefine and expand public responsibility and enlarge the collective stake in the community. The attending emphasis on collaborative behavior and common action assumed form in the context of the hurricane, by which hierarchies of values were arranged to meet the requirements of individual well-being and collective recovery within the larger setting of community needs. "Some people have compared disasters to a drama which grips people's imaginations," Dynes astutely observes, "heightens the sense of importance of human action, and facilitates emotional identification. Such events become important in the collective memories of a community and provide major reference points by which other events become compared and rated. Since a disaster is such a public event, all those who have shared in it are brought together by their common participation in a dramatic event."[7]

The research by Harry Moore is similarly suggestive and has direct implications for Cuba. Examining the impact of Hurricane Carla on the Texas Gulf Coast in 1961, Moore came to appreciate the larger social significance of the experience and actually suggested that there existed something akin to a "disaster culture" that was "characteristic of the Gulf Coast and, perhaps, other areas exposed to frequent storms." At the core of this disaster culture, Moore argued, was the development of "a community of interests growing out of experiences common to the participants but uncommon, or unknown, to the larger society."[8]

The larger implications of hurricanes in nineteenth-century Cuba stand in sharp relief. The recurring experience of common hardships contributed to the memories by which the meaning of community assumed accessible form, the terms by which local triumphs and tragedies provided an all-encompassing narrative of a shared past as a source of binding affinities. But this was not only a matter of a common past, for it implied, too, a future in which all were inextricably bound. Hurricanes would surely recur, and once more the community would be threatened; again, all members would be obliged to join together for the common good. This was precisely the meaning of Rafael Montoro's reflections in the wake of the hurricane of October 1888. "We arrive at the comforting conclusion," Montoro observed of the relief donated by residents of Havana, "that this society is and has been generous, good, and self-sacrificing, despite the hardships to which it has been subject. . . . Societies save themselves with will power and perseverance in work. . . . As long as there is the will and moral force, man always finds in his spirit the necessary energy to recover from all forms of adversities through honorable efforts." Montoro concluded: "When time has passed and the industrious worker sees there in the fields, at present devastated, once more filled with bountiful harvests produced through the sweat of his brow, where on the horizon will be found once more a rebuilt home from which will rise a column of smoke signifying the happiness of a tranquil home, perhaps the helpful hand that was extended from Havana will be recognized."[9]

The terms by which nationality acquired definition were further ratified through the presentation of a past that celebrated the triumph of collective resolve, either as an expression of regional virtue or of national valor and sometimes both. The character of Cuban was thus extolled explicitly as a function of resilience and resolve over powerful and otherwise uncontrollable forces of nature. The process by which Cubans came to terms with the recurring hazards of their physical environment necessarily implied the need for cultural adaptation to adversity. If, indeed, it was to be the inescapable fate of Cuba to experience periodically the perils of the hurricane, it was only through the indomitable collective resolve that the survival of the nation could be guaranteed.

It was thus necessary to cultivate and celebrate those attributes required to survive the hurricane, attributes fostered as a larger cultural ideal that over time insinuated themselves into the larger normative systems around which the proposition of nationality formed. The hurricane came to represent something of a recurrent circumstance around which appropriate cultural responses took shape. The nation thus lives on alert for six months of the year in anticipation of the fury of natural forces.

This fact of life has contributed mightily to the creation of a context from which to take measure of the national condition. Jon Anderson offers a theoretical framework within which to further explore the means by which the recurring threat of disaster is "normalized" as a "culture-building process." "Where the threat is chronic," Anderson suggests, "it may be considered an aspect of the environment to which the culture must permanently accommodate." He adds: "By accommodating . . . the threat is culturally defined, and, to this extent becomes a 'normal' experience. As part of the culture's body of knowledge it can be transmitted to others as one of the recognized hazards of life, even before it is actually experienced. . . . Chronic threats are accommodated in the more salient and enduring concerns of a culture." The process is thus completed when "people have had an opportunity to accommodate to hazards and integrate them conceptually into the overall scheme of their culture."[10]

The formulation of *cubanidad*, that is, of what it means to be Cuban, had to incorporate the experience of the hurricane as a facet of nationality. Reflecting on those things that comprise the national traits and idiosyncrasies of the nation, Gustavo Pittaluga included "excessive faith in luck," which was mostly related to experience with the unexpected—specifically, "the surrender of the spirit to the uncertainty of the future." Pittaluga explained: "I refer to the hurricane as an example of the chance factors that exercise an influence over the collective psychology. It is known that there is little one can do, from the point of view of planning, against the hurricane. . . . The country thus proceeds a little too much confiding in luck." Mercedes Cros Sandoval suggested that Cubans possessed a "quasi-mystical attitude toward life," adding: "There was a fatalistic acceptance of the view that men were subjugated to supernatural forces. . . . Cubans believe in luck as a factor affecting human life. Success was attributed to luck more than to diligence, which of course made failure more tolerable than in societies when control over nature is assumed."[11] In his meditation on the nature and sources of cubanidad, Fernando Ortiz gave proper acknowledgment to the hurricane: "*Cubanidad* is principally the peculiar quality of a culture: that of Cuba. . . . Cubanidad is a condition of the soul, a complex of sentiments, ideas, and attitudes. But there is still a more all-inclusive cubanidad. . . . It is something that makes us susceptible to the affection of our breezes and arouses us to the excitement of our hurricanes."[12]

The past itself is enlisted in behalf of this larger purpose, an instrumental construct designed to celebrate behaviors that were at once a reflection of the necessities of reality and the requirements of the nation. In addressing the recurring threat to the collective well-being of the nation, the historical narrative on the hurricane was thus framed as loaded with meanings simultaneously descriptive and prescriptive. In his 1955 history of Las Villas, Rafael Rodríguez Altunaga wrote: "Hurricanes have been the most constant enemy of the development and well-being of our province of Las Villas . . . [and] set in relief the valor and character of the spirit of *villareños*. No other region in Cuba has been and continues to be more brutally treated by Nature, but in no other place does one see men struggle with more resolve. . . . They devote their courage and labor to the improved reconstruction of their homes and their fields." Juan Almeida Bosque reflected on some of the larger implications of Hurricane Flora in 1963, and for him there was no doubt about what mattered most. Almeida Bosque later asserted: "[The people] were able to display great valor. . . . That is how absolutely all conducted themselves, those in the moment of danger were disposed to help, to evacuate, and save their brothers. That is how the people conducted themselves during this disaster. For them the pain was shared, the strength was one, the sacrifice was shared. And the victory was shared." Fernando Boytel Jambú similarly declared in 1978 with considerable pride that Cuba, "with the passage of time, as a result of the will of its people, has apprized itself of the problems of the hurricane, perhaps the most powerful natural disturbance of the national environment."[13]

/ / / / /

The idea of the hurricane insinuated itself deeply into Cuban sensibilities. Popular usage of the words *huracán* and *ciclón* early developed as a standard of measure, embedded in national idioms derived from shared experiences: the encodings by which the temperament of a people was revealed. Usage drew on an imagery that implied scale and scope and evoked the vastness of the force. In his 1906 analysis of Cuban character, M. Márquez Sterling condemned national intellectual traditions as "corrupted by a current of falsehood that makes us at times feel the anticipated sensation of an impending hurricane." Sergio Carbó, a journalist, in 1958 despaired over the deepening civil war, the murders and the assassinations, the torture and terror, and could only describe the national crisis as a "cyclone of vengeance and death" (*ciclón de venganza y muerte*). Luis Suardíaz characterized the tumultuous first three decades of the Cuban revolution as "treinta huracanados años." It entered the *naturaleza* of being Cuban, what in Omara Portuondo's song lyric "Vale la Pena" affirmed that it was indeed worth "ver pasar un ciclón" (to see a hurricane pass) in order to live in Cuba.[14]

The proposition of hurricane implied a metaphor, a means of context and comparison, often as a frame of reference for a state of mind. Its invocation implied the measure of a mood, an accessible reference point possessed of a unique cultural resonance. "A Revolution is a force more powerful than Nature," affirmed Fidel Castro in October 1963, only days after the passing of Hurricane Flora. "Hurricanes and all those things are trivial [*son una bobería*] when compared to what a Revolution is." He explained: "A Revolution possesses forces superior to all existing natural phenomena and cataclysms. A Revolution is a social cataclysm; it is also the people running over. A Revolution inundates everything, invades everything, and is capable of demolishing everything that is put in its way and all the obstacles that are put in its path. That is a Revolution."[15] On the other hand, Aurelio N. Torrente in 1977 wrote a short story from exile in Miami about "the devastating and continuing destruction of a hurricane called 'Fidel' ":

> In the beginning of the year 1959 it was a complete and well formed hurricane . . . which already began to move slowly toward the western part of the Isla. . . . The path of hurricane Fidel planted death and desolation in the mountains, plains, valleys and cities of Cuba. . . . Thousands fled in fear by sea and air and thousands of others, less fortunate, perished attempting to escape the uncontrollable fury of the fearful hurricane Fidel. But the great majority . . . remained trapped among the ruins of the great devastation caused by the hurricane.[16]

In prose and poetry alike, the proposition of hurricane passed directly into the realm of allegory to evoke turbulence and tumult. The theme of Cuban insularity—the island at sea—and the hurricane served as the principal story line of Luis Adrián Betancourt's novel *Huracán* (1976).[17] The hurricane was also emblematic of inner turmoil and disquiet. "I have passed through desperate hours before starting these lines," the narrator explains in Hortensia de Varela's short story "Irredento." "After the impetuous and inexplicable hurricane that has stirred my very being, calm has returned, and now, serenely, I write you." This was, moreover, the function assigned to the hurricane in Alfonso Hernández Catá's short story "La tempestad." Arístides Fernández Vázquez invokes hurricane imagery in still another fashion. "[S]omething vast, powerful, overpowered my will," the protagonist affirms in "Caminaban sin prisa por la acera," "like a hurricane that buffets the frail leaf."[18] Armando Leyva used the hurricane as backdrop in a coming-of-age autobiographical short story, "El Ciclón": "One night—twenty? twenty-five years ago?—we went to bed . . . under the threat of an approaching hurricane. . . . So many years ago! And yet: my memory, that fails me with the even most recent events, has not lost a single detail." Leyva continued:

> At dawn the sky was gray and the wind howling through the lonely streets. I felt an unusual joy, a happiness that did not have a name, a sensation that I had never experienced. A desire to go to the coast—I, the timid small boy who was taken by the hand to school by an old black lady— to go to the rocky shore, where the boats were located, where the sailors were discussing the passing hurricane. And I went. Proud and afraid of my daring. . . . And there the spectacular sight of the churning and raging sea, coughing up the white rage upon the coast. I don't know how long I stood there. Neither do I know when a calloused hand grabbed me by the arm and returned me to my home. What I will never forget, what [will] always come to mind when a hurricane is announced, is that my first rebellion, my first act of liberation in life, the first thing I confronted to challenge was a hurricane.[19]

And then there was *Ciclón*, an avant-garde literary review published in Havana during 1955–59, described by José Antonio Portuondo as an effort "to break with cultural structures" and inspired, in the words of Graciela Pogolotti, with a "provocative spirit."[20]

Hurricanes have been a recurring presence in Cuban fiction, as setting and backdrop, as source of high drama and heroic outcomes. In Jorge Velázquez Ramayo's *Vórtice* (1977), Hurricane Flora provided the setting for an account of heroism and courage during the early years of the Cuban revolution. Miguel de Marco's *Fotuto* (1948) turns on the hurricane of 1926 in Havana. Indeed, it has been at the hands of novelists that experience of the hurricane of October 20, 1926, has obtained some of its most compelling renderings.[21] Similarly, Ofelia Rodríguez Acosta in her *Sonata interrumpida* (1943) provided a moving account of the 1932 hurricane in Santa Cruz del Sur. Annually the National Observatory warned of impending hurricanes, the novel's narrator explains, to which most people reacted "with sarcastic criticism and an indifference idiosyncratically Cuban"—and the stage is thus set: "In that year of 1932, it fell to the fishing village of Santa Cruz del Sur, in the province of Camagüey, to suffer the terrible consequences of its irresponsible attitude of fearlessness." The narrative continues: "The [imminent] danger of the deadly combination of the fury of the hurricane with that of sea surge had been announced. But neither the warning nor the justified alarm of some of the fisherman who, with an infallible instinct, sensed that things were going to get ugly, was sufficient to prepare the people of the town and induce them to take appropriate precautionary measures." Rodríguez Acosta provides a chilling portrayal of what followed:

> It developed like a thousand whirlwinds. . . . The fierce headwaters enveloped the houses, penetrating them in what appeared at first like an exploratory filtration, followed by inundation, and finally a destructive force unleashed. . . . The sea charged headlong like a roaring animal, like an eruption, upon the helpless little town. Its furious rage bellowed, hurling all the solid underwater mass, now in the form of an eruption, in an uncontrollable apocalyptic gallop toward the exposed shore. A gigantic avalanche, hurling its waves relentlessly in ferocious succession. The monstrous sea was spewing fire: it fumed with rage, it flared as if it were electrified, as if its mysterious convulsive floor were a huge cauldron.[22]

Isa Caraballo titled her published collection of poems, *Vendimia de huracanes* (1939), using the imagery of a gathering of hurricanes to convey the power of her poetry. "What matters," Caraballo affirmed in her introduction, "is the force, the hurricane within, that informs the words."[23]

/ / / / /

It was, indeed, through poetry that the meaning of the hurricane obtained some of its most enduring representations. This was poetry conveying reverence and respect: the hurricane as awe-inspiring, as a means with which to give narrative resonance to the power of natural forces and thereby placing in perspective the human place in the great scheme of things. In many ways, poetry combines two facets of earlier literary genres: poetry as a paean to propitiate the angry gods and poetry as the invention of new narrative structures to give familiarity to the experience similar to the sixteenth-century chronicles. José María Heredia's encounter with a hurricane in September 1822 was reflected at length in "En una tempestad" (1832), in which the poet surrenders to the storm:

> Al fin, mundo fatal, nos separamos;
> el huracán y yo solos estamos.
> Sublime tempestad! ¡Cómo en tu seno,
> de tu solemne inspiración henchido,
> al mundo vil y miserable olvido,
> y alzo la frente, de delicia lleno!

¿Dó está el alma cobarde
que teme tu rugir. . . ? Yo en ti me elevo
al trono del Señor; oigo en las nubes
el eco de su voz; siento a la tierra
escucharle y temblar. Ferviente lloro
desciende por mis pálidas mejillas,
y su alta majestad trémulo adoro.[24]

Some poems were rendered explicitly as offerings, including such works as Francisco Orgaz's epics "El huracán" and "Invocación a los huracanes" (1838) and Néstor Cepeda's "Al huracán" (1865).[25] Other poets bore witness to the destruction of one particular hurricane, such as Sarfino's lengthy ode, *El huracán: Temporal del 4 y 5 de octubre de 1844* (1845), and the poems inspired by the hurricane of 1846, including José María Pérez's "El huracán" and Manuel Orgallez's "El huracán."[26] Gustavo Cardelle remembered October 1926 in "Huracán del 26":

Desde el Mar de las Antillas
viene el huracán furioso
y su ira se derrama
por el país venturoso
maltratando el panorama
sin que lo impida, piadoso,
el Cielo, por el que clama,
la guajira de rodillas.[27]

Francisco Poveda's epic poem, "El día de la tormenta" (1855), is a chronicle of one community under siege during a hurricane. In "Noche tempestuosa," Juan Clemente Zenea memorialized one nineteenth-century hurricane:

Murió la luna; el ángel de las nieblas
Su cadáver recoge en blanca gasa;
Y en su manto de rayos y tinieblas
El Dios del huracán envuelo pasa.

Llueve y torna a llover; el hondo seno
Resga la nube en conmoción violenta,
y en las sendas incógnitas del trueno
Combate la legión del la tormenta.

¡Qué oscuridad! ¡Que negros horizontes!
¡Hora fatal de angustias y pesares!

¡Ay de aquellos que viajan por los montes!
¡Ay de aquellos que van sobre los mares!

¡Cuántos niños habrá sin pan ni techo
Que se lamenten de dolor profundo!
¡Cuánta pobre mujer sin luz ni lecho!
¡Cuánta pobre mujer sola en el mundo![28]

Much of the poetic imagination has been dedicated to chronicling the variety of forms in which hurricane forces reveal themselves. The poems of José Sánchez-Boudy ("El ciclón"), Halio Orovio ("El huracán y la palma"), Cintio Vitier ("El ciclón"), Renael González Batista ("Ciclón"), Edith Llerena ("El ciclón"), Coralina Sánchez de Cabrera ("Tempestad"), Felipe Pichardo Moya ("Ciclón"), and Eliseo Diego ("Huracán") all dwell on the fury of the hurricane.[29] Julio Marzán vividly recalled his first hurricane in "Temporal":

El viento que apagó la luz eléctrica
e hizo que Tití cocinara en el hornillo,
picando el polo junto a un quinqué
ahora le hacía rezar que Dios ampare
todos los campos con casas de madera,
como tenía mi tío Juan de Santa Olaya.
Sonó, e furia de soplos, un desgarro,
el palo de aguacate, alguien gritó, y temí
vuelos de árboles y casas en pedazos. Así
acampado entre el miedo y la fascinación pase
me primer huracán, comiendo arroz con pollo
mientras caía la casa de Juanito en Santa Olaya.[30]

Much of the poetry inspired by hurricanes also dwells on the moment of revelation, the signs through which the impending storm makes its presence first known, an event, of course, in which weather forecasting has no role to play. The first stanza of Ruben Martínez Villena's "Tempestad" imagines the hurricane descending on the countryside:

La selva temerosa parece que presiente
con un temblor de frondas la próxima refriega,
y una ráfaga helada cruza el cálido ambiente,
portadora del reto de huracán que llega.[31]

One stanza in Roberto Fernández Retamar's "El ciclón" gives voice to the experience of the Cuban peasant:

El guajiro lo ve bajar a tumbos desde el monte;
Es el ciclón, con una capa de viento destructor.
Como un toro celeste, viene mugiendo sin descanso
Detrás del agua, de esas anticipadas, duras lágrimas.[32]

In similar fashion, Esperanza Rubido's short verse "Génesis del huracán" offers access to an inner dialogue on the approaching storm:

El corazón temblando
en labios abiertos.

Aire muriéndose

Las hojas sin destino.
Un pensamiento inerte.
Vorágine de ansias.
Tempestades y vientos.

Confusion en las venas.

¡Cómo se ríe el viento! [33]

Two very different views of the passing of the hurricane are found in Nena Diez de Ramos's "Después de la tormenta" and Edith Llerena's "Después del ciclón," with Diez de Ramos celebrating life and the opportunity for renewal in the aftermath, culminating in her last stanza:

Pero en la inmensa comba azul del cielo,
renace un Sol de rayos refulgentes
que, dorando la Tierra con anhelo,
la llena de verdores de repente . . .

Llerena offers her poem as an introspective lament:

Después del ciclón
ningún pájaro se arriesga
a que lo abriguen.
Una vez descubierto el tiempo,
duele la lluvia.
Me ha despilfarrado,
lo sabe el júcaro y
lo sabe el río.[34]

The notion of *ciclón* has also made its way into the popular lexicon as a *cubanismo:* metaphorical, to be sure, at times playful and whimsical, often as a combination of cynicism and brashness around which national humor resonates. To be a ciclón ("ser un ciclón") is either to be very active or to be totally unscrupulous and thus a person with whom others cannot deal, the way a hurricane obliterates everything in sight. For a woman to be a ciclón ("ser una mujer un ciclón") implies that the pronounced movement of her hips is a function of her gait. For a ciclón to descend upon someone ("caerle a alguien arriba un ciclón") signifies the sudden appearance of big trouble. "Botarse de ciclón" suggests dancing especially well. Writers can also jest about the annual specter of the impending hurricane as a facet of the Cuban condition. "The word 'October' written in the calender in capital letters," commented Gilberto Pérez Castillo, "is the most terrible omen: OCTOBER. OCTOBER! The hurricane is coming."[35]

Affirmations of levity, in fact, belied still one more meaning assigned to the hurricane, namely, a circumstance to which to stand up to and affirm resolve that implied defiance in the face of adversity. The experience signified an occasion in which to test character and courage under peculiarly Cuban conditions. In his ode to Cuban youth in the face of Hurricane Flora in 1963, Alfredo Echarry Ramos depicted the terms of the encounter explicitly: "As in every occasion that the enemy lances his blows, [Cubans] knew how to resist the attacks of the meteorological phenomenon, without abandoning their positions. This history . . . is a simple homage not only to those who participated in the historic undertaking against the unleashed forces of nature, but also to all who have been similarly heroic in different situations and epochs."[36]

Cuban responses assumed a variety of cultural forms endowed with ritual and prescriptive behaviors, insinuated themselves into popular sensibilities, and eventually acquired a place in the realm of tradition. That some responses may have appeared—and, indeed, were often self-consciously proclaimed to be—festive should not obscure their important function to sustain networks of kin and friends during times of anticipated adversity.

In their most popular expressions of self-representation, these practices assumed the form of brashness and bravado. Eladio Secades, one of the most astute chroniclers of popular forms in Cuba, reflected in 1952 on the ways that the hurricane entered the conventions of popular culture. Hurricanes provided a reason to party. "People invite friends to await the arrival of the hurricane in their homes," Secades wrote, "as if it were an occasion for celebration. The Cuban believes that Christmas eve and the hurricane are occasions in which to be reunited with all the family. The tradition is complete and even delightful when the married children arrive." This signified, too, the stockpiling of canned foods, preserves, and crackers. "The hurricane is an accumulation of foodstuffs," Secades observed. The post-hurricane period also had its conventions. "After the Cuban hurricane all of us are pleased with the way we have behaved. We seek out anyone willing to listen to us recount our experiences. . . . We go out into the streets to see the effects, with an old sweater and the honest sensibility of a yankee tourist. . . . To travel around the city and stop before each fallen wall and every destroyed roof." Over the years and across generational lines, veterans of hurricanes have engaged in animated debates over which hurricane was the worst. Dynes's observation that a disaster "generates topics for conversation" is reinforced by Secades's comments. Secades wrote of the ongoing polemic among habaneros, between those who recalled 1926 and those who experienced 1944. "The craziest of all are those defending the furies of the hurricane of 1944," Secades remarked, "those who declare themselves to be irreconcilable opponents of the previous storm. That is how the debates between one side and the other go, ending with both sides hating each other. Which is, in short, to give to meteorology the same fervor expressed between fans of the Almendares and Habana baseball clubs."[37]

Hurricanes have thus served as the circumstance by which meanings of Cuban, national as well as individual, institutional as well as idiosyncratic, acquire some of their most enduring forms. So much in the character of economic conditions, social relationships, and cultural forms bear the distinctive imprint of the hurricane. The very notion of nationality, no less than the idea of nation, evolved from the experience of the encounter and contributed in decisive ways to the people Cubans have become.

Notes

ABBREVIATIONS
ANC   Archivo Nacional de Cuba, Havana
GR/State/NA General Records of the U.S. Department of State,
             National Archives, Washington, D.C.
RG   Record Group

INTRODUCTION

1. Dolores María de Ximeno, "Aquellos tiempos: Memorias de Lola María," *Revista Bimestre Cubana* 22 (January–February 1927): 69–70. A slightly different version of this account appears in María de Ximeno, *Memorias de Lola María* (Havana, 1983), pp. 75–76.

2. Oscar Lewis, Ruth M. Lewis, and Susan Rigdon, eds., *Four Women: Living the Revolution: An Oral History of Contemporary Cuba* (Urbana, Ill., 1977), p. 349.

3. Francisco Llorente to Lieutenant Governor General, Matanzas, March 30, 1871, file 13, no. 7, Fondo Gobierno Provincial (Cementerio), Archivo Histórico Provincial de Matanzas, Matanzas. For detailed first-person accounts of the 1870 hurricane, see Henry Hall to John Davis, October 15, 1870, Dispatches from U.S. Consuls in Havana (1783–1906), U.S. Consular Agent, Cárdenas, to Secretary of State (October 17, 1870), George L. Washington to Henry Hall (October 19, 1870), and James H. Homer to Secretary of State (October 17, 1870), RG 59, GR/State/NA.

4. Guardia Civil, Comandancia de Vuelta Abajo, "Estractos de los servicios prestados por la fuerza de esta comandancia durante el temporal acaecido en los días 4 y 5 del actual," September 19, 1888, file 194, no. 11026, Fondo Gobierno General, ANC. For Pinar del Río, see also Juan Maldonado, "Documentos sobre noticias acerca del huracán ocurrido en los días 4 y 5 de septiembre de 1888," and Juan Madán to Governor General, September 7, 12, 1888, both in file 194, no. 11026, Fondo Gobierno General, ANC. For Sagua la Grande, see Daniel Mullen to George L. Rives, September 6, 1888, Dispatches from U.S. Consuls in Sagua la Grande, RG 59, GR/State/NA, and Antonio Miguel Alcover y Beltrán, *Historia de la villa de Sagua la Grande y su jurisdicción* (Sagua la Grande, 1905), p. 302. For the devastation in Cárdenas as well, see Carlos Hellberg, *Historia estadística de Cárdenas* (1893; reprint, Cárdenas, 1957), pp. 141–42, and Herminio Portell Vilá, *Historia de Cárdenas* (Havana, 1928), p. 167.

5. Pablo Medina, *Exiled Memories: A Cuban Childhood* (Austin, Tex., 1990), p. 38. For another first-person account of the October 1926 hurricane, see Carlton Baily Hurst, *The Arms above the Door* (New York, 1932), pp. 325–29. As chief of

the U.S. Consulate in Havana, Hurst cabled the Department of State at the time that an estimated 30,000 bohíos had been destroyed by the storm. See also Hurst, "Various Damages by the Hurricane of October 20, 1926," 837.48/84, Records Relating to the Internal Affairs of Cuba, 1910–29, RG 59, GR/State/NA.

6. M. Gutiérrez Lanza, *Génesis y evolución del huracán del 20 de octubre de 1926* (Havana, 1927), p. 13; Fernando Inclán Lavastida, *Historia de Marianao* (Marianao, 1943), p. 149. Among the better accounts of the October 1926 hurricane, see José Carlos Millás, "El huracán de La Habana de 1926," *Boletín del Observatorio Nacional* 22 (October 1926): 185–225, and "El ciclón del día 20 de octubre," *Boletín de Obras Públicas* 1 (October 1926): 312–25; and Eduardo Robreño, "El ciclón del 26," *Cualquier tiempo pasado fué. . . .* (Havana, 1981), pp. 129–30.

7. José Mauricio Quintero y Almeyda, *Apuntes para la historia de la Isla de Cuba con relación a la ciudad de Matanzas desde el año de 1693 hasta el 1877* (Matanzas, 1878), pp. 817–18; Fernando Boytel Jambú, *Hombres y huracanes* (Santiago de Cuba, 1978), pp. 110–11; Mariano Gutiérrez Lanza, "Génesis y evolución del huracán del 20 de octubre de 1926," in Simón Sarasola, ed., *Los huracanes en las Antillas* (Madrid, 1928), pp. 209–33; Juan Almeida Bosque, *Contra el agua y el viento* (Havana, 1985), p. 86.

8. Federico Villoch, "Los ciclones," *Carteles* 25 (November 12, 1944): 6.

9. Xavier Cugat, *Rumba Is My Life* (New York, 1948), p. 21.

10. Samuel Eliot Morison, *Admiral of the Ocean Sea: A Life of Christopher Columbus*, 2 vols. (Boston, 1942), 2:158.

11. Herbert Ingram Priestley, *Tristán de Luna: Conquistador of the Old South* (Glendale, Calif., 1936), pp. 108–9.

CHAPTER ONE

1. John Oldmixon, *The British Empire in America, Containing the History of the Discovery, Settlement, Progress and State of the British Colonies on the Continent and Islands of America* 2 vols. (1708; reprint, London, 1741), 2:280. Europeans soon acquired sufficient experience in the Caribbean to develop a strikingly similar catalog of signs of the impending winds. "The inhabitants within their track are seldom taken unprepared," Edward Long wrote from Jamaica in 1774, "as there are several prognostics of their approach. . . . On their near approach, a turbulent appearance of the sky. The sun unusually red. The air perfectly calm. . . . The stars at night with large burs round them. The sky towards the North West looking very black and foul. The sea smelling unusually strong, and rolling on the coast, and into harbours, with a great swell. On the full of the moon, a bur is seen round her orb, and sometimes a halo round the sun. These signs should be carefully watched, in August, September, and October." Long, *The History of Jamaica*, 3 vols. (1774; reprint, New York, 1972), 3:320.

2. For a general discussion on tropical hurricanes, see José Carlos Millás Hernández, "Génesis y marcha de los huracanes antillanos," *Proceedings of the Second Pan American Congress* (Washington, D.C., 1917), pp. 42–55, "Sobre la recurva en lazo en trayectorias de ciclones tropicales," *Boletín del Observatorio*

Nacional 22 (April 1926): 49–61, and "Cloud Motions and Sea Swells in Hurricane Detection and Analysis," in *Final Report of the Caribbean Hurricane Seminar Held at Ciudad Trujillo, Dominican Republic, February 16–25, 1956* (Ciudad Trujillo, 1956), pp. 109–21; Arnold E. True, "La estructura de los ciclones tropicales," *Boletín del Observatorio Nacional* 2 (January–April 1937): 10–20; and E. Palmen, "On the Formation and Structure of Tropical Hurricanes," *Geophysica* 3 (1948): 26–38, and "On the Dynamics of Tropical Hurricanes," in *Final Report of the Caribbean Hurricane Seminar . . . 1956*, pp. 34–55.

3. Rudolph Schuller, "El 'huracán': Dios de la tormenta, y el Popol-Vuh," *Archivos del Folklore Cubano* 4 (April–June 1929): 113–88; A. de Angulo y Guiridi, "Huracanes en las Antillas," *El Prisma* 1 (October 1846): 151–53. For indigenous sources of the word "huracán," see Manuel Alvar Ezquerra, *Vocabulario de indigenismos en las crónicas de Indias* (Madrid, 1997), pp. 206–7, and Joan Corominas and José A. Pascual, *Diccionario crítico etimológico castellano e hispánico*, 6 vols. (Madrid, 1980), 3:429.

4. *Memorias de la Academia Mexicana*, 3 vols. (Mexico, 1876–86), 3:29–36. Among the Quiché Maya of Guatemala, "huracán" signified the Heart of Heaven. See *Popol Vuh: The Sacred Book of the Ancient Quiché Maya*, translated by Adrián Recinos, Delia Goetz, and Sylvanus G. Morley (Norman, Okla., 1950), pp. 82, 85, 87.

5. "This idea of strength and might is of course," wrote Daniel N. Brinton, "very appropriate to the deity who presides over the appalling forces of the tropical thunder-storm, who flashes the lightning and hurls the thunderbolts." Brinton further suggests that the proposition of *hurakan* as a *diablo* was prevalent throughout the circum-Caribbean region. Brinton, *Essays of an Americanist* (1890; reprint, New York, 1970), pp. 122–23.

6. Gonzalo Fernández de Oviedo, *De la natural historia de las Indias*, edited by Enrique Alvarez López (Madrid, 1942), pp. 84–85.

7. Pedro Mártir de Anglería, *Décadas del Nuevo Mundo* (1511) (Madrid, 1989), pp. 45–46.

8. Bartolomé de las Casas, *Historia de las Indias*, edited by André Saint-Lu, 3 vols. (1575; Caracas, 1986), 1:446; Gonzalo Fernández de Oviedo, *Historia general y natural de las Indias, islas y tierra firme de la mar océano*, 4 vols. (Madrid, 1951), 1:146, 148. See also José Carlos Millás Hernández, "Un ensayo sobre los huracanes de las Antillas," *Revista Bimestre Cubana* 23 (May–June 1928): 513–15.

9. Pedro Simón, *Noticias historiales de las conquistas de Tierra Firme en las Indias Occidentales*, 9 vols. (Bogotá, 1953), 5:70–71.

10. See Peter Martyr, *The Decades of the New World, or West India*, translated by Richard Eden (1555; reprint, Birmingham, 1885); Edward Arber, ed., *The First Three English Books on America [?1511–55]* (Birmingham, 1885), pp. 61–200; *Oxford English Dictionary*, 2d ed., 20 vols. (Oxford, 1989), 7:506.

11. Las Casas, *Historia de las Indias*, 1:323–24; William Strachey, "A True Reportory of the Wreck and Redemption of Sir Thomas Gates, Knight" (1610), in Louis B. Wright, ed., *A Voyage to Virginia in 1609: Two Narratives* (Charlottesville, 1964), pp. 4–6.

12. Bryan Edwards, *The History, Civil and Commercial, of the British Colonies in the West Indies*, 4 vols. (1793; reprint, 4th ed., Philadelphia, 1805), 1:10.

13. Alexander Hamilton to the *Royal Danish American Gazette*, September 6, 1772, in Hamilton, *The Papers of Alexander Hamilton*, edited by Harold C. Syrett and Jacob E. Cooke, 27 vols. (New York, 1961–87), 1:35.

14. Admiral Lord George Rodney to Philip Stephens, December 10, 1780, in Rodney, *Letters-Books and Order-Book of George, Lord Rodney, Admiral of the White Squadron, 1780–1782*, 2 vols. (New York, 1932), 1:91. It is striking how often earthquakes were associated with hurricanes. Describing a hurricane in Tobago in October 1847, Henry Iles Woodcock wrote: "[A]bout ten o'clock at night, the raging wind blowing from the northwest, rain in torrents, the loud thunder and the vivid lightning, awakened all to the dire reality that a hurricane of irresistible violence was desolating the land. A severe earthquake is said to have preceded the first outbreak; and in such a war of elements it is not unlikely or unusual to find the earthquake contributing its force to increase the general devastation." Woodcock, *A History of Tobago* (1867; reprint, New York, 1971), pp. 106–7.

15. George Wilson Bridges, *The Annals of Jamaica*, 2 vols. (London, 1828), 2:177–78. Years after the Barbados hurricane, Bryan Edwards wrote: "The capital of this island was torn from its foundations, and the whole country made a scene of desolation. . . . [D]amage to the country was computed at £1,320,564 sterling." Edwards, *History . . . of the British Colonies in the West Indies*, 2:38.

16. Christopher Jeaffreson to Mrs. Peacock, November 10, 1681, in Jeaffreson, *A Young Squire of the Seventeenth Century*, edited by John Cordy Jeaffreson, 2 vols. (London, 1878), 1:280.

17. Quoted in Robert H. Schomburgk, *The History of Barbados, Compromising a Geographical and Statistical Description of the Island* (1848; reprint, London, 1971), pp. 59–60. See also Henry Capadose, *Sixteen Years in the West Indies*, 2 vols. (London, 1845), 2:26.

18. For the phenomenon of the storm surge, see David Longshore, *Encyclopedia of Hurricanes, Typhoons, and Cyclones* (New York, 1998), pp. 291–95.

19. Oldmixon, *The British Empire in America*, 2:363.

20. The excerpted journal of Bryan Young appeared in Schomburgk, *History of Barbados*, pp. 55–58. See also Robert H. Simpson and Herbert Riehl, *The Hurricane and Its Impact* (Baton Rouge, 1981), pp. 2–94.

21. James E. Alexander, *Transatlantic Sketches*, 2 vols. (London, 1833), 1:171–72.

22. Ibid., 172.

23. Schomburgk, *History of Barbados*, p. 40; Alexander Hamilton to the *Royal Danish American Gazette*, September 6, 1772, in Hamilton, *Papers*, 1:35.

24. A. E. Moss, "Effect on Trees of Wind-Driven Salt Water," *Journal of Forestry* 38 (May 1940): 421–25.

25. Andrew Halliday, *The West Indies* (London, 1837), p. 39; William Reid, *An Attempt to Develop the Law of Storms* (London, 1838), p. 320. Robert Schomburgk (*History of Barbados*, p. 40), who had experienced a hurricane in St. John Island in August 1830, recalled blasts of air carrying "numerous small pebbles

which struck with some force against my face." David E. Fisher described the grim effects of the driving wind of the 1935 hurricane in the Florida Keys: "People caught out in the open were sandblasted, quite literally: the sand was lifted from the beaches and blasted them with such force that it stripped their clothing away and scoured their skin. Corpses were found with nothing left but their leather belts and shoes—and when I say 'with nothing' I mean not even their skin remained." Fisher, *The Scariest Place on Earth: Eye to Eye with Hurricanes* (New York, 1994), p. 110. Jay Barnes, writing about hurricanes in Florida, comments that "automobiles have had their paint completely stripped away—down to bare metal—by wind-driven sand." Barnes, *Florida's Hurricane History* (Chapel Hill, 1998), p. 21.

26. Louis J. Battan, *The Nature of Violent Storms* (Garden City, N.Y., 1961), pp. 100–116; R. Cecil Gentry, "Nature and Scope of Hurricane Damage," in American Society for Oceanography, *Hurricane Symposium* (Houston, 1966), pp. 233–53; Ivan Ray Tannehill, *Hurricanes* (Princeton, 1944); David L. Niddrie, "Hurricanes," *Geographical Magazine* 32 (July 1964): 228–34.

27. Alexander, *Transatlantic Sketches*, 1:166–67. More than 22,000 persons perished during the October 1780 hurricane as it battered its way across the full length of the Caribbean archipelago.

28. James Power, "Building Construction and Precautionary Maintenance in Hurricane Areas," in *Final Report of the Caribbean Hurricane Seminar . . . 1956*, pp. 291–301.

29. James M. Phillippo, *The United States and Cuba* (London, 1857), pp. 425–26; "Letter from a Resident at Cuba," *New Monthly Magazine and Universal Register* (London) 14 (August 1, 1820): 170.

30. See Andrés Poey, "A Chronological Table, Comprising 400 Cyclonic Hurricanes Which Have Occurred in the West Indies and in the North Atlantic within 362 Years, from 1493 to 1855," *Journal of the Royal Geographic Society* 25 (1855): 291–328; Edward B. Garriott, *West Indian Hurricanes* (Washington, D.C., 1900); William C. Redfield, *Observations on the Hurricanes and Storms of the West Indies* (New Haven, 1833); Simón Sarasola, *Los ciclones en las Antillas* (Madrid, 1928); José Carlos Millás Hernández, "Un ensayo sobre los huracanes de las Antillas," *Boletín del Observatorio Nacional* 24 (January 1928): 3–19 and (February 1928): 27–42; David M. Ludlum, *Early American Hurricanes, 1492–1870* (Boston, 1963); José Carlos Millás Hernández, *Hurricanes of the Caribbean and Adjacent Regions, 1492–1800* (Miami, 1968).

31. William Shakespeare, *The Tempest*, edited by Stephen Orgel (Oxford, 1987), pp. 101–12.

32. Enrique del Monte, "Los ciclones," *Revista Cubana* 20 (September 1894): 265–74.

33. Fernando Boytel Jambú, *Hombres y huracanes* (Santiago de Cuba, 1978), pp. 148–52; Abiel Abbot, *Letters Written in the Interior of Cuba* (Boston, 1829), p. 96. In 1969 Armando Cárdenas recalled his life along the Contramaestre River in Oriente province: "[T]he Contramaestre River would back up, flooding an enormous field almost 2,000 meters long. They called it 'the graveyard' because

the carcasses of drowned animals were thrown there for the river to carry away. Where the Cauto and Contramaestre rivers pour their waters into the sea, living animals and whole families were swept to hell into the floods." Quoted in Oscar Lewis, Ruth M. Lewis, and Susan M. Rigdon, eds., *Neighbors: Living the Revolution: An Oral History of Contemporary Cuba* (Urbana, Ill., 1978), p. 162.

34. Alvar Núñez Cabeza de Vaca, *Naufragios y comentarios, con dos cartas y relación de Hernando de Ribera* (5th ed., Madrid, 1971), pp. 14–15.

35. Edward N. Rappaport and José J. Fernández-Partagás, "History of the Deadliest Atlantic Tropical Cyclones since the Discovery of the New World," in Henry F. Díaz and Roger S. Pulwarty, eds., *Hurricanes: Climate and Socioeconomic Impact* (Berlin, 1997), pp. 93–108.

36. Jacobo de la Pezuela, *Ensayo histórico de la Isla de Cuba* (New York, 1842), pp. 238–39.

37. Everett Hayden, *West Indian Hurricanes* (New York, 1889), p. 7; Carlos Theye, "Trayectorías de los ciclones durante el mes de octubre," *Anales de la Academia de Ciencias Médicas, Físicas y Naturales de La Habana* 24 (1886): 341–45; Francisco Jimeno, "Huracanes acaecidos en la isla de Cuba en los meses de septiembre y octubre," *La Ilustración Cubana* 1 (September 1885): 211.

38. Félix Erenchún, *Anales de la Isla de Cuba*, 4 vols. (Havana, 1859), 2:1951.

39. José María de la Torre, *Lo que fuimos y lo que somos, o La Habana antigua y moderna* (Havana, 1857), pp. 163–64; Manuel Pérez-Beato, *Habana antigua: Apuntes históricos* (Havana, 1936), p. 27.

40. Jacobo de la Pezuela, *Historia de la Isla de Cuba*, 4 vols. (Madrid, 1868–78), 2:16.

41. On the 1767 hurricane, see "Carta dirigida a Bartolomé Sánchez, sobre el temporal que abatió a Mayarí durante tres días seguidos," n.d., Fondo Correspondencia de los Capitanes Generales, file 25, no. 76, ANC; and Jines Pomares to Marqués de Casa Cagigal, December 6, 1767, Fondo Correspondencia de los Capitanes Generales, file 16, no. 45, ANC. On the 1778 hurricane, see Ultramar, "Carta aprobando el auxilio dado a la ciudad de Santiago de Cuba con motivo del temporal que sufrió," 1778, Fondo Reales Cédulas y Ordenes, file 14, no. 1040, ANC.

42. Mary Cruz del Pino, *Camagüey: Biografía de una provincia* (Havana, 1955), pp. 54–54; Juan de Quesada, "Informes relativos a los considerables daños que causó a la villa de Puerto Príncipe el huracán que experimentó el 4 de octubre de 1780," file 2, no. 198, Fondo Asuntos Políticos, ANC.

43. Thomas Southey, *Chronological History of the West Indies*, 3 vols. (London, 1827), 3:48; Manuel Martínez Escobar, *Historia de Remedios* (Havana, 1944), p. 149.

44. Antonio Bucareli to Marqués de Casa Cagigal, October 20, 1768, Fondo Correspondencia de los Capitanes Generales, file 19, no. 76, ANC; Real Consulado y Junta de Fomento, "Expediente formado para dar cuenta a S.M. del temporal acaecido en la noche del 2 al 3 del corriente," October 6, 1796, Fondo Real Consulado y Junta de Fomento, file 1, no. 14, ANC; Emilio Blanchet, *Compendio de la historia de Cuba* (Matanzas, 1866), p. 78.

45. *Memorias de la Real Sociedad Económica de La Habana*, 2d. ser., 1 (January 1846): 44–45; Manuel de Mediavilla to Gobernador Capitán General, June 8, 1832, and Manuel de Mediavilla, "Relación de los buques que habían en este puerto la noche del 5 del presente mes y lo que padecieron todos a causa del gran huracán que hubo en ella y partida la mañana del seis," June 7, 1832, Fondo Intendencia, file 1069, no. 24, ANC. For the effects of the 1810 hurricane, see "Carta relativa a los daños ocasionados por el temporal de 25 de octubre último," December 27, 1810, Fondo Reales Cédulas y Ordenes, file 43, no. 172, ANC. On the 1812 hurricane in Trinidad, see Juan Ruiz de Apodaca to Ayuntamiento of Havana, Fondo Donativos y Remisiones, file 561, no. 23, ANC. On 1821, see Ricardo V. Rousset, *Historial de Cuba*, 3 vols. (Havana, 1918), 3:60. For an account of the devastation of the 1825 storm, see "Comunicación del Capitán General al Gobernador de [Santiago de] Cuba . . . sobre donativos voluntarios para auxiliar víctimas del huracán en Sancti-Spíritus, Villa Clara, etc.," November 19, 1825, Fondo Gobierno Superior Civil, file 1675, no. 83753, ANC. For the most complete descriptions of hurricanes in Cuba between the late fifteenth century and the early nineteenth century, see Desiderio Herrera, *Memoria sobre los huracanes en la Isla de Cuba* (Havana, 1847); Manuel Fernández de Castro, *Estudios sobre los huracanes ocurridos en la Isla de Cuba* (Madrid, 1871); and José Martínez-Fortún y Foyo, "Ciclones en Cuba," *Revista Bimestre Cubana* 50 (2d Semester 1942): 232–58. For later storms, see Mariano Gutiérrez Lanza, "Ciclones que han pasado por la Isla de Cuba, o tan cerca que hayan hecho sentir en ella sus efectos con alguna fuerza, desde 1865 a 1926," *Boletín Oficial del Observatorio* 23 (January 1927): 195–208.

46. Jorge Juárez Cano, *Apuntes de Camagüey* (Camagüey, 1929), p. 79; Manuel Dionisio González, *Memoria histórica de la villa de Santa Clara y su jurisdicción* (Villaclara, 1858), pp. 266–68; Rafael Rodríguez Altunaga, *Las Villas: Biografía de una provincia* (Havana, 1955), pp. 119–20.

47. Alexander, *Transatlantic Sketches*, 1:382.

48. Las Casas, *Historia de las Indias*, 1:417; Fernández de Oviedo, *Historia general y natural de las Indias*, 1:148.

49. The "Ad repellendas tempestates" invocation appealed for divine protection "to keep the evil spirits and the malevolent winds away from our house." Quoted in Fernando Ortiz, *El huracán* (Mexico, 1947), pp. 81–82. On the island of Nevis, planters observed three public fasts annually in supplication of divine protection against hurricanes. See Robert Dirks, *The Black Saturnalia: Conflict and Its Ritual Expression on British West Indian Slave Plantations* (Gainesville, Fla., 1987), p. 82.

50. For a representative selection of articles published in the *Papel Periódico*, see Cintio Vitier, Fina García Marruz, and Roberto Friol, eds., *La literatura en el Papel Periódico de la Havana* (Havana, 1990).

51. The monthly *Anales de Ciencias, Agricultura, Comercio y Artes* published a regular meteorological section dedicated to commentary on rainfall, temperature, wind, and weather forecasts. See also Rafael Madrigal, "Clima y su influencia en la agricultura," *El Prisma* 1 (July 1846): 75–78 and (August 1846): 79–81.

CHAPTER TWO

1. José Ahumada y Centurión, *Memoria histórica de la Isla de Cuba* (Havana, 1874), p. 39; William R. Lux, "French Colonization in Cuba, 1791–1809," *The Americas* 29 (1972): 57–61; Olga Portuondo Zúñiga, *Santiago de Cuba: Los colonos franceses y el fomento cafetalero, 1798–1809* (Santiago de Cuba, 1992); Alain Yacou, "Los franceses de Saint Domingue en el cinturón cafetalero de Santiago de Cuba," *Revista de Ciencias Sociales* 30 (1993): 91–107; Alain Yacou, " 'Santiago de Cuba a la hora de la revolución de Santo Domingo (1790–1804)," *Del Caribe* 26 (1997): 73–81.

2. Ramón de la Sagra, *Historia económico-política y estadística de la Isla de Cuba* (Havana, 1830), pp. 71–76; "Real Resolución sobre terrenos y baldíos, comunicada por el Ministro de Hacienda de Indias a la Intendencia de Ejército," July 16, 1819, in José María Zamora y Coronado, *Biblioteca de legislación ultramarina*, 6 vols. (Madrid, 1846), 6:56–57.

3. Benjamin M. Norman, *Rambles by Land and Water, or Notes of Travel in Cuba and Mexico* (New York, 1845), pp. 50–51; Eugene Ney, *Cuba en 1830: Diario de viaje de un hijo del Mariscal Ney*, translated by Miguel F. Garrido (Miami, 1973), p. 18; Jacinto de Salas y Quiroga, *Viages: Isla de Cuba* (Madrid, 1840), pp. 101–2; John G. Wurdemann, *Notes on Cuba* (Boston, 1844), p. 68. See also Robert Francis Jameson, *Letters from the Havana during the Year 1820 Containing an Account of the Present State of the Island of Cuba* (London, 1821), pp. 86–105.

4. Cuba, Capitanía General, *Cuadro estadístico de la Siempre Fiel Isla de Cuba, correspondiente al año de 1827* (Havana, 1829), n.p., and *Cuadro estadístico de la Siempre Fiel Isla de Cuba, correspondiente al año de 1846* (Havana, 1847), p. 6; Leví Marrero, *Cuba: Economía y sociedad*, 15 vols. (Madrid, 1972–88), 10:77.

5. Cuba, Capitanía General, *Cuadro estadístico . . . al año 1827*, n.p.

6. Doria González Fernández, "Acerca del mercado cafetalero cubano durante la primera mitad del siglo XIX," *Revista de la Biblioteca Nacional "José Martí"* 31, 3d period (May–August 1989): 151–59; Ramiro Guerra y Sánchez, *Mudos testigos: Crónica del ex-cafetal Jesús Nazareno* (1948; reprint, Havana, 1974), pp. 68–69; H. E. Friedlaender, *Historia económica de Cuba* (Havana, 1944), p. 211.

7. Cuba, Capitanía General, *Cuadro estadístico . . . al año 1827*, n.p.; "Resumen general de partidos, número de negros de la dotación de los ingenios . . . y de los cafetales que se hallan en el Obispado de La Habana," 1832–33, file 3772, no. Añ, Fondo Miscelánea de Expedientes, ANC.

8. Julio J. LeRiverend Brusone, *La Habana: Biografía de una provincia* (Havana, 1960), pp. 238–39; Marrero, *Cuba*, 10:89, 11:109–10; Alexander Humboldt, *The Island of Cuba*, translated by J. S. Thrasher (New York, 1856), p. 282; Friedlaender, *Historia económica de Cuba*, p. 207.

9. "Ingenios y cafetales," 1832–33, 1834–35, Fondo Miscelánea de Expedientes, file 3772, no. Añ, ANC; Orlando García Martínez, "Estudio de la economía cienfueguera desde la fundación de la colonia Fernandina de Jagua hasta mediados del siglo XIX," *Islas* 55–56 (September 1976–April 1977): 132; Susan Schroeder, *Cuba: A Handbook of Historical Statistics* (Boston, 1982), p. 246.

10. Marrero, *Cuba*, 11:109; Abiel Abbot, *Letters Written in the Interior of Cuba* (Boston, 1829), p. 139; "Topografía vegetal del partido de Alquízar," *Anales de Ciencias, Agricultura, Comercio y Artes* 1 (March 1828): 259–70.

11. Cirilo Villaverde, *Cecilia Valdés: O la loma del angel*, 2 vols. (1839–82; reprint, Havana, 1923), 2:32.

12. Guerra y Sánchez, *Mudos testigos*, p. 49. *Mudos testigos* is an outstanding case study of the history of one coffee estate in Havana province through the nineteenth century. See also José Rafael Lauzán, *Historia colonial ariguanabense* (Havana, 1994), p. 23.

13. Ramón de la Sagra, *Historia física, política y natural de la Isla de Cuba*, 12 vols. (Paris, 1842–66), 2:266, 277.

14. Marrero, *Cuba*, 11:124.

15. Ramón de Palma, "Una pascua en San Marcos," in de Palma, *Cuentos cubanos*, edited by A. M. Eligio de la Puente (Havana, 1928), p. 36; Anselmo Suárez y Romero, "Ingenios," 1840, in Anselmo Suárez y Romero, *Colección de artículos* (1859; reprint, Havana, 1963), pp. 236–37.

16. "Consejos a los dueños de cafetales de la Isla de Cuba," *Anales de Ciencias, Agricultura, Comercio y Arte* 2 (June 1829): 358–61.

17. *Tasación y venta del cafetal Valiente en el partido de Güines* (N.p., 1821); José María Fernández, *Agricultura cubana: Tratado del cultivo del café* (Havana, 1862), pp. 23–28; William H. Ukers, *All About Coffee* (New York, 1935), pp. 136–37.

18. J. D. Dunlop, "A Scotsman in Cuba, 1811–1812," edited by Raymond A. Mohl, *The Americas* 29 (October 1972): 242; Wurdemann, *Notes on Cuba*, pp. 139–40, 145; Xavier Marmier, "Cuba en 1850: Cartas sobre América," *Revista Bimestre Cubana* 54 (2d Semester 1944): 217.

19. Benjamin M. Norman, *Rambles by Land and Water, or Notes of Travel in Cuba and Mexico* (New York, 1845), pp. 52–53; William Henry Hulbert, *Gan-Eden, or Pictures of Cuba* (Boston, 1854), pp. 146–47. See also James Rawson, *Cuba* (New York, 1847), pp. 46–53, and Ney, *Cuba en 1830*, pp. 68–69.

20. Maturin M. Ballou, *History of Cuba, or Notes of a Traveller in the Tropics* (Boston, 1854), p. 148.

21. Abbot, *Letters*, pp. 140, 223–24; M. Isidro Méndez, "Tres tipos de cafetales en San Marcos de Artemisa," *Revista Bimestre Cubana* 59 (1st Semester 1947): 217–24; M. Isidro Méndez, "Biografía del cafetal Angerona," *Revista de la Biblioteca Nacional* 3 (July–September 1952): 56; David Turnbull, *Travels in the West: Cuba, with Notices of Porto Rico, and the Slave Trade* (London, 1840), pp. 294–95; Richard R. Madden, *The Island of Cuba: Its Resources, Progress, and Prospects* (London, 1853), pp. 172–73; Wurdemann, *Notes on Cuba*, pp. 104–5.

22. Cuba, *Cuadro estadístico de la Siempre Fiel Isla de Cuba, correspondiente al año de 1827* (Havana, 1829), n.p.; Cuba, *Cuadro estadístico de la Siempre Fiel Isla de Cuba, correspondiente al año 1846* (Havana, 1846), n.p.; Sagra, *Historia económico-política y estadística*, pp. 92–114.

23. Antonio Abad Anido, "Del cultivo del cacao en la villa de San Juan de los Remedios," *La Cartera Cubana* 2 (February 1839): 80–84; "Expediente sobre

fomentar y proteger el cultivo del cacao en esta Isla," 1832–33, Fondo Real Consulado y Junta de Fomento, file 201, no. 8937, ANC.

24. Antonio Bachiller y Morales, "Cultivo del trigo en Cuba," *Memoria de la Real Sociedad Económica de La Habana*, 2d ser., 5 (May 1848): 316–24; "Arroz," *Memoria de la Real Sociedad Económica de La Habana* 19 (March 1845): 319–24; Ramiro Guerra y Sánchez et al., *Historia de la nación cubana*, 10 vols. (Havana, 1952), 3:211.

25. Norman, *Rambles by Land and Water*, pp. 54, 61–62. See also Antonio Bachiller y Morales, *Prontuario de agricultura general para el uso de los labradores i hacendados de la Isla de Cuba* (Havana, 1856); José Alvarez et al., *A Study on Cuba* (Coral Gables, Fla., 1965), p. 77; Marrero, *Cuba*, 11:46–48, 134; Sagra, *Historia económico-política y estadística*, pp. 114–21.

26. Humboldt, *The Island of Cuba*, p. 271; Manuel Moreno Fraginals, *El ingenio: Complejo económico social cubano del azúcar*, 3 vols. (Havana, 1978), 1:137–48; "Historia geográfica, topográfica y estadística de la villa de Cienfuegos y su jurisdicción," *Memorias de la Real Sociedad Económica de La Habana*, 2d ser., 1 (April 1846): 204–11; Pedro Oliver y Bravo, *Memoria histórica, geográfica y estadística de Cienfuegos y su jurisdicción* (Cienfuegos, 1846), pp. 30–46; Hernán Venegas Delgado, "Apuntes sobre la decadencia trinitaria en el siglo XIX," *Islas* 46 (September–December 1973): 184; García Martínez, "Estudio de la economía cienfueguera," pp. 137–38, 147–63; José García de Arboleya, *Manual de la Isla de Cuba: Compendio de su historia, geografía, estadística y administración*, 2d ed. (Havana, 1859), pp. 138–39; Marrero, *Cuba*, 10:278.

27. "Agricultura: Cultivo de la caña y fabricación del azúcar," *Memorias de la Real Sociedad Económica de La Habana*, 2d ser., 5 (April 1848): 240–58.

28. Alicia García, "De la historia de Trinidad," *Islas* 43 (September–December 1972): 58–60; Guerra y Sánchez, *Historia*, 3:178–79; Humboldt, *The Island of Cuba*, pp. 215–16.

29. Norman, *Rambles by Land and Water*, p. 54. See also "Estadística de la jurisdicción de Güines, 1846," file 423, no. 20314, Fondo Gobierno General, ANC.

30. See Oscar Zanetti Lecuona and Alejandro García Alvarez, *Caminos para el azúcar* (Havana, 1987), pp. 11–66.

31. Cuba, Capitanía General, *Resumen del censo de población de la Isla de Cuba a fin del año de 1841* (Havana, 1842), pp. 19–26.

32. Abbot, *Letters*, p. 113.

33. Cuba, Capitanía General, *Resumen del censo de población*, pp. 24–26; Felipe Poey, *Compendio de la geografía de la Isla de Cuba* (Havana, 1839), pp. 50–51; Antonio José Valdés, *Historia de la Isla de Cuba y en especial de la Habana* (1813; reprint, Havana, 1964), p. 335; José M. de la Torre, *Lo que fuimos y lo que somos, o La Habana antigua y moderna* (1857; reprint, Havana, 1913), pp. 23–47; Manuel Pérez-Beato, *Habana antigua: Apuntes históricos* (Havana, 1936), pp. 374–83; LeRiverend Brusone, *La Habana: Biografía de una provincia*, pp. 252–54.

34. "Observaciones sobre los progresos de la población, agricultura y comercio de Matanzas," *Anales de Ciencias, Agricultura, Comercio y Artes* 1 (November

1827): 143–48; Francisco Jimeno Fuentes, "Matanzas, estudio histórico estadístico: Dedicado a la Exma: Diputación Provincial de Matanzas," *Revista de la Biblioteca Nacional*, 2d ser., 8 (January–March 1957): 11–99; Francisco J. Ponte y Domínguez, *Matanzas: Biografía de una provincia* (Havana, 1959), pp. 94–95; Moreno Fraginals, *El ingenio*, 1:140–41; Sagra, *Historia económico-política y estadística*, pp. 183–84, and *Historia física, política y natural*, 2:28–30.

35. Abbot, *Letters*, p. 78.

36. José de la Concha, *Memorias sobre el estado política, gobierno y administración de la Isla de Cuba* (Madrid, 1855), p. 13; Jacobo de la Pezuela, *Diccionario geográfico estadístico, histórico de la Isla de Cuba*, 4 vols. (Madrid, 1863–66), 2:61–63; Schroeder, *Cuba: A Handbook*, p. 246; Guerra y Sánchez, *Historia*, 3:211; Humboldt, *The Island of Cuba*, pp. 289, 292–93.

37. Sagra, *Historia económico-política y estadística*, pp. 339–45; Pedro José Imbernó, *Guía geográfica y administrativa de la Isla de Cuba* (Havana, 1891); Guerra y Sánchez, *Historia*, 3:180–84. For an excellent first-person account of demographic developments in the province of Pinar del Río during these years, see the travelogue by novelist Cirilo Villaverde, *Excursión a Vuelta Abajo* (Havana, 1891). Villaverde's travel accounts were first published as two essays, one that appeared in *El Album* in 1838 and the second in two installments in *El Faro Industria de La Habana* of May and June 1842.

38. Cuba, Capitanía General, *Resumen del censo de población de la Isla de Cuba a fin del año de 1841* (Havana, 1842), pp. 19–21.

39. Hubert H. S. Aimes, *A History of Slavery in Cuba, 1511 to 1868* (1907; reprint, New York, 1967), p. 100; Cuba, Capitanía General, *Cuadro estadístico de la Siempre Fiel Isla de Cuba, correspondiente al año de 1827* (Havana, 1829), p. 26; Sagra, *Historia física, política y natural*, 1:298; "Resumen general de partidos, número de negros de la dotación de los ingenios . . . y de los cafetales que se hallan en el Obispado de La Habana," 1832–33, Fondo Miscelánea de Expedientes, file 3772, no. Añ, ANC; Gloria García Rodríguez, *La esclavitud desde la esclavitud: La visión de los siervos* (Mexico, 1996), p. 21; González Fernández, "Acerca del mercado cafetalero cubano," p. 155.

40. Laird W. Bergad, *Cuban Rural Society in the Nineteenth Century: The Social and Economic History of Monoculture in Matanzas* (Princeton, 1990), pp. 36, 39.

41. See Cuba, Real Hacienda, *Balanza general del comercio de la Isla de Cuba en 1843* (Havana, 1844).

42. Guerra y Sánchez, *Historia*, 3:175.

CHAPTER THREE

1. These two storms are briefly described in Desiderio Herrera, *Memoria sobre los huracanes en la Isla de Cuba* (Havana, 1847), p. 54; Manuel Fernández de Castro, *Estudio sobre los huracanes ocurridos en la Isla de Cuba* (Madrid, 1871), p. 127; and Edward B. Garriott, *West Indian Hurricanes* (Washington, D.C., 1900), p. 58.

2. *El Faro Industrial de La Habana*, August 22, 1844, p. 2.

3. José Ahumada y Centurión, *Memoria histórica de la Isla de Cuba* (Havana, 1874), p. 253; Ricardo V. Rousset, *Historial de Cuba*, 3 vols. (Havana, 1918), 3:39.

4. John Glanville Taylor, *The United States and Cuba: Eight Years of Change and Travel* (London, 1851), pp. 242–44.

5. Enrique Edo, *Memoria histórica de la villa de Cienfuegos y su jurisdicción* (1861; reprint, Havana, 1943), p. 75.

6. Three years later Tobago also experienced a nocturnal hurricane. Henry Iles Woodcock wrote: "We are told that the lightning was of such frequent occurrence, and so vivid during the storm, as to prove of much service to persons escaping from falling houses and seeking someplace of refuge; and that its benefits were acknowledged by those on board the vessels that were stranded, as without it greater damage than was occasioned must have been sustained both to life and property." Woodcock, *A History of Tobago* (1847; reprint, New York, 1971), p. 107.

7. *El Faro Industrial de La Habana*, October 21 (p. 3), 30 (p. 2), 1844.

8. Francisco Zoyestino to Governor General, November 2, 1844, Fondo Donativos y Remisiones, file 93, no. 10, ANC. See also Edo, *Memoria histórica de la villa de Cienfuegos*, pp. 75–76.

9. David Turnbull, *Travels in the West: Cuba, with Notices of Porto Rico, and the Slave Trade* (London, 1840), p. 199.

10. William C. Redfield, *On Three Several Hurricanes of the Atlantic and Their Relations to the Northers of Mexico and Central America* (New Haven, 1846), p. 44.

11. Robert McClure to Editor, October 9, 1844, *Nautical Magazine* (London), 1845, pp. 15–16.

12. Ramón Zembrana, "Memoria," June 16, 1846, *Repertorio Económico de Medicina, Farmacia y Ciencias Naturales* 1 (July 1851): 306–7.

13. *El Faro Industrial de La Habana*, October 7, 1844, p. 2. See also "Expediente sobre el estrago que hizo el huracán el día 5 de octubre de 1844," file 63, no. 3760, Fondo Gobierno Superior Civil, ANC; "Expediente sobre la urgente reparación que necesitaban los faroles del alumbrado público por los estragos que causó el huracán del 5 de octubre de 1844," file no. 63, no. 3760), ibid.; and Redfield, *On Three Several Hurricanes*, p. 44.

14. *El Faro Industrial de La Habana*, October 9 (p. 2), 10 (p. 2), 1844; Desiderio Herrera, *Memoria sobre los huracanes en la Isla de Cuba* (Havana, 1847), p. 55; Fernando Inclán Lavastida, *Historia de Marianao* (Marianao, 1943), pp. 32–33; Redfield, *On Three Several Hurricanes*, pp. 40–43. For the destruction of Vereda Nueva, see José Rivero Muñiz, *Vereda Nueva* (Havana, 1964), pp. 62–64. The report on Santiago de las Vegas is from *El Faro Industrial de La Habana*, October 20, 1844, p. 2.

15. *El Faro Industrial de La Habana*, October 8, 1844, p. 2.

16. T. M. Rodney to J. C. Calhoun, December 16, 1844, Dispatches from U.S. Consuls in Matanzas, 1820–89, RG 59, GR/State/NA. For destruction in Matanzas, see "Expediente que trata sobre la reparación del estrago que causó en los faroles del alumbrados el huracán del mes de octubre de 1844" and "Expediente que trata sobre la reparación de los estragos que causó el huracán del mes de octubre de 1844," file 108, no. 5474, Fondo Gobierno Superior Civil, ANC.

17. *El Faro Industrial de La Habana*, October 12, 1844, p. 3.

18. Francisco Zoyestino to Governor General, November 2, 1844, Fondo Donativos y Remisiones, file 93, no. 10, ANC. See also José Ahumada y Centurión, *Memoria histórica de la Isla de Cuba* (Havana, 1874), p. 253.

19. Robert McClure to Editor, October 9, 1844, *Nautical Magazine*, p. 15.

20. *El Faro de La Habana*, October 8, 1844, p. 2.

21. *El Faro Industrial de La Habana*, October 10, 1844, p. 2.

22. Cuba, Capitanía General, *Relación de los estragos causados por el temporal del once de octubre del corriente año* (Havana, 1846), pp. 21–24; Francisco Pérez de la Riva, *El café: Historia de su cultivo y explotación en Cuba* (Havana, 1944), p. 70. The diary of Joseph Goodwin provides a graphic first-person account of the devastation inflicted on one coffee estate in Matanzas by a hurricane in 1823. See Goodwin, Diary, June 26, 1820 to March 6, 1827, New-York Historical Society, New York.

23. Miguel del Aldama to Domingo del Monte, October 10, 1844, in Academia de la Historia de Cuba, *Centón epistolario de Domingo del Monte*, edited by Domingo Figarola-Caneda, Joaquín Llaverías y Martínez, and Manuel I. Mesa Rodríguez, 6 vols. (Havana, 1923–53), 6:113.

24. Herrera, *Memoria sobre los huracanes*, pp. 55–57.

25. Taylor, *The United States and Cuba*, pp. 144–245, 250.

26. Ibid., pp. 245–46.

27. *Diario de La Habana*, October 6, 1846, p. 2.

28. Miguel Rodríguez Ferrer, *Naturaleza y civilización de la grandiosa Isla de Cuba*, 2 vols. (Madrid, 1876–87), 1:365–66.

29. Sociedad Económica de Amigos del País, *Memorias*, 4th ser., 2 (1846): 304.

30. *La Aurora de Matanzas*, October 22, 1846, p. 2.

31. Manuel Fernández de Castro, *Estudio sobre los huracanes ocurridos en la Isla de Cuba* (Madrid, 1871), p. 129; Samuel Hazard, *Cuba with Pen and Pencil* (Hartford, 1871), p. 80; David Longshore, *Encyclopedia of Hurricanes, Typhoons, and Cyclones* (New York, 1998), pp. 150–51.

32. *Diario de la Marina*, October 14, 1846, p. 2.

33. Ibid., October 15 (pp. 2–3), 17 (p. 2), 1846; Juan Torres Lasquete, *Colección de datos históricos-geográficos y estadísticos de Puerto del Príncipe [sic] y su jurisdicción* (Havana, 1888), pp. 45–46.

34. *Diario de la Marina*, October 8, 1846, p. 3.

35. *Diario de La Habana*, October 17, 1846, p. 2.

36. Leopoldo O'Donnell to Ministro del Ultramar, October 12, 1846, file 156, no. 315, Fondo Reales Cédulas y Ordenes, ANC; Cuba, Capitanía General, *Relación de los estragos causados*, pp. 3–5.

37. [*El Faro Industrial de La Habana*], *Huracán de 1846: Reseñas de sus estragos en la Isla de Cuba y relación ordenada de la pérdidas y desgracias sufridas en las poblaciones y puertos que visitó el memorable día 11 de octubre* (Havana, 1846), pp. 10–11.

38. Leopoldo O'Donnell to Ministro del Ultramar, October 12, 1846, file 156, no. 315, Fondo Reales Cédulas y Ordenes, ANC. For a list of the coastwise ves-

sels lost in Havana harbor, see Cuba, Capitanía General, *Relación de los estragos causados*, pp. 19–20.

39. J. Tabares Sosa, "La Habana Vieja: Datos históricos," *La Lucha*, September 5, 1926, p. 3; *Diario de la Habana*, October 27, 1846, p. 2.

40. "Destruyó un huracán el edificio del Teatro Principal de La Habana," *Carteles* 35 (April 24, 1954): 100; Alfredo Saurulle to Governor General, October 12, 1846, "Expediente sobre los daños causados en el Hospital de San Lázaro por el huracán de 1846," file 3, no. 63, Fondo Gobierno General, ANC; "Expediente sobre la reparación del estrago que el huracán de 11 de octubre de 1846 causó en la casa que sirve a hospital militar," January 8, 1847, file 1636, no. 82266, Fondo Gobierno Superior Civil, ANC; Félix Vidal y Girera, *Historia de la villa de Guanabacoa* (Havana, 1887), p. 84.

41. [*Diario de la Marina*], *Resumen de los desastres ocurridos en el puerto de La Habana y sus jurisdicciones inmediatos del Departamento Occidental de la Isla de Cuba, días 10 y 11 de Octubre de 1846* (Havana, 1846), p. 19.

42. *El Faro Industrial de La Habana*, November 17, 1846, p. 1; *Diario de la Marina*, October 11, 1846, p. 2; Rodríguez Ferrer, *Naturaleza y civilización*, 1:369.

43. Robert B. Campbell to Secretary of State James Buchanan, October 15, 1846, Dispatches from U.S. Consuls in Havana, 1783–1906, RG 59, GR/State/NA; Carlos Martí to Juan de la Granja, November 2, 1846, William G. Stewart Papers, Manuscript Department, New-York Historical Society, New York.

44. *Diario de la Marina*, October 13, 1846, p. 3.

45. [*El Faro Industrial de La Habana*], *Huracán de 1846*, pp. 53–59.

46. For a list of the coastwise vessels destroyed in Matanzas harbor, see Cuba, Capitanía General, *Relación de los estragos causados*, pp. 14–15.

47. *El Faro Industrial de La Habana*, October 25, 1846, p. 2.

48. Pedro Antonio Alfonso, *Memorias de un matancero Apuntes para la historia de la Isla de Cuba, con relación a la ciudad de San Carlos y San Severino de Matanzas, principiados en 1830 y continuados para ofrecer un presente al Bazar matancero* (Matanzas, 1854), p. 225; *Aurora de Matanzas*, October 11 (p. 1), 13 (p. 2), 1846. See also *Diario de La Habana*, October 13, 1846, p. 1. For an official report of the damage to Matanzas shipping and port facilities, see José Montojo, "Partes recibidos en la comandancia general de marina," *El Faro Industrial de La Habana*, October 15, 1846, p. 1.

49. Bartolomé Junqué to Pastor y Barnet, October 12, 1846, in Cuba, Capitanía General, *Relación de los estragos causados*, p. 12.

50. Manuel de Garay y Echeverría, *Historia descriptiva de la villa de San Antonio de los Baños y su jurisdicción* (Havana, 1859), p. 19; Cuba, Capitanía General, *Relación de los estragos causados*, pp. 9, 14, 23.

51. *Diario de La Habana*, October 15, 1846, p. 1; *Diario de la Marina*, October 13, 1846, p. 3; [*El Faro Industrial de La Habana*], *Huracán de 1846*, pp. 53–59; Diego Fernández Herrera, "Comunicado," October 17, 1846, in Cuba, Capitanía General, *Relación de los estragos causados*, p. 30; Garay y Echeverría, *Historia descriptiva de la villa de San Antonio*, pp. 89–90.

52. *Diario de La Habana*, October 14 (p. 2), 15 (p. 1), 1846.

53. *Diario de la Marina*, October 17, 1846, p. 2.

54. Leopoldo O'Donnell to Ministro del Ultramar, October 12, 1846, file 156, no. 315, Fondo Reales Cédulas y Ordenes, ANC.

55. Cuba, Capitanía General, *Relación de los estragos causados*, p. 16.

56. Ibid.

57. Diego Fernández Herrera, "Comunicado," October 17, 186, p. 27.

58. *Aurora de Matanzas*, October 13, 1846, p. 2.

59. Cuba, Capitanía General, *Relación de los estragos causados*, p. 24.

60. *Aurora de Matanzas*, October 16, 1844, p. 1.

61. Diego Fernández Herrera, "Comunicado," October 17, 1846, p. 28.

62. Cuba, Capitanía General, *Relación de los estragos causados*, p. 26.

63. Levi Marrero, *Cuba: Economía y sociedad*, 15 vols. (Madrid, 1972–88), 12:114.

64. *Aurora de Matanzas*, October 13, 1846, p. 2; *El Faro Industrial de La Habana*, October 15, 1846, p. 1.

65. *Aurora de Matanzas*, October 13, 1846, p. 1.

66. *Diario de la Marina*, October 20, 1846, p. 3.

67. Cuba, Capitanía General, *Relación de los estragos causados*, p. 42; Pérez de la Riva, *El cafe*, pp. 71–72; *El Faro Industrial de La Habana*, October 15, 1846, p. 1; "Estado que manifiesta los deterioros sufridos por el temporal de 1846 en Artemisa," *El Faro Industrial de La Habana*, November 7, 1846, p. 2.

68. *Aurora de Matanzas*, October 22, 1846, p. 1; *El Faro Industrial de La Habana*, October 15, 1846, p. 2.

69. Leopoldo O'Donnell to Ministro de Ultramar, October 31, file 156, no. 344, Fondo Reales Cédulas y Ordenes, ANC.

70. [*El Faro Industrial de La Habana*], *Huracán de 1846*, p. 12.

CHAPTER FOUR

1. *Diario de La Habana*, October 24, 1846, p. 2.

2. José García de Arboleya, *Manual de la Isla de Cuba: Compendio de su historia, geografía, estadística y administración*, 2d ed. (Havana, 1859), pp. 56–58; John Glanville Taylor, *The United States and Cuba: Eight Years of Change and Travel* (London, 1851), p. 245. In Humboldt's *Island of Cuba*, John Thrasher noted that "[d]uring both these hurricanes, the wind veered to every point of the compass, and the salt spray was carried fifteen or twenty miles inland, blackening vegetation as though fire had passed over it." Alexander Humboldt, *The Island of Cuba*, translated by John S. Thrasher (New York, 1856), p. 170.

3. *Diario de La Habana*, October 16 (p. 1), 26 (p. 2), 1846.

4. Esteban Pichardo, *Geografía de Cuba* (Havana, 1854), pp. 254–55; García de Arboleya, *Manual*, p. 153; Cuba, Capitanía General, *Cuadro estadístico de la Siempre Fiel Isla de Cuba, correspondiente al año de 1827* (Havana, 1827), n.p.; Leví Marrero, *Cuba: Economía y sociedad*, 15 vols. (Madrid, 1972–88), 10:92; José R. Simoni, *Apuntes para la apicultura cubana* (Puerto Príncipe, 1865), p. 3.

5. Francisco Campo to Editor, *El Faro Industrial de La Habana*, October 25, 1846, p. 1.

6. *Diario de La Habana,* October 14, 1846, p. 1.

7. Ramón de la Sagra, *Cuba, 1860: Selección de artículos sobre agricultura cubana* (Havana, 1963), p. 156.

8. William C. Bryant, "Letters from Cuba," *Littell's Living Age* 22 (July 1849): 14, and *Letters of a Traveller* (New York, 1850), p. 372.

9. William H. Ukers, *All About Coffee,* 2d ed. (New York, 1935), pp. 501, 526.

10. José Rivero Muñiz, *Vereda Nueva* (Havana, 1964), pp. 62–64.

11. Domingo Malpica la Barca, "El cafetal," *Revista Cubana* 11 (March 1890): 209–27.

12. Francisco Campo to Editor, *El Faro Industrial de La Habana,* October 25, 1846, p. 1; "Expediente sobre el mal estado en que se halla el cafetal Arcadia," September 1848, Fondo Gobierno Superior Civil, file 945, no. 33335, ANC.

13. *Diario de La Habana,* October 15, 1846, p. 2.

14. Ibid., October 30, 1846, p. 2.

15. See *Diario de la Marina,* November, December 1846.

16. Bryant, "Letters from Cuba," p. 14; Bryant, *Letters of a Traveller,* pp. 376–77.

17. Carlton H. Rogers, *Incidents of Travel in the Southern States and Cuba* (New York, 1862), pp. 125, 127.

18. Simeon M. Johnson to James Buchanan, August 27, 1847, Dispatches from U.S. Consuls in Matanzas, 1820–89, RG 59, GR/State/NA.

19. Cuba, Capitanía General, *Cuadro estadístico . . . al año de 1827,* n.p., *Cuadro estadístico de la Siempre Fiel Isla de Cuba correspondiente al año de 1846* (Havana, 1847), n.p., and *Noticias estadísticas de la Isla de Cuba en 1862* (Havana, 1864), n.p.; García de Arboleya, *Manual,* pp. 141–42; Jacobo de la Pezuela, *Diccionario geográfico, estadístico, histórico de la Isla de Cuba,* 4 vols. (Madrid, 1863–66), 1:225; Doria González Fernández, "Acerca del mercado cafetalero cubano durante la primera mitad del siglo XIX," *Revista de la Biblioteca Nacional "José Martí"* 31, 3d period (May–August 1989): 167–68; Marrero, *Cuba,* 12:137.

20. Cuba, Capitanía General, *Cuadro estadístico . . . al año de 1827,* n.p., *Cuadro estadístico . . . al año de 1846,* n.p., and *Noticias estadísticas,* n.p.; Félix Erenchún, *Anales de la Isla de Cuba,* 4 vols. (Havana, 1856–61), 1:266.

21. Marrero, *Cuba,* 11:124.

22. Cuba, Capitanía General, *Noticias estadísticas,* n.p.; Marrero, *Cuba,* 11:124; Francisco Pérez de la Riva, *El café: Historia de su cultivo y explotación en Cuba* (Havana, 1944), p. 78; Mariano Torrente, *Bosquejo económico político de la Isla de Cuba,* 2 vols. (Madrid, 1852–53), 1:144.

23. M. Isidro Méndez, "Tres tipos de cafetales en San Marcos de Artemisa," *Revista Bimestre Cubana* 59 (1st Semester 1947): 221; Cuba, Capitanía General, *Cuadro Estadístico de la Siempre Fiel Isla de Cuba, correspondiente al año de 1827* (Havana, 1829), *Cuadro estadístico de la Siempre Fiel Isla de Cuba, correspondiente al año de 1846* (Havana, 1847), and *Noticias estadísticas;* Pezuela, *Diccionario geográfico, estadístico, histórico,* 1:38–39; José Rafael Lauzán, *Historia colonial ariguanabense* (Havana, 1994), p. 26; Ramiro Guerra y Sánchez et al.,

Historia de la nación cubana, 10 vols. (Havana, 1953), 4:147; H. E. Friedlaender, *Historia económica de Cuba* (Havana, 1944), p. 208.

24. Ramiro Guerra y Sánchez, *Mudos testigos: Crónica del ex-cafetal Jesús Nazareno* (1948; reprint, Havana, 1974), pp. 80–112.

25. Fredrika Bremer, *The Homes of the New World: Impressions of America*, translated by Mary Howitt, 2 vols. (1853; reprint, New York, 1968), 2:404–5.

26. Manuel de Garay y Echeverría, *Historia descriptiva de la villa de San Antonio de los Baños y su jurisdicción* (Havana, 1859), p. 23.

27. Julio J. LeRiverend Brusone, *La Habana: Biografía de una provincia* (Havana, 1960), pp. 239–41.

28. García de Arboleya, *Manual*, p. 142.

29. Ramón de la Sagra, *Cuba en 1860, o sea cuadro de sus adelantos en la población, la agricultura, el comercio y las rentas públicas* (Paris, 1863), p. 144.

30. Cuba, Capitanía General, *Cuadro estadístico . . . al año de 1846*, n.p., and *Noticias estadísticas*, n.p.

31. John G. Wurdemann, *Notes on Cuba* (Boston, 1844), p. 190. More than forty years later, one Havana magazine published a long-view photograph of Angerona, with the caption: "The entrance to the Angerona *potrero*." See *La Ilustración Cubana* 3 (December 10, 1887): 387.

32. José María de la Torre and Tranquilino Sandalio de la Noda, "Marien [Mariel]: Noticias históricas, geográficas y estadísticas de esta jurisdicción," *Memorias de la Real Sociedad Económica de La Habana*, 2d ser., 4 (September 1847): 165–66; William Howell Reed, *Reminiscences of Elisha Atkins* (Cambridge, Mass., 1890), pp. 72–73; Bryant, *Letters of a Traveller*, p. 385; Richard Henry Dana Jr., *To Cuba and Back: A Vacation Voyage* (Boston, 1859), pp. 117–18. On the Adriana cafetal, see Pérez de la Riva, *El café*, p. 81.

33. Taylor, *The United States and Cuba*, p. 288.

34. Francisco Letamendi to Domingo del Monte, May 12, 1840, Academia de la Historia de Cuba, *Centón epistolario de Domingo del Monte*, edited by Domingo Figarola-Caneda, Joaquín Llaverías y Martínez, and Manuel Mesa Rodríguez, 6 vols. (Havana, 1923–53), 4:147.

35. L. Leonidas Allen, *The Island of Cuba, or Queen of the Antilles* (Cleveland, 1852), p. 21.

36. H. W. Bates, *Central America, the West Indies and South America* (London, 1878), p. 157.

37. Laird W. Bergad, *Cuban Rural Society in the Nineteenth Century: The Social and Economic History of Monoculture in Matanzas* (Princeton, 1990), p. 117; Henry Latham, *Black and White: A Journal of a Three Months' Tour in the United States* (London, 1867), pp. 213–14; W. M. L. Jay [Julia Louisa Matilda Woodruff], *My Winter in Cuba* (New York, 1871), pp. 259–60.

38. Cuba, Capitanía General, *Cuadro estadístico . . . al año de 1846*, n.p., and, *Noticias estadísticas*, n.p.

39. Marrero, *Cuba*, 11:49.

40. Abiel Abbot, *Letters Written in the Interior of Cuba* (Boston, 1829), p. 137.

41. Cuba, Capitanía General, *Cuadro estadístico . . . al año de 1846*, n.p., and *Noticias estadísticas*, n.p.

42. José Alvarez Díaz et al., *A Study on Cuba* (Coral Gables, Fla., 1965), p. 67; Guerra y Sánchez, *Historia*, 4:153–54; Cuba, Capitanía General, *Cuadro estadístico . . . al año de 1846*, n.p., and *Noticias estadísticas*, n.p.

43. Cuba, Capitanía General, *Cuadro estadístico . . . al año de 1846*, n.p., and *Noticias estadísticas*, n.p.; Miguel Rodríguez Ferrer, *El tabaco habano: Su historia, su cultivo, sus vicisitudes, sus mas afamadas vegas en Cuba* (Madrid, 1854), pp. 57–58.

44. Alvarez Díaz, *A Study on Cuba*, p. 73; Sagra, *Cuba*, 1860, pp. 169–70.

45. José Rivero Muñiz, *Tabaco: Su historia en Cuba*, 2 vols. (Havana, 1965), 2:269–70, 277.

46. Manuel Moreno Fraginals, *El ingenio: Complejo económico social cubano del azúcar*, 3 vols. (Havana, 1978), 3:36; Marrero, *Cuba*, 12:114.

47. "Commerce and Resources of Cuba," *Merchants' Magazine* 21 (July 1849): 34–35.

48. *Diario de La Habana*, October 14 (p. 1), 23 (p. 2), 26 (p. 2), 1846.

49. Nicolás Heredia, *Leonela* (1893; reprint, Havana, 1972), pp. 264–65.

50. Cuba, Capitanía General, *Cuadro estadístico . . . al año de 1846*, n.p.; Sagra, *Cuba en 1860*, p. 105; Carlos Rebello, *Estados relativos a la producción azucarera de la Isla de Cuba* (Havana, 1860), p. 108; Pezuela, *Diccionario geográfico, estadístico, histórico*, 1:39. For a useful discussion on the transformation of the Cuban planter class, see Ramiro Guerra y Sánchez, *Sugar and Society in the Caribbean: An Economic History of Cuban Agriculture*, translated by Marjory M. Urquidi (New Haven, 1964).

51. Arthur F. Corwin, *Spain and the Abolition of Slavery in Cuba, 1817–1886* (Austin, Tex., 1967), pp. 35–91; Franklin W. Knight, *Slave Society in Cuba during the Nineteenth Century* (Madison, Wis., 1970), pp. 47–58; Luis Martínez-Fernández, *Fighting Slavery in the Caribbean: The Life and Times of a British Family in Nineteenth-Century Havana* (Armonk, N.Y., 1998).

52. Corwin, *Spain and the Abolition of Slavery in Cuba*, pp. 69–91.

53. Roland T. Ely, *Cuando reinaba su majestad el azúcar* (Buenos Aires, 1963), p. 564.

54. Edward Sullivan, *Rambles and Scrambles in North and South America* (London, 1852), p. 253.

55. "Agricultura: Cultivo de la caña y fabricación del azúcar," *Memorias de la Sociedad Económica de La Habana*, 2d ser., 5 (April 1848): 254.

56. *On Sugar Cultivation in Louisiana, Cuba, &c. and the British Possessions* (London, 1848), pp. 3–73; Oscar Zanetti and Alejandro García, *Caminos para el azúcar* (Havana, 1987), pp. 46–66; Gert J. Oostindie, "La burguesía cubana y sus caminos de hierro, 1830–1868," *Boletín de Estudios Latinoamericanos y del Caribe* 37 (December 1984): 99–115; Francisco J. Ponte Domínguez, *Matanzas: Biografía de una provincia* (Havana, 1959), pp. 111–12.

57. Francisco Diago to Henry A. Coit, March 29, 1841, in Ely, *Cuando reinaba su majestad el azúcar*, p. 608; "Importancia de los ferrocarriles en la Isla

de Cuba," *Memorias de la Real Sociedad Económica de La Habana*, 2d ser., 6 (February 1849): 409.

58. "Sumario por el Capitán de Guanajay sobre indicios de sublevación por la negrada del Ingenio La Carolina," 1844, file 939, no. 33129, Fondo Gobierno Superior Civil, ANC, and Leopoldo O'Donnell, "Testimonio de la tenencia sobre la conspiración de varias negradas en la jurisdicción de Matanzas," 1844, file 943, no. 33287, ibid. For informative historical accounts of the slave insurrections during the 1830s and 1840s, see Fernando Ortiz, *Los negros esclavos* (1916; reprint, Havana, 1975), pp. 359–94, and José Luciano Franco, *Rebeldías negras en los siglo XVIII y XIX* (Havana, 1975).

59. Jacobo de la Pezuela, *Historia de la Isla de Cuba*, 4 vols. (Madrid, 1868–78), 4:364; Miguel de Aldama to Domingo del Monte, November 9, 1843, in Academia de la Historia de Cuba, *Centón epistolario*, 5:147–50; Manuel Barcia Paz, *La resistencia esclava en las plantaciones cubanas* (Havana, 1998); *Las rebeldías de esclavos en Matanzas* (Havana, 1976), pp. 23–33.

60. Domingo del Monte, "Memorial dirigido al Gobierno de España sobre el estado de Cuba en 1844," *Escritos*, edited by José A. Fernández de Castro, 2 vols. (Havana, 1929), 1:162.

61. José Luis Alfonso to Domingo del Monte, December 10, 1843, in Academia de la Historia de Cuba, *Centón epistolario*, 5:181.

62. Robert L. Paquette, *Sugar Is Made with Blood: The Conspiracy of La Escalera and the Conflict between Empires over Slavery in Cuba* (Middletown, Conn., 1988), pp. 209–32; Miguel del Aldama to Domingo del Monte, March 10, 1844, in Academia de la Historia de Cuba, *Centón epistolario*, 6:12. See also Rita Llanes Miqueli, *Víctimas del año del cuero* (Havana, 1984), pp. 101–12. The records of the Fondo Comisión Militar in the Cuban National Archives are filled with the files of many hundreds of slaves and free people of color who were implicated in the conspiracies and rebellions of the 1840s.

63. Miguel de Aldama to Domingo del Monte, April 9, 1844, in Academia de la Historia de Cuba, *Centón epistolario*, 6:19–20.

64. In contrast, slave mortality rates on coffee estates in the jurisdiction of Havana were estimated at 4 percent. See Moreno Fraginals, *El ingenio*, 3:85–90, and Ramón de la Sagra, *Historia económico-política y estadística de la Isla de Cuba* (Havana, 1831), p. 22.

65. David Turnbull, *Travels in the West: Cuba, with Notices of Porto Rico, and the Slave Trade* (London, 1840), pp. 281–82.

66. Sagra, *Cuba en 1860*, pp. 42–43; "Inmigración de asiáticos en esta Isla," *Anales de la Real Junta de Fomento* 4 (1851): 183–98; José Luciano Franco, "Aspectos económicos del tráfico de culiés chinos a Cuba, 1853–1874," *El barracón y otros ensayos* (Havana, 1975), pp. 255–81; Mary Turner, "Chinese Contract Labour in Cuba, 1847–1874," *Caribbean Studies* 14 (July 1974): 66–81; Duvon Clough Corbitt, *A Study of the Chinese in Cuba, 1847–1947* (Wilmore, Ky., 1971), pp. 1–86.

67. For useful discussions on the decline of the slave population, see Kenneth F. Kiple, *Blacks in Colonial Cuba, 1774–1899* (Gainesville, Fla., 1976), pp. 52–53, and Jack Ericson Eblen, "On the Natural Increase of Slave Populations: The Ex-

ample of the Cuban Black Population, 1776–1900," in Stanley L. Engerman and Eugene D. Genovese, eds., *Race and Slavery in the Western Hemisphere: Quantitative Studies* (Princeton, 1975), pp. 232–33.

68. Miguel de Aldama to Domingo del Monte, January 9, 1845, in Academia de la Historia de Cuba, *Centón epistolario*, 6:148.

69. "Proyecto de demolición de los ingenios San Juan y San Cristobal pertenecientes a los bienes de regulares en beneficio de los mismos objetos de su institution," *Memorias de la Real Sociedad Económica de La Habana*, 2d ser., 6 (February 1849): 313–14; Joseph J. Dimock, *Impressions of Cuba in the Nineteenth Century: The Travel Diary of Joseph J. Dimock*, edited by Louis A. Pérez Jr. (Wilmington, 1998), p. 97; Marrero, *Cuba*, 11:121–23; Torrente, *Bosquejo económico político*, 1:148.

70. De la Torre and Sandalio de la Noda, "Marien [Mariel]," pp. 165–66.

71. See "Cuaderno de las entradas y gastos del cafetal San Lorenzo," 1849, and "Cuaderno para los años 1852 y 1853, cafetal San Lorenzo" (MSS, Cuban Collection, Biblioteca Nacional José Martí, Havana).

72. Miguel de Aldama to Domingo del Monte, September 10, 1845, in Academia de Historia de Cuba, *Centón epistolario*, 6:240.

73. Moreno Fraginals, *El ingenio*, 1:273–74. Excerpts from the British commissary judge report of January 1849 are found as an appendix in Richard R. Madden, *The Island of Cuba: Resources, Progress, and Prospects* (London, 1853), pp. 193–96.

74. Robert Baird, *Impressions and Experiences of the West Indies and North America in 1849*, 2 vols. (Edinburgh, 1850), 2:266–27.

75. Miguel de Aldama to Domingo del Monte, August 9, 1845, in Academia de la Historia de Cuba, *Centón epistolario*, 6:230.

76. Jacob Omnium to Lord John Russell, October 24, 1847, in *London Times*, October 27, 1847, p. 6.

77. Federico Roncali to Ministro, Ultramar, 1849, in Marrero, *Cuba*, 11:122.

78. Torrente, *Bosquejo económico político*, 1:147–48.

79. Susan Schroeder, *Cuba: A Handbook of Historical Statistics* (Boston, 1982), pp. 260–61.

80. Instituto de Historia de Cuba, *Historia de Cuba: La colonia: Evolución socioeconómica y formación nacional de los orígenes hasta 1867* (Havana, 1994), pp. 369–70.

81. Ibid., pp. 259–62.

82. For a suggestive discussion of the role of natural disasters and the distribution of wealth and income, see J. L. Anderson and E. L Jones, "Natural Disasters and the Historical Response," *Australian Economic History Review* 28 (March 1988): 3–20.

83. "Export Trade of the Island of Cuba," *Merchants' Magazine* 16 (January 1847): 110; "Exports of Havana from 1837 to 1848," *Merchants' Magazine* 20 (May 1849): 545; "Export of Sugar from Havana and Matanzas," *Merchants' Magazine* 21 (November 1849): 561; Schroeder, *Cuba*, pp. 265, 413; Alvarez Díaz, *A Study on Cuba*, p. 75.

CHAPTER FIVE

1. "In general," Terry Cannon has persuasively written, "disasters are not natural: they happen to people who are put at risk as a result of their *vulnerability*." Cannon, "Vulnerability Analysis and the Explanation of 'Natural' Disasters," in Ann Varley, ed., *Disasters, Development and Chichester, Environment* (Chichester, England, 1994), pp. 13–30. For a thorough treatment of the relationship between social and economic conditions and natural disasters, see Piers Blaikie, Terry Cannon, Ian Davis, and Ben Wisner, *At Risk: Natural Hazards, People's Vulnerability, and Disasters* (London, 1994), and Rolando V. Garcia, *Nature Pleads Not Guilty* (Oxford, 1981). Stuart B. Schwartz provides a very useful examination of some of the implications of these conditions in "The Hurricane of San Ciriaco: Disaster, Politics, and Society in Puerto Rico, 1899–1901," *Hispanic American Historical Review* 72 (August 1992): 303–34.

2. Cuba, Capitanía General, *Resumen del censo de población de la Isla de Cuba a fin del año de 1841* (Havana, 1842), p. 19.

3. Felipe de Fonsdeviela (Marqués del Torre), "Bando sobre dentro de dos año se fabriquen de otros materiales las casas de guano," June 25, 1776, *Memorias de la Real Sociedad Económica de La Habana* 18 (July 1844): 168–69; Cuba, Capitanía General, *Cuadro estadístico de la Siempre Fiel Isla de Cuba, correspondiente al año de 1827* (Havana, 1827), p. 46.

4. [El Faro Industrial de La Habana], *Huracán de 1846: Reseñas de sus estragos en la Isla de Cuba y relación ordenada de las pérdidas y desgracias sufridas en las poblaciones y puertos que visitó el memorable día 11 de octubre* (Havana, 1846), p. 22.

5. Fredrika Bremer, *The Homes of the New World: Impressions of America*, translated by Mary Howitt, 2 vols. (1853; reprint, New York, 1968), 2:274.

6. Cuba, Capitanía General, *Relación de los estragos causados por el temporal del once de octubre del corriente año* (Havana, 1846), p. 4.

7. [El Faro de La Habana], *Huracán de 1846*, p. 22; "Libro en el que se encuentran numerosas observaciones meteorológicas tomadas en su mayoría en los años 1825–1892" (MS, Biblioteca Nacional José Martí, Havana, n.d.), p. 22; [*Diario de la Marina*], *Resumen de los desastres ocurridos en el puerto de La Habana y sus jurisdicciones inmediatos del Departamento Occidental de la Isla de Cuba, días 10 y 11 de octubre de 1846* (Havana, 1846), p. 16.

8. Julio J. LeRiverend, *Patología especial de la Isla de Cuba* (Havana, 1858), p. 68.

9. *El Faro Industrial de La Habana*, September 6, 1842, p. 3.

10. Ibid., October 7, 1844, p. 2; *Diario de la Marina*, October 11, 1846, p. 2; Francisco Cartas, *Recopilación histórica y estadística de la jurisdicción de La Habana por distritos . . .* (Havana, 1856), p. 80.

11. [*Diario de la Marina*], *Resumen de los desastres ocurridos en el puerto de La Habana*, p. 16; José García de Arboleya, *Manual de la Isla de Cuba: Compendio de su historia, geografía, estadística y administración*, 2d ed. (Havana, 1859), pp. 57–58; Emilio Blanchet, *Compendio de la historia de Cuba* (Matanzas, 1866), p. 117; "Comunicación del Sor Presidente en que pide al Real Acuerdo voto consultivo,

acerca del haber propuesto a S.E. el Ayuntamiento de esta ciudad, como medida que puede aliviar los males esperimentados por el último huracán," October 13, 1846, file 1101, no. 3, Fondo Intendencia, ANC.

12. Cuba, Capitanía General, *Resumen del censo de población de la Isla de Cuba a fin del año de 1841* (Havana, 1842), p. 25.

13. *Diario de la Marina*, October 12, 1846, p. 4.

14. Cuba, Capitanía General, *Relación de los estragos causados*, pp. 3–5.

15. *Diario de La Habana*, October 12, 1846, p. 1.

16. Francisco Cardozo to Leopoldo O'Donnell, January 26, 1847, file 258, no. 9146, Fondo Gobierno Superior Civil, ANC.

17. Isabel Landín to Junta de Socorro, February 3, 1847, file 257, no. 9145, ibid.; José de Sogo to Leopoldo O'Donnell, November 1846, file 257, no. 9144, ibid.

18. Miguel Sánchez to Leopoldo O'Donnell, January 4, 1847, file 257, no. 9145, ibid.

19. Francisca de Sila to Leopoldo O'Donnell, March 11, 1847, file 258, no. 9147, ibid.; Manuel and Rosalía de Zayas to Junta de Socorro, January 15, 1847, file 257, no. 9144, ibid.; Ramón López to O'Donnell, January 21, 1847, file 258, no. 91457, ibid.; Juan Sánchez to O'Donnell, October 16, 1846, file 257, no. 9144, ibid.

20. Juanita Oliver to Leopoldo O'Donnell, February 1, 1847, file 257, no. 9145, ibid.

21. Antonio Sánchez to Junta de Socorro, November 10, 1846, file 257, no. 9144, ibid.; Blasa del Val to Leopoldo O'Donnell, November 9, 1846, file 257, no. 9144, ibid.

22. Josefa López to Leopoldo O'Donnell, February 12, 1847, file 257, no. 9145, ibid.; María del Carmen Verna to O'Donnell, January 25, 1847, file 257, no. 9145, ibid.; Eugenia Rivero to O'Donnell, February 10, 1847, file 256, no. 9143, ibid.; Elena Herrera to O'Donnell, January 29, 1847, file 256, no. 9143, ibid.; Ramona González to O'Donnell, January 25, 1847, file 258, no. 9147, ibid.; Apolonia María de Miranda de Fernández to O'Donnell, June 24, 1848, file 256, no. 9143, ibid.

23. María Josefa Romo to Leopoldo O'Donnell, November 1846, Comprobantes de Pagos, file 257, no. 9144, ibid.; Caridad Romero to O'Donnell, February 1, 1847, Comprobantes de Pago, file 256, no. 9143, ibid.; Gabriela Torres to O'Donnell, January 25, 1847, file 258, no. 9146, ibid.; Josefa Montero Gutiérrez to O'Donnell, January 27, 1847, file 257, no. 9145, ibid. Orphans, retired and civil military officials living off modest pensions, and countless heads of households with dependent children were also reduced to destitution on the streets of the capital. See Luis del Valle to Junta de Socorro, March 11, 1847, file 257, no. 9145, ibid.; Carolina Rey to O'Donnell, January 28, 1847, file 256, no. 9143, ibid.; Juan Maqueira to O'Donnell, January 12, 1847, file 257, no. 9145, ibid.

24. *Diario de La Habana*, October 23, 1846, p. 2.

25. Instituto de Historia de Cuba, *Historia de Cuba: La colonia: Evolución socioeconómica y formación nacional de los orígenes hasta 1867* (Havana, 1994), pp. 276–81.

26. *El Faro Industrial de La Habana*, October 9, 1844, p. 2.

27. Manuel de Garay y Echeverría, *Historia descriptiva de la villa de San Antonio de los Baños y su jurisdicción* (Havana, 1859), p. 89; Cuba, Capitanía General, *Relación de los estragos causados*, p. 31. In one contemporary history of Santa Clara, Manuel Dionisio González wrote that a hurricane in October 1837 "destroyed more than 170 houses, among which were included 87 that belong to poor families." Dionisio González, *Memoria histórica de la villa de Santa Clara y su jurisdicción* (Villaclara, 1858), p. 266.

28. *Diario de La Habana*, October 26, 1846, p. 2; *El Faro Industrial de La Habana*, October 10, 1844, p. 2.

29. Cuba, Capitanía General, *Resumen del censo de población*, p. 19.

30. Cuba, Capitanía General, *Relación de los estragos causados*, p. 28.

31. Junta de Fomento, "Expediente formado para dar cuenta a S.M. del temporal acaecido en la noche del 2 al 3 del corriente," October 6, 1796, file 1, no. 14, Fondo Real Consulado y Junta de Fomento, ANC; Abiel Abbot, *Letters Written in the Interior of Cuba* (Boston, 1829), p. 148.

32. *Diario de La Habana*, October 15, 1846, p. 1.

33. Robert Dirks, *The Black Saturnalia: Conflict and Its Ritual Expression on British West Indian Slave Plantations* (Gainesville, Fla., 1987), p. 81.

34. George Wilson Bridges, *The Annals of Jamaica*, 2 vols. (London, 1828), 2:179; Richard B. Sheridan, "The Crisis of Slave Subsistence in the British West Indies during and after the American Revolution," *William and Mary Quarterly* 33 (October 1976): 632–33 (M'Neill); William Dickson, ed., *Mitigation of Slavery in Two Parts: Part I: Letters and Papers of the Late Hon. Joshua Steel — Part II: Letters to Thomas Clarkson* (1814; reprint, Miami, 1969), pp. 61, 314, 431; Lowell Joseph Ragatz, *The Fall of the Planter Class in the British Caribbean, 1763–1863* (1928; reprint, New York, 1977), pp. 159, 191.

35. *Diario de La Habana*, October 23, 1846, p. 2.

36. *El Faro Industrial de La Habana*, October 14, 1844, p. 2, October 15, 1846, p. 1; *El Diario de La Habana*, October 13 (p. 2), 24 (p. 2), 1846; Edward B. Garriott, *West Indian Hurricanes* (Washington, D.C., 1900), p. 60; Junta de Fomento, "Expediente sobre estragos causados por el huracán del 11 del corriente en la casa en que estaba alojada la negrada de las obras de calzadas en San Francisco de Paula," October 18, 1846, file 120, no. 6028, Fondo Real Consulado y Junta de Fomento, ANC; Manuel Pérez Delgado, "Colecturía de la Manda Pia: Forzosa y derechos de sepulturas," in Cuba, Capitanía General, *Relación de los estragos causados*, pp. 9–10.

37. See *Diario de la Marina* and *Faro Industrial de La Habana*, October–December 1844 and 1846.

38. Miguel de Aldama to Domingo del Monte, October 10, 1844, in Academia de la Historia de Cuba, *Centón epistolario de Domingo del Monte*, edited by Domingo Figarola-Caneda, Joaquín Llaverías y Martínez, and Manuel I. Mesa Rodríguez, 6 vols. (Havana, 1923–53), 6:113; *El Faro Industrial de La Habana*, October 13, 1846, p. 1; Cuba, Capitanía General, *Relación de los estragos causados*, p. 4.

39. *Diario de La Habana*, October 26, 1846, p. 2.

40. Thomas Fowell Buxton, *The African Slave Trade and Its Remedy* (London, 1840), p. 33. I am indebted to Gabino la Rosa Corzo for the information concerning the Angerona coffee estate.

41. Robert Baird, *Impressions and Experiences of the West Indies and North America in 1849*, 2 vols. (Edinburgh, 1850), 2:225.

42. In an interview by Richard Madden, Domingo del Monte estimated that the average slave mortality rate was 8 percent on a sugar plantation and 2 percent on a coffee estate. When asked if births exceeded deaths on the ingenios, del Monte responded: "Oh, no!" and on cafetales, "On many coffee plantations they do." See the appendix in Richard R. Madden, ed., *Poems by a Slave in the Island of Cuba, Recently Liberated. . . . with the History of the Early Life of the Negro Poet, Written by Himself, to Which Are Prefixed Two Pieces Descriptive of Cuban Slavery and the Slave-Traffic*, edited by Edward J. Mullen (1840; reprint, Hamden, Conn., 1981), pp. 130–31; Abbot, *Letters*, p. 28.

43. David Turnbull, *Travels in the West: Cuba, with Notices of Porto Rico, and the Slave Trade* (London, 1840), pp. 293–94; Abbot, *Letters*, p. 144.

44. Completed between 1838 and 1839, *Francisco* was published posthumously in New York in 1880.

45. Anselmo Suárez y Romero to José Jacinto Milanés, November 12, 1838, *Revista de la Biblioteca Nacional*, 2d ser., 5 (January–March 1954): 47; Anselmo Suárez y Romero, "Ingenios," 1840, in Anselmo Suárez y Romero, *Colección de artículos* (1859; reprint, Havana, 1963), p. 237. "In vain does one leave the *ingenio* to travel to another *finca*," Suárez y Romero wrote from Güines the following year, "for slaves and masters are everywhere, everywhere there are *mayorales*, which is the same thing as saying that everywhere there groans a race of exploited men under the power of another happier race that inhumanely takes advantages of their sweat and labor." Suárez y Romero to Domingo del Monte, March 15, 1839, in Academia de la Historia de Cuba, *Centón epistolario*, 4:38.

46. John G. F. Wurdemann, *Notes on Cuba* (Boston, 1844), pp. 104, 144–45. W. M. L. Jay made similar if more exaggerated observations: "The operations of the *cafetal* present nothing of the hard and repulsive features of the *ingenio*. It is simply an easy and beautiful system of horticulture, on a most extensive scale. . . . There is no occasion for night labor, and the negroes looked altogether heartier and happier than those of the *ingenio*." See W. M. L. Jay [Julia Louisa Matilda Woodruff], *My Winter in Cuba* (New York, 1871), p. 258.

47. Abbot, *Letters*, p. 144. For an informative history of the Angerona coffee estate, see M. Isidro Méndez, "Biografía del cafetal Angerona," *Revista de la Biblioteca Nacional* 3 (July–September 1952): 49–65.

48. Ramiro Guerra y Sánchez, *Mudos testigos: Crónica del ex-cafetal Jesús Nazareno* (1948; reprint, Havana, 1974), p. 74; Gerardo Brown Castillo, *Cuba colonial: Ensayo histórico social de la integración de la sociedad cubana* (Havana, 1952), p. 46; Gloria García Rodríguez, *La esclavitud desde la esclavitud: La visión de los siervos* (Mexico, 1996), p. 95.

49. Richard Henry Dana Jr., *To Cuba and Back: A Vacation Voyage* (Boston, 1859), p. 121.

50. Francisco de Paula Serrano, *Agricultura cubana o tratado sobre los ramos principales de su industria rural* (Havana, 1837), p. 45.

51. Marqués de Campo Florido, "Representation del Marqués de Campo Florido con motivo de la circular para la construcción del barracones en las fincas," August 21, 1843, and "Expediente: Representaciones de varios hacendados, esponiendo los inconvenientes y perjuicios que resultan de llevarse a cabo la construcción de barracones en las como se previno por circular," 1843, Fondo Miscelánea de Expedientes, file 3585, no. Cu, ANC.

52. José Montalvo y Castillo to Governor General, August 25, 1843, ibid.

53. Alvaro Reynoso, *Estudios progresivos sobre varias materias científicas, agrícolas e industriales* (Havana, 1861), pp. 328–29; Joseph John Gurney, *A Winter in the West Indies* (London, 1841), p. 210. One of the better accounts of the barracón is found in Juan Pérez de la Riva, "El barracón de ingenio en la época esclavista," *El barracón y otros ensayos* (Havana, 1975), pp. 15–74.

54. Richard Robert Madden, *The Island of Cuba: Its Resources, Progress, and Prospects* (London, 1853), pp. 174–75; Bremer, *Homes of the New World*, 2:332.

55. Jacob Omnium to Lord John Russell, October 24, 1847, in *London Times*, October 27, 1847, p. 6.

56. "Expediente sobre el levantamiento de los negros pertenecientes a la dotación del cafetal Perseverancia," September 1842, file 941, no. 33195, Fondo Gobierno Superior Civil, ANC; "Expediente sobre el alzamiento de los negros del cafetal de Don José Canto Valdespino situado entre los partidos de la Seyba del Agua y Vereda Nueva," July 1840, file 939, no. 33191, ibid. For details of an insurrection on the Recurso cafetal in Jibacoa, see file 3, no. 9, Fondo Comisión Militar, ANC.

57. H. E. Friedlaender, *Historia económica de Cuba* (Havana, 1944), pp. 168–239, 454–55.

58. "Our union with Spain," planter José del Castillo insisted in 1838, "does not depend entirely on Spanish will or force. It does depend on the interest and the will of the most influential part of our population, of the devotion of our aristocracy . . . to its proper interests, to its physical and moral existence." José del Castillo to Andrés de Arango, May 1838, in Academia de la Historia, *Centón Epistolario*, 3:150.

59. Domingo del Monte, "Proyecto de Memorial a S.M. la Reina, en nombre del Ayuntamiento de La Habana, pidiendo leyes especiales para la Isla de Cuba," 1838, in Domingo del Monte, *Escritos*, edited by José Fernández de Castro, 2 vols. (Havana, 1929), 1:74. See also Urbano Martínez Carmenate, *Domingo del Monte y su tiempo* (Matanzas, 1992), pp. 288–348.

60. Little information appeared either in 1844 or in 1846 about posthurricane illness and disease. The one exception was a news story that appeared in *Diario de La Habana* on October 31, 1846, p. 2: "The abundance of rain, alternating with the heat and humidity that we have had, have given rise to an increased number of fevers, and most of all to the increase of yellow fever."

61. Joaquín Gómez, "Cuenta general de los donativos colectados con motivo del huracán acaecido en esta ciudad y otros puntos de Isla de 4 al 5 de octubre y su

distribución para socorro de las más necesidades," n.d., file 1537, no. 70976, Fondo Gobierno Superior Civil, ANC; Gómez, "Cuentas de los donativos colectados con motivo del huracán acaecido del 10 al 11 de octubre de 1846 y su distribución para socorrar a los más necesitados," n.d., file 1537, no. 70976, ibid.; Gómez to Leopoldo O'Donnell, July 24, 1848, file 1537, no. 70976, ibid.; *Gaceta de Madrid*, December 5, 1844, p. 1; Ultramar, Madrid, "Se manifiesta que ha dispuesto se abra en la Peninsula una suscripción en beneficio de que los que sufrieron pérdidas en el huracán en esta Isla in October," December 5, 1844, file 135, no. 55, Fondo Reales Cédulas y Ordenes, ANC; García de Arboleya, *Manual*, pp. 58–59.

62. "Propuestas de los comisarios de barrios para nombrar los comisarios que han de recaudar los donativos," January 1848, file 1537, no. 70976, Fondo Gobierno Superior Civil, ANC. For solicitation of donations, see *El Faro Industrial de La Habana*, October 15, 1846, p. 1.

63. *Diario de La Habana*, October 24 (p. 2), November 3 (p. 2), 1846.

64. Ibid., October 15, 1846, p. 3.

65. "Documento referente a una fiesta religiosa en la Catedral en acción al Todopoderoso por haber salvado nuestras vidas del terrible huracán que acaba de sufrir esta parte de la Isla," October 16, 1846, file 386, no. 18434, Fondo Gobierno General, ANC; Enrique Edo, *Memoria histórica de la villa de Cienfuegos y su jurisdicción* (1861; reprint, Havana, 1943), pp. 98–99; Ayuntamiento of Havana, *Memoria de las tareas del ayuntamiento de La Habana en los dos años de 1847 y 1848* (Havana, 1850), p. 4.

66. Cuba, Real Junta de Fomento, *Memoria presentada a la Real Junta de Fomento, Agricultura y Comercio de la Siempre Fiel Isla de Cuba* (Madrid, 1851), pp. 28–52; Carlos de Sedano y Cruzat, *Cuba desde 1850 a 1873* (Madrid, 1873), p. 25.

67. Sección de Comercio y Ultramar, Ministerio de Comercio, to Gobernador Capitán General, October 26, 1842, file 165, no. 141, Fondo Reales Cédulas y Ordenes, ANC; Ultramar, Madrid, "Se aprueba la conducta de las autoridades con motivo del huracán," December 4, 1844, file 135, no. 45, ibid.

68. Leopoldo O'Donnell to Ministro de Ultramar, December 31, 1846, file 135, no. 45, ibid.

69. "Comunicación del Sor Presidente en que pide al Real Acuerdo voto consultivo, acerca de haber prospuesto a S.E. el Ayuntamiento de esta ciudad, como medida que puede aliviar los males esperimentados por el último huracán," October 13, 1846, file 1101, no. 3, Fondo Intendencia, ANC.

70. Audiencia de La Habana, "Respuesta," November 9, 1846, ibid.

71. Leopoldo O'Donnell, "Manifestando haber dado cuenta oportunamente del huracán y que adoptó las medidas convenientes para el posible alivio de los males," December 31, 1846, file 156, no. 403, Fondo Reales Cédulas y Ordenes, ANC.

72. Cuba, Capitanía General, *Cuadro estadístico . . . al año de 1846*, app., p. 26; "Commerce and Resources of Cuba," *Merchants' Magazine* 21 (July 1849): 34.

73. *El Faro Industrial de La Habana*, January 6, 1848, p. 1.

74. "Commerce of the Island of Cuba, in 1844," *Merchants' Magazine*, 13 (October 1845): 381–82.

75. Ministerio de Ultramar to Intendant, Havana, December 29, 1844, file 171, no. 141, Fondo Reales Cédulas y Ordenes, ANC; "Real Orden desaprobando la medida acordada por la Junta Directiva," December 29, 1844, file 135, no. 112, ibid.; Francisco Jimeno, "Huracanes acaecidos en la isla de Cuba en los meses de septiembre y octubre," *La Ilustración Cubana* 1 (September 1885): 211.

76. Miguel de Aldama to Domingo del Monte, March 4, 1845, in Academia de Historia de Cuba, *Centón epistolario*, 6:167. Nearly ten years earlier, del Monte himself had observed: "Spain, at some 1,700 leagues distance from us, cannot and does not know how to govern us except despotically." Domingo del Monte to Salustiano de Olózaga, April 26, 1836, in del Monte, *Escritos*, 1:40–41.

CHAPTER SIX

1. Bartolomé de las Casas, *Historia de las Indias*, edited by André Saint-Lu, 3 vols. (Caracas, 1986), 1:416; Fredrika Bremer, *The Homes of the New World: Impressions of America*, translated by Mary Howitt, 2 vols. (1853; reprint, New York, 1968), 2:298. For similar tendencies in the British West Indies, see Peter Hulme, *Colonial Encounters: Europe and the Native Caribbean, 1492–1797* (London, 1986), pp. 94–101.

2. Eduardo F. Plá, "El primer observatorio meteorológico de Cuba," *Revista Bimestre Cubana* 9 (November–December 1914): 401–35.

3. "Huracán en las Antillas en agosto de 1856," *Crónica Naval de España* 4 (1856): 129–55, 257–80, 396–415, 532–46; Benito Viñes, *Huracanes del 7 y 19 de octubre de 1870* (Havana, 1870); *El huracán de Vuelta-Abajo: Curiosa recopilación de todo lo que de más notable ha publicado la prensa con motivo de aquella tremenda catástrofe* (Havana, 1882); Enrique H. del Monte, *La tormenta tropical de octubre de 1904 y la armonía entre dos centros tempestuosos* (Havana, 1905); Carlos Theye, *El huracán de octubre de 1910* (Havana, 1911); Luis García y Carbonell, *Huracán del 9 al 10 de septiembre de 1919* (Havana, n.d.); Mariano Gutiérrez Lanza, *El huracán de septiembre 1919* (Havana, 1919); Mariano Gutiérrez Lanza, "Ciclones que han pasado por la Isla de Cuba, o tan cerca que hayan hecho sentir en ella sus efectos con alguna fuerza desde 1865 a 1926," *Boletín del Observatorio Nacional* 23 (1927): 195–208.

4. Carlos Manuel Céspedes, *El diario perdido*, edited by Eusebio Leal Spengler (Havana, 1994), pp. 109–10.

5. Ricardo A. Delgado to Gonzalo de Quesada, October 30, 1895, in León Primelles, ed., *La revolución del 95 según la correspondencia de la delegación cubana en Nueva York*, 5 vols. (Havana, 1932–37), 2:230.

6. Russell R. Dynes, *Organized Behavior in Disaster* (Lexington, Mass., 1970), p. 84.

7. Ibid., p. 99.

8. Harry Estill Moore, *. . . and the Winds Blew* (Austin, Tex., 1964), pp. 195–203. In an older but still suggestive essay, Lowell Juilliard Carr argued that "the essence of disaster" was to be found in "cultural collapse," to which communities were perforce obliged to adapt, concluding that "[e]very disaster tends to set up individual, interactive, and eventually cultural readjustments." Lowell Juilliard

Carr, "Disaster and the Sequence-Pattern Concept of Social Change," *American Journal of Sociology* 38 (September 1932): 213–14. See also Harry Estill Moore, "Toward a Theory of Disaster," *American Sociological Review* 21 (December 1956): 733–37, and William I. Torry, "Natural Disasters, Social Structure and Change in Traditional Societies," *Journal of Asian and African Studies* 13 (July–October 1978): 167–83.

9. Rafael Montoro, "Las víctimas del huracán," October 8, 1888, *Obras*, 4 vols. (Havana, 1930), 2:191–93.

10. Jon W. Anderson, "Cultural Adaptation to Threatened Disaster," *Human Organization* 27 (Winter 1968): 300–305.

11. Gustavo Pittaluga, *Diálogos sobre el destino* (Havana, 1954), pp. 388–89; Mercedes Cros Sandoval, *Mariel and Cuban National Identity* (Miami, 1986), p. 61. See also Salvador Massip, *Factores geográficos de la cubanidad* (Havana, 1941), and Calixto Masó y Vázquez, *El carácter cubano: Apuntes para un ensayo de psicología social* (1941; reprint, Miami, 1996), pp. 31–32.

12. Fernando Ortiz, "Los factores humanos de la cubanidad," *Revista Bimestre Cubana* 45 (1st Semester 1940):165.

13. Rafael Rodríguez Altunaga, *Las Villas: Biografía de una provincia* (Havana, 1955), p. 120; Juan Almeida Bosque, *Contra el agua y el viento* (Havana, 1985), p. 112; Fernando Boytel Jambú, *Hombres y huracanes* (Santiago de Cuba, 1978), p. 229.

14. M. Márquez Sterling, *Alrededor de nuestra psicología* (Havana, 1906), p. 101; *Bohemia* 50 (February 9, 1958), supp. 8; Roberto Pérez León, *Tiempo de 'Ciclón'* (Havana, 1995), p. 118; Omara Portuondo, "Vale la pena vivir," *Omara Portuondo con Adalberto Alvarez*, Compact Disc, Egrem, CD 0163, 1984.

15. *Revolución*, October 24, 1963, p. 2.

16. Aurelio N. Torrente, "Un huracán llamado 'Fidel,'" *Chubascos del exilio* (Miami, 1977), pp. 143–44.

17. Luis Adrián Betancourt, *Huracán* (Havana, 1976).

18. Hortensia de Varela, "Irredento," *Cuentos* (Havana, 1932), p. 132; Alfonso Hernández Catá, "La tempestad," *Cuentos y noveletas*, edited by Salvador Bueno (Havana, 1983), pp. 212–25; Arístides Fernández Vázquez, "Caminaban sin prisa por la acera," *Cuentos* (Havana, 1959), p. 98.

19. Armando Leyva, "El ciclón," *La provincia, las aldeas* (Santiago de Cuba, n.d.), pp. 140–42.

20. Pérez León, *Tiempo de "Ciclón,"* pp. 83, 87.

21. Jorge Velázquez Ramayo, *Vórtice* (Havana, 1976); Miguel de Marcos, *Fotuto* (1948; reprint, Havana, 1976), pp. 296–327. See also Eduardo Robreño, "El ciclón del 26," *Cualquier tiempo pasado fue . . .* (Havana, 1981), pp. 128–32.

22. Ofelia Rodríguez Acosta, *Sonata interrumpida* (Mexico, 1943), pp. 196–96.

23. Isa Caraballo, *Vendimia de huracanes: Antología poética, 1934–1939* (Havana, 1939), p. 14.

24. José María Heredia, *Poesías completas*, edited by Angel Aparicio Laurencio (Miami, 1970), pp. 154–55.

25. Francisco Orgaz, "Invocación a los huracanes," in José Lezama Lima, ed.,

Antología de la poesía cubana, 3 vols. (Havana, 1965), 2:435–40; Néstor Cepeda, "Al huracán," in Cintio Vitier and Fina García Marruz, eds., *Flor oculta de poesía cubana, Siglos XVIII y XIX* (Havana, 1978), pp. 202–4.

26. Sarfino, *El huracán: Temporal del 4 y 5 de octubre de 1844: Poema* (Havana, 1845); José María Pérez, "El huracán," *Diario de la Marina*, November 9, 1846, p. 3; Manuel Orgallez, "El huracán," *Diario de La Habana*, October 28, 1846, p. 2.

27. Gustavo Cardelle, "Huracán del 26," *Reflejos sobre la nieve* (New York, 1978), pp. 15–19.

28. Francisco Poveda, "El día de la tormenta," in Samuel Feijóo, ed., *Romances cubanos del siglo XIX* (Havana, 1977), pp. 150–57; Juan Clemente Zenea, "Noche tempestuosa," in Mirta Aguirre, ed., *Poesía social cubana* (Havana, 1980), pp. 107–8.

29. José Sánchez-Boudy, *Tiempo congelado: Poemario de una isla ausente* (Miami, 1979), p. 13; Halio Orovio, *El huracán y la palma* (Havana, 1980); Cintio Vitier, *Antología poética* (Havana, 1981), pp. 9–10; Renael González Batista, *Guitarra para dos islas* (Havana, 1981), p. 20; Edith Llerena, *Las catedrales del agua* (Madrid, 1981), pp. 29–30; Coralina Sánchez de Cabrera, "Tempestad," in *107 poetas cubanos del exilio* (Miami, 1988), p. 386; Felipe Pichardo Moya, *La ciudad de los espejos: Antología poética*, edited by Luis Suardíaz (Havana, 1992), p. 56; Eliseo Diego, *Poesía* (Havana, 1983), p. 234.

30. Julio Marzán, *Puerta de tierra* (San Juan, 1998), p. 11.

31. Rubén Martínez Villena, *La pupila insomne* (Havana, n.d.), p. 133.

32. Roberto Fernández Retamar, *Poesía reunida, 1948–1965* (Havana, 1966), pp. 62–63.

33. Esperanza Rubido, *Más allá del azul* (Miami, 1975), p. 26.

34. Nena Diez de Ramos, "Después de la tormenta," in *107 poetas cubanos del exilio*, p. 143; Edith Llerena, *La piel de la memoria* (Madrid, 1976), p. 93.

35. José Sánchez Boudy, *Diccionario de cubanismos más usuales*, 3 vols. (Miami, 1978–86), 1:100, 3:19; Gilberto Pérez Castillo, "¡El ciclón viene!," *Bohemia* 27 (November 10, 1935): 89.

36. Alfredo Echarry Ramos, *Gloria entre aguas* (Havana, 1972), p. 20.

37. Eladio Secades, "Los ciclones," *Bohemia* 44 (November 9, 1952): 9, 136.

Bibliographical Essay

Hurricanes in the Caribbean have long been a subject of intense interest and sustained research. An extensive literature, with antecedents early in the nineteenth century, has emerged dealing with virtually all facets of the tropical hurricane. This essay is designed to provide the reader with a general guide to the books and articles that offer additional information on those aspects of hurricanes most directly relevant to this work.

Most of the literature responds to the proposition that the hurricane is a natural force to be reckoned with, something to be understood so as to better control — or at least contain — the damage wrought by the mighty storms. There is an immediacy to this literature, much of which has to do with the desire to understand the origins of the hurricane, to forecast its course, and to understand its destructive capacity in the past in order to minimize destruction in the future. For the most part, these writings reflect the perspective of meteorology, oceanography, geophysics, and the allied weather sciences whose pursuit of knowledge about the hurricane has direct implications. The research has drawn on the interests and needs various constituencies, including government agencies, regional planners, and the countless thousands of communities in scores of countries that lie in the known paths of hurricanes.

The accumulated literature provides a vast range of information about the character of the hurricane, the sources of its force, and the circumstances of its development. Among the most complete discussions of the hurricane in all its multiple facets are the informative volumes prepared by David Longshore, *Encyclopedia of Hurricanes, Typhoons, and Cyclones* (New York, 1998), and Stephen H. Schneider, ed., *Encyclopedia of Climate and Weather* (Oxford, 1996).

Descriptive chronologies of hurricanes provide a useful historical overview of the cycle and course of the storms. The most informative accounts include David M. Ludlow, *Early American Hurricanes, 1492–1870* (Boston, 1963); David L. Niddrie, "Hurricanes," *Geographical Magazine* 23 (July 1964): 228–34; R. Cecil Gentry, "Nature and Scope of Hurricane Damage," in American Society for Oceanography, *Hurricane Symposium* (Houston, 1966), pp. 233–53; and Edward N. Rappaport and José J. Fernández-Partagás, "History of the Deadliest Atlantic Tropical Cyclones since the Discovery of the New World," in Henry F. Díaz and Roger S. Pulwarty, eds., *Hurricanes: Climate and Socioeconomic Impact* (Berlin, 1997), pp. 93–108.

A number of general works on hurricanes offer highly useful information. These include M. S. Douglas, *Hurricane* (New York, 1958); Louis J. Battan, *The Nature of Violent Storms* (Garden City, N.Y., 1961); Thomas Helm, *Hurricane:*

Weather at Its Worst (New York, 1967); Robert H. Simpson and Herbert Riehl, *The Hurricane and Its Impact* (Baton Rouge, 1981); David E. Fisher, *The Scariest Place on Earth: Eye to Eye with Hurricanes* (New York, 1994); Jerome Gold, *Hurricanes* (Seattle, 1994); and the two books by Jay Barnes, *North Carolina's Hurricane History* (Chapel Hill, 1995) and *Florida's Hurricane History* (Chapel Hill, 1998). Older but still helpful volumes are Isaac Monroe Cline, *Tropical Cyclones* (New York, 1926), and Ivan Ray Tannehill, *Hurricanes* (Princeton, 1944).

Older works, particularly nineteenth-century treatises on storms, give insights into the historical development of the science of meteorology and provide important perspectives on past perceptions of the origins and nature of hurricanes. They are particularly valuable as a source for the evolution of knowledge about hurricanes. These works were the science of their time but can be read today as useful sources for an understanding of the ways that hurricanes insinuated themselves into the nineteenth-century scientific imagination. Among the most informative are William C. Redfield, "Observations on the Hurricanes and Storms of the West Indies and the Coast of the United States," *American Journal of Science and Arts* 25 (January 1834): 114–21; William Reid, *An Attempt to Develop the Law of Storms* (London, 1838); Edward Elwar, *West Indian Hurricanes and Other Storms* (London, 1907); and Oliver L. Fassig, *Hurricanes of the West Indies* (Washington, D.C., 1913).

Some of the more specialized works on hurricanes are particularly useful in understanding how the natural forces associated with hurricanes affect local economies and population centers. A number of articles provide informative discussions of winds, tides, rain, flooding, and storm surges—among them, José Carlos Millás Hernández, "Cloud Motions and Sea Swells in Hurricane Detection and Analysis," *Final Report of the Caribbean Hurricane Seminar Held at Ciudad Trujillo, Dominican Republic, February 16–25, 1956* (Ciudad Trujillo, 1956), pp. 109–21; A. E. Moss, "Effect on Trees of Wind-Driven Salt Water," *Journal of Forestry* 28 (May 1940): 421–25; Herbert S. Saffir, "The Effects of Structures of Winds of Hurricane Force," *American Society of Civil Engineering Proceedings* 79 (July 1953): 206/1–19; E. Palmén, "On the Formation and Structure of Tropical Hurricanes," *Geophysica* 3 (1948): 26–38, and "On the Dynamics of Tropical Hurricanes," *Final Report of the Caribbean Hurricane Seminar . . . , February 16–25, 1956*, pp. 34–55; James Power, "Building Construction and Precautionary Maintenance in Hurricane Areas," *Final Report of the Caribbean Hurricane Seminar . . . February 16–25, 1956*, pp. 291–301; Ernest Gherzi, "Methodology in the Study of the Origin and Motion of Tropical Cyclones," *Final Report of the Caribbean Hurricane Seminar . . . February 16–25, 1956*, pp. 19–33; Gordon E. Dunn, "History and Development of Hurricane Forecasting in the Atlantic Area," *Final Report of the Caribbean Hurricane Seminar . . . February 16–25, 1956*, pp. 95–104; and Billye Brown and Walter R. Brown, *Hurricanes and Tornadoes* (Reading, Mass., 1972). A short but suggestive article on the environmental implications of hurricanes is William Schulz, "The Sweeping Effects of Hurricane Gilbert on Tropical Forests," *Smithsonian Institution Research Reports*, no. 58 (Autumn 1989): 1, 8.

The long-term economic consequences of hurricanes in the circum-Caribbean is the subject of three informative articles: Arnold L. Sugg, "Economic Aspects of Hurricanes," *Monthly Weather Review* 95 (March 1967): 143–46; David C. Weaver, "The Hurricane as an Economic Catalyst," *Journal of Tropical Geography* 27 (December 1968): 6–71; and Richard A. Lobdell, "The Economic Consequences of Hurricanes in the Caribbean: A Report on a Work in Progress," *Review of Latin American Studies* 3 (1990): 178–96.

/ / / / /

Much of the hurricane literature concerning the Caribbean assumes the form of descriptive chronological compendiums of the hurricane experience. Perhaps the most complete for the period it considers is José Carlos Millás Hernández, *Hurricanes of the Caribbean and Adjacent Regions, 1492–1800* (Miami, 1968), which provides an annotated chronology of every hurricane known to have passed through the circum-Caribbean region between 1492 and 1800. A similar format is used in Andrés Poey, "A Chronological Table, Comprising 400 Cyclonic Hurricanes Which Have Occurred in the West Indies and in the North Atlantic within 362 Years, from 1493 to 1855," *Journal of the Royal Geographic Society* 25 (1855): 291–328, and Simón Sarasola, *Los ciclones en las Antillas* (Madrid, 1928).

The literature on hurricanes in the Caribbean is especially rich and deals with a variety of themes, including seasonal variations, the movement of winds and seas, and the historic trajectories followed by hurricanes. Among the older works are William C. Redfield, *On Three Several Hurricanes of the Atlantic and Their Relations to the Northers of Mexico and Central America* (New Haven, 1846); Henry Piddington, *Conversations about Hurricanes* (London, 1852); Everett Hayden, *West Indian Hurricanes and the March Blizzard* (New York, 1889); and Edward B. Garriott, *West Indian Hurricanes* (Washington, D.C., 1900). These four treatises are useful not only for the information they contain about hurricanes of the last century, but also as an important source of how meteorologists approached hurricanes in the early phase of scientific research on weather and climate. Other useful discussions of nineteenth-century hurricanes in the Caribbean include "Huracanes en las Antillas," *El Prisma* 1 (October 1846): 151–53; Andrés Poey, *Bibliographie cyclonique*, 2d ed. (Paris, 1866); Benito Viñes, *Investigaciones relativas a la circulación y traslación ciclónica en los huracanes de las Antillas* (Havana, 1895); and Carlos Theye, "Trayectorías de los ciclones durante el mes de octubre," *Anales de la Academia de Ciencias Médicas, Físicas y Naturales de La Habana* 24 (1886): 341–45.

For the twentieth-century literature, see Maxwell Hall, "West Indian Cyclones and the Local Wind," *Quarterly Journal of the Royal Meteorological Society* 42 (1916): 183–89; the three installments of José Carlos Millás Hernández, "Un ensayo sobre los huracanes de las Antillas," *Boletín del Observatorio Nacional* 24 (January 1928): 3–19, (February 1928): 27–42, and (May–June 1928): 513–15; Carlos Millás Hernández, "Génesis y marcha de los huracanes antillanos," *Proceedings of the Second Pan American Congress* (Washington, D.C., 1917), pp. 42–55, and "Sobre la recurva en lazo en trayectorías de ciclones tropicales," *Boletín del Observatorio Nacional* 22 (April 1926): 49–61; Arnold E. True, "La estructura de los ciclones tropicales," *Boletín del Observatorio Nacional* 2 (January–April 1937): 10–20; J. S. Sawyer, "Notes on the Theory of the Tropical Cyclones," *Quarterly Journal of the Royal Meteorological Society* 73 (1947): 101–26; and T. Bergeron, "The Problem of the Tropical Hurricanes," *Quarterly Journal of the Royal Meteorological Society* 80 (1954): 131–64.

/ / / / /

The general literature on hurricanes in Cuba has its antecedents in the nineteenth century and in the aggregate constitutes an impressive body of writings. An outstanding anthropological approach to the study of hurricanes is found in Fernando Ortiz, *El huracán* (Mexico, 1947), a treatise exploring the relationship of hurricanes to pre-Columbian cultures in the Caribbean with an emphasis on mythology and religious ritual. Perhaps the best general survey of hurricanes in Cuba is Fernando Boytel Jambú, *Hombres y huracanes* (Santiago de Cuba, 1978).

Among the older but still valuable general studies are Desiderio Herrera, *Memoria sobre los huracanes en la Isla de Cuba* (Havana, 1847); Marcos de J. Melero, "Los huracanes de la Isla de Cuba: Bajas y ondas barométricas observadas," *Anales de la Academia de Ciencias Médicas, Físicas y Naturales* 7 (November 1870): 329–35, and "Los huracanes y el barómetro en la isla de Cuba," *El Genio Científico* 2 (January 1874): 11–23; Manuel Fernández de Castro, "Sobre las bajas y ondas barométricas observadas en los huracanes de la Isla de Cuba," *Anales de la Academia de Ciencias Médicas, Físicas y Naturales* 8 (July 1871): 57–61, and *Estudio sobre los huracanes ocurridos en la Isla de Cuba* (Madrid, 1871); Francisco Jimeno, "Huracanes acaecidos en la isla de Cuba en los meses de septiembre y octubre," *La Ilustración Cubana* 1 (September 1885): 211; and Enrique del Monte, "Los ciclones," *Revista Cubana* 20 (September 1894): 265–74. The more informative twentieth-century accounts include Mariano Gutiérrez Lanza, "Ciclones que han pasado por la isla de Cuba, o tan cerca que hayan hecho sentir en ella sus efectos con alguna fuerza, desde 1865 a 1926," *Boletín Oficial del Observatorio* 23 (January 1927): 195–208, and José Martínez-Fortún y Foyo, "Ciclones en Cuba," *Revista Bimestre Cubana* 50 (2d Semester 1942): 232–58.

A characteristic feature of the Cuban hurricane literature—of both the nineteenth and twentieth centuries—has been its tendency to give monographic attention to specific hurricanes. A number of works deal entirely with the hurricane of 1846, providing detailed accounts of the scope and severity of the storm across western Cuba. One of the most comprehensive volumes, prepared by the colonial government, is Cuba, Capitanía General, *Relación de los estragos causados por el temporal del once de octubre del corriente año* (Havana, 1846). The newspaper *El Faro Industrial de La Habana* drafted a highly informative compendium of the damages resulting from the 1846 hurricane, focusing on Havana and Matanzas but also giving attention to interior provincial towns, entitled *Huracán de 1846: Reseñas de sus estragos en la Isla de Cuba y relación ordenada de la pérdidas y desgracias sufridas en las poblaciones y puertos que visitó el memorable día 11 de octubre* (Havana, 1846). Similar in format, and equally useful, is the synopsis prepared by the newspaper *Diario de la Marina* and published as *Resumen de los desastres ocurridos en el puerto de La Habana y sus jurisdicciones inmediatos del Departamento Occidental de la Isla de Cuba, días 10 y 11 de Octubre de 1846* (Havana, 1846).

A literature of substantial proportions has taken form around the study of individual hurricanes. These include the four-part study, "Huracán en las Antillas en agosto de 1856," *Crónica Naval de España* 4 (1856): 129–55, 257–80, 396–415, 532–46; the most important works of Benito Viñes, director of the Belén Meteorological Observatory: *Huracanes del 7 y 19 de octubre de 1870* (Havana, 1870), "Temporal del 6 de octubre de 1873," *Anales de la Academia de Ciencias Médicas, Físicas y Naturales* 10 (October 1873): 171–77, (January 1874): 280–300, *Apuntes relativos a los huracanes de las Antillas en septiembre y octubre de 1875 y 76* (Havana, 1877), and *El huracán de Vuelta-Abajo: Curiosa recopilación de todo lo que de más notable ha publicado la prensa con motivo de aquella tremenda catástrofe* (Havana, 1882); Enrique H. del Monte, *La tormenta tropical de octubre de 1904 y la armonía entre dos centros tempestuosos* (Havana, 1905); Carlos Theye, *El huracán de octubre de 1910* (Havana, 1911); Luis García y Carbonell, *Huracán del 9 al 10 de septiembre de 1919* (Havana, n.d.); three works by Mariano Gutiérrez Lanza: *El huracán de septiembre 1919* (Havana, 1919), *Huracán sin precedente, Octubre de 1924* (Havana, 1924), and *Génesis y evolución del huracán del 20 de octubre de 1926* (Havana, 1927); and two articles by José Carlos Millás, "El huracán de La Habana de 1926," *Boletín del Observatorio Nacional* 22 (October 1926): 185–225, and "El ciclón del día 20 de octubre," *Boletín de Obras Públicas* 1 (October 1926): 312–25.

/ / / / /

The sources for the historical study of hurricanes in Cuba and the circum-Caribbean are available in many forms and located in many places. The Archivo Nacional in Havana, as well as provincial archives in Matanzas, Cienfuegos, Holguín, and Santiago de Cuba, among others, offer a rich collection of manuscripts and locally published serial literature.

Also of considerable value are the works of the many scribes who provided a written record of the early European presence in the New World. For one thing, they provide data useful in reconstructing the history of hurricanes in the region. In many cases, they are themselves first-person accounts of the experience of hurricanes; in other instances, they draw on the firsthand experience of others with whom the early chroniclers were in contact. Regardless, these accounts provide an ample documentary base for the study of the early European encounter with tropical hurricanes. In addition, they offer fascinating literary form to this experience. Some of the most engaging—and, indeed, occasionally some of the most compelling—descriptions of hurricanes are found in the prose of sixteenth- and seventeenth-century chroniclers, as Europeans endeavored to give a previously unknown phenomenon narrative familiarity. The prose is rich with creative metaphor and imaginative allegory, using imagery to make comprehensible what was inconceivable. Some of the better accounts are found in Gonzalo Fernández de Oviedo, *De la natural historia de las Indias*, edited by Enrique Alvarez

López (Madrid, 1942), and *Historia general y natural de las Indias, islas y tierra firme de la mar océano,* 4 vols. (Madrid, 1951); Pedro Mártir de Anglería, *Décadas del Nuevo Mundo* (Madrid, 1989); Bartolomé de las Casas, *Historia de las Indias* (1575), edited by André Saint-Lu, 3 vols. (Caracas, 1986); Alvar Núñez Cabeza de Vaca, *Naufragios y comentarios, con dos cartas y relación de Hernando de Ribera* (5th ed., Madrid, 1971); and Pedro Simón, *Noticias historiales de las conquistas de Tierra Firme en las Indias Occidentales,* 9 vols. (Bogotá, 1953).

In similar fashion, and for many of the same reasons, some of the most informative accounts of hurricanes are found in the contemporary histories of the West Indies, most of which were written between the seventeenth and nineteenth centuries. A number of these histories are themselves first-person accounts of hurricanes; others were written sufficiently soon thereafter to include eyewitness accounts of the storms. The better contemporary histories in the British West Indies include Richard Blome, *A Description of the Island of Jamaica, with the Other Isles and Territories in America to Which the English are Related* (London, 1672); John Oldmixon, *The British Empire in America, Containing the History of the Discovery, Settlement, Progress and State of the British Colonies on the Continent and Islands of America,* 2 vols. (1708; reprint, London, 1741); Edward Long, *The History of Jamaica,* 3 vols. (1774; reprint, New York, 1972); John A. Fowler, *A General Account of the Calamities Occasioned by the Late Tremendous Hurricanes and Earthquakes in the West-Indian Islands* (London, 1781); Thomas Southey, *Chronological History of the West Indies,* 3 vols. (London, 1827); George Wilson Bridges, *The Annals of Jamaica,* 2 vols. (London, 1828); Robert H. Schomburgk, *The History of Barbados, Compromising a Geographical and Statistical Description of the Island* (1848; reprint, London, 1971); and Henry Iles Woodcock, *A History of Tobago* (1867; reprint, New York, 1971).

The most informative contemporary histories of Cuba during the nineteenth century include the two works by Ramón de la Sagra, *Historia económico-política y estadística de la Isla de Cuba* (Havana, 1830) and *Historia física, política y natural de la Isla de Cuba,* 12 vols. (Paris, 1842–66); José María de Andueza, *Isla de Cuba: Pintoresca, histórica, política, literaria, mercantil, e industrial, recuerdos, apuntes, impresiones de dos épocas* (Madrid, 1841); the two important studies by Jacobo de la Pezuela, *Ensayo histórico de la Isla de Cuba* (New York, 1842) and *Historia de la Isla de Cuba,* 4 vols. (Madrid, 1868–78); Félix Erenchún, *Anales de la Isla de Cuba,* 4 vols. (Havana, 1859); José García de Arboleya, *Manual de la Isla de Cuba: Compendio de su historia, geografía, estadística y administración* (2d ed., Havana, 1859); Emilio Blanchet, *Compendio de la historia de Cuba* (Matanzas, 1866); Carlos de Sedano y Cruzat, *Cuba desde 1850 a 1873* (Madrid, 1873); José Ahumada y Centurión, *Memoria histórica de la Isla de Cuba* (Havana, 1874); and Miguel Rodríguez Ferrer, *Naturaleza y civilización de la grandiosa Isla de Cuba,* 2 vols. (Madrid, 1876–87). A very useful guide to the historiography of nineteenth-century Cuba is José Manuel Pérez Cabrera, *Historiografía de Cuba* (Mexico, 1962), especially pp. 137–333.

First-person accounts of nineteenth-century conditions in Cuba abound in the form of travel literature. Cuba was a much-visited island, for its location at the middle latitudes of the Western Hemisphere, at the crossroads of the principal sea lanes of the Caribbean and the Gulf of Mexico, made a visit to the island all but obligatory to many travelers to the New World. Cuba was within easy reach of North American travelers, who with increasing frequency visited the island through much of the period that is the focus of this book. Travelers were often shrewd observers and faithful chroniclers of time and place. It is the good fortune, indeed, of researchers to have available such textured first-person accounts of Cuban life in the nineteenth century. As a genre of literature and a source of historical writing, the nineteenth-century travelogues are, of course, uneven in quality, and like other sources must be used with circumspection. But when they do "work," they work magnificently.

Travel accounts thus provide insight into the impact and implications of hurricanes. Travelers paid attention to detail, they moved freely among Cubans of all classes, visited homes and workplaces, walked on city streets and traveled country roads, recorded conversations, and collected local statistics. Anecdotes often supply valuable data that might otherwise have been lost. These accounts provide graphic testimony to the lasting effects of the hurricanes of the first half of the nineteenth century. The most useful include J. D. Dunlop, "A Scotsman in Cuba, 1811–1812," edited by Raymond A. Mohl, *The Americas* 29 (October 1972): 232–45; Robert Francis Jameson, *Letters from the Havana during the Year 1820 Containing an Account of the Present State of the Island of Cuba* (London, 1821); Abiel Abbot, *Letters Written in the Interior of Cuba* (Boston, 1828); James E. Alexander, *Transatlantic Sketches*, 2 vols. (London, 1833); Jacinto de Salas y Quiroga, *Viages: Isla de Cuba* (Madrid, 1840); David Turnbull, *Travels in the West: Cuba, with Notices of Porto Rico, and the Slave Trade* (London, 1840); Joseph John Gurney, *A Winter in the West Indies* (London, 1841); John G. Wurdemann, *Notes on Cuba* (Boston, 1844); Henry Capadose, *Sixteen Years in the West Indies*, 2 vols. (London, 1845); Benjamin M. Norman, *Rambles by Land and Water, or Notes of Travel in Cuba and Mexico* (New York, 1845); Andrew Halliday, *The West Indies* (London, 1837); James Rawson, *Cuba* (New York, 1847); John Glanville Taylor, *The United States and Cuba: Eight Years of Change and Travel* (London, 1851); Fredrika Bremer, *The Homes of the New World: Impressions of America*, translated by Mary Howitt, 2 vols. (1853; reprint, New York, 1968); Richard Robert Madden, *The Island of Cuba: Its Resources, Progress, and Prospects* (London, 1853); Maturin M. Ballou, *History of Cuba, or Notes of a Traveller in the Tropics* (Boston, 1854); William Henry Hulbert, *Gan-Eden, or Pictures of Cuba* (Boston, 1854); James M. Phillippo, *The United States and Cuba* (London, 1857); Xavier Marmier, "Cuba en 1850: Cartas sobre América," *Revista Bimestre Cubana* 54 (2d Semester 1944): 215–40; L. Leonidas Allen, *The Island of Cuba, or Queen of the Antilles* (Cleveland, 1852); Edward Sullivan, *Rambles and Scrambles in North and South America* (London, 1852); Richard Henry Dana Jr., *To Cuba and Back: A Vacation Voyage* (Boston, 1859); Carlton H. Rogers, *Incidents of Travel in the Southern States and Cuba* (New York, 1862); Henry Latham, *Black and White: A Journal of a Three Months' Tour in the United States* (London, 1867); and W. M. L. Jay [Julia Louisa Matilda Woodruff], *My Winter in Cuba* (New York, 1871). The best general guide to this vast travel literature is found in Rodolfo Tro, *Cuba: Viajes y descripciones, 1493–1943* (Havana, 1950).

/ / / / /

Local and regional histories are another source of information and insight regarding the impact of hurricanes on Cuban communities. Nuance and subtlety are often blurred in the large aggregate categories employed in national histories. Wide-ranging generalizations employed to characterize collective experience tend to overlook the details and urgency registered at the municipal or provincial level. In local histories, on the other hand, hurricanes of the magnitude experienced in 1844 and 1846, for example, assume a place of prominence. The experience is understood to have had a profound and lasting effect on the local economy and local customs, as well as on the well-being of almost all of the area's residents.

It is thus in local and regional histories that some of the most useful insights into the impact of hurricanes on the life of communities appear. The better histories of Havana include Francisco Cartas, *Recopilación histórica y estadística de la jurisdicción de la Habana por distritos, hallandose en cada barrio las noticias de historia que le corresponden como asimismo el censo de población* (Havana, 1856); José María de la Torre, *Lo que fuimos y lo que somos, o La Habana antigua y moderna* (Havana, 1857); Julio J. LeRiverend Brusone, *La Habana: Biografía de una provincia* (Havana, 1960); Fernando Inclán Lavastida, *Historia de Marianao* (Marianao, 1943); and Elpidio de la Guardia, *Historia de Guanabacoa: 1511–1946* (Guanabacoa, 1946).

The history of Matanzas is well examined in Francisco Jimeno Fuentes, "Matanzas, estudio histórico estadístico: Dedicado a la Exma: Diputación Provincial de Matanzas," *Revista de la Biblioteca Nacional*, 2d ser., 8 (January–March 1957): 11–99; Pedro Alfonso, *Memorias de un matancero: Apuntes para la historia de la Isla de Cuba, con relación a la ciudad de San Carlos y San Severino de Matanzas, principiados en 1830 y continuados para ofrecer un presente al bazar matancero* (Matanzas, 1854); Mauricio Quintero y Almeyda, *Apuntes para la historia de la Isla de Cuba con relación a la ciudad de Matanzas desde el año 1693 hasta el de 1877* (Matanzas, 1878); and Francisco J. Ponte Domínguez, *Matanzas: Biografía de una provincia* (Havana, 1959).

Works on Pinar del Río include José María de la Torre and Tranquilino Sandalio de Noda, "Marien [Mariel]: Noticias históricas, geográficas y estadísticas de esta jurisdicción," *Memorias de la Real Sociedad Económica de La Habana*, 2d ser., 4 (September 1847): 165–81, and Emeterio S. Santovenia, *Pinar del Río* (Mexico, 1946). Camagüey province is examined in Juan Torres Lasqueti, *Colección de datos históricos-geográficos y estadísticos de Puerto Príncipe* (Havana, 1888); Jorge Juárez Cano, *Apuntes de Camagüey* (Camagüey, 1929); and Mary Cruz del Pino, *Camagüey: Biografía de una provincia* (Havana, 1955).

The region that came to constitute Las Villas province is best represented by Manuel Dionisio González, *Memoria histórica de la villa de Santa Clara y su jurisdicción* (Villaclara, 1858); Rafael Rodríguez Altunaga, *Las Villas: Biografía de una provincia* (Havana, 1955); Rafael Félix Pérez Luna, *Historia de Sancti-Spíritus*,

2 vols. (Sancti-Spíritus, 1888–89); Manuel Martínez-Moles, *Epítome de la historia de Sancti-Spíritus* (Havana, 1936); Antonio Miguel Alcover, *Historia de Sagua y su jurisdicción* (Sagua, 1906); and Manuel Martínez Escobar, *Historia de Remedios* (Havana, 1944). Two areas of Las Villas to have received special attention have been Cienfuegos and Trinidad. Important monographs that deal with Cienfuegos include "Historia geográfica, topográfica y estadística de la villa de Cienfuegos y su jurisdicción," *Memorias de la Real Sociedad Económica de La Habana*, 2d ser., 1 (April 1846): 204–11; Pedro Oliver y Bravo, *Memoria histórica, geográfica y estadística de Cienfuegos y su jurisdicción* (Cienfuegos, 1846), pp. 30–46; Enrique Edo, *Memoria histórica de la villa de Cienfuegos y su jurisdicción* (1861; reprint, Havana, 1943); and Orlando García Martínez, "Estudio de la economía cienfue-guera desde la fundación de la colonia Fernandina de Jagua hasta mediados del siglo XIX," *Islas* 55–56 (September 1976–April 1977): 117–68. Two informative works on the history of Trinidad are Francisco Marín Villafuerte, *Historia de Trini-dad* (Havana, 1945), and Hernán Venegas Delgado, "Apuntes sobre la decadencia trinitaria en el siglo XIX," *Islas* 46 (September–December 1973): 159–251.

Other municipal and provincial histories that provide insights on hurricanes' effects locally include Manuel de Garay y Echeverría, *Historia descriptiva de la villa de San Antonio de los Baños y su jurisdicción* (Havana, 1859); Francisco Fina García, *Historia de Santiago de Las Vegas* (Santiago de Las Vegas, 1954); Juan Jerez Villarreal, *Oriente: Biografía de una provincia* (Havana, 1960); José Rivero Muñiz, *Vereda Nueva* (Havana, 1964); and José Rafael Lauzán, *Historia colonial ariguanabense* (Havana, 1994).

/ / / / /

The study of hurricanes as a condition of the Caribbean has largely escaped the attention of modern historians, an oversight made all the more remarkable in view of the decisive impact that hurricanes have often had in the region. The out-standing exception is the model essay by Stuart B. Schwartz, "The Hurricane of San Ciriaco: Disaster, Politics, and Society in Puerto Rico, 1899–1901," *Hispanic American Historical Review* 72 (August 1992): 303–34, which provides suggestive approaches to and important information on the phenomenon of hurricanes in the Caribbean past. A general discussion of hurricanes set within the larger historical geography of the Caribbean is found in David Watts, *The West Indies: Patterns of Development, Culture, and Environmental Change since 1492* (Cambridge, 1987).

A useful approach to the larger study of hurricanes, finally, is suggested in the sociological literature that has accumulated on the subject of disaster, in which hurricanes usually are considered together with tornadoes, earthquakes, flood-ing, and drought. This literature has assumed immense proportions. The purpose here is to direct the reader to titles most relevant to hurricanes.

A point of departure are two collections of essays edited by E. L. Quarantelli: *Disaster: Theory and Research* (Beverly Hills, Calif., 1978) and *What Is a Disas-ter?: Perspectives on the Question* (London, 1998). Lowell Juilliard Carr's "Disaster and the Sequence-Pattern Concept of Social Change," *American Journal of Soci-ology* 38 (September 1932): 207–18, is an important pioneer work. A highly suggestive essay, Harry Estill Moore's "Toward a Theory of Disaster," *American Sociological Review* 21 (December 1956): 733–37, should be consulted in conjunction with J. L. Anderson and E. L. Jones's "Natural Disasters and the Historical Response," *Australian Economic History Review* 28 (March 1988): 3–20. The impact of disasters on existing social systems is explored in William I. Torry, "Natural Disasters, Social Structure and Change in Traditional Societies," *Journal of Asian and African Studies* 13 (July–October 1978): 167–83, and Gary A. Krebs, "Disaster and Social Order," *Sociological Theory* 3 (Spring 1985): 49–64. A valuable and, indeed, very suggestive approach to the study of the impact of tropical hurricanes in the Caribbean is found in Jon W. Anderson, "Cultural Adaption to Threatened Disaster," *Human Organization* 27 (Winter 1968): 298–307. Also of value is Terry Cannon, "Vulnerability Analysis and the Explanation of 'Natural' Disasters," in Ann Varley, ed., *Disasters, Development and Environment* (Chichester, 1994), pp. 13–30. For a thorough treatment of the relationship between social and economic conditions and natural disasters, see Piers Blaikie, Terry Cannon, Ian Davis, and Ben Wisner, *At Risk: Natural Hazards, People's Vulnerability, and Disasters* (London, 1994), and Rolando V. García, *Nature Pleads Not Guilty* (Oxford, 1981).

Index

46, 89, 91–92; and sugar production, 48, 49; population growth of, 50; and hurricane of 1842, 59; and hurricanes of 1844 and 1846, 61–62, 69, 71–73, 110, 111, 112–20
Havana Philharmonic Society, 67, 69
Heredia, Nicolás, 97

Jamaica, 21–22, 23–24, 123
Jovellanos, 48, 99

Las Casas, Bartolomé, 19, 20, 34, 140

Marco, Miguel de, 149
Mariel, 66, 75
Mártir de Anglería, Pedro, 18–19
Matanzas, 69, 140; and hurricane of 1870, 5, 6, 7; and hurricane of 1730, 33; and economic development, 40; and coffee production, 41, 46–47, 89, 140; and sugar production, 48–49, 51–52; population growth of, 51; and hurricane of 1842, 59; and hurricanes of 1844 and 1846, 63, 69, 74, 80, 89, 92; and railroads, 99; and slavery, 100, 101
Mayan Indians, 17

Nuevitas, 48
Núñez Cabeza de Vaca, Alvar, 29–30

O'Donnell, Leopoldo, 67; and hurricanes of 1844 and 1846, 70, 71, 76, 81; and hurricane relief, 134, 135, 136
Ortiz, Fernando, 18, 146

Palma, Ramón de, 43
Papel Periódico de La Habana, 36
Pezuela, Jacobo de la, 30
Pinar del Río, 69, 142; and hurricane of 1888, 6; and hurricane of 1910, 6; and hurricane of 1730, 33; and

hurricane of 1810, 33; and coffee production, 41, 46–47; population growth of, 51; and hurricanes of 1844 and 1846, 63, 75, 78, 80; and tobacco production, 95; and hurricane of 1895, 142
Pittaluga, Gustavo, 146
Population, 50–52
Puerto Príncipe, 48; and hurricane of 1780, 32–33; and hurricane of 1831, 34; and hurricane of 1846, 69

Railroads, 48, 49–50, 98–99
Real Consulado y Junta de Fomento, 33
Real Sociedad Económica de La Habana, 34, 98–99, 100
Remedios, 47, 48, 53; and hurricane of 1703, 33
Rodríguez Acosta, Ofelia, 149
Roncali, Federico, 106

Sagra, Ramón de la, 54, 91, 95
Sagua la Grande, 34, 48; and hurricane of 1888, 6; and hurricane of 1730, 33; and hurricane of 1791, 33; and sugar production, 48; and hurricane of 1846, 69
St. Christopher, 16, 22
St. Croix, 20–21, 25
St. Domingue, 9, 38–39; slave insurrection at, 38–39
Sancti-Spíritus, 51
Santa Clara, 34, 51
Santa Cruz del Sur, and hurricane of 1932, 6–7, 149–50
Shipping, 26–27; and hurricanes, 8, 66–67, 70–71
Simón, Pedro, 19
Slavery, 43, 44, 54, 88, 90, 99, 103, 105, 111; in St. Domingue, 38; and slave trade, 97–98, 102, 103, 132; and hurricanes of 1844 and 1846, 98, 121–25, 129–31; and slave